SINGING AND WELLBEING

Singing and Wellbeing provides evidence that the benefits of a melodious voice go far beyond pleasure, and confirms the importance of singing in optimum health. A largely untapped resource in the healthcare professions, the singing voice offers rewards that are closer than ever to being fully quantified by advances in neuroscience and psychology. For music, pre-med, bioethics, and medical humanities students, this book introduces the types of ongoing research that connect behaviour and brain function with the musical voice. It also synthesizes medical findings with Western music history, musical ethics, aesthetics, and ethnomusicology.

The centrality of the inflected voice in human existence will be examined through the lenses of anthropological, evolutionary, historical, musicological, philosophical, psychological, and emerging medical evidence. The book contributes to the interdisciplinary bridge-building already underway among musicians, music therapists, healthcare researchers and providers, and caregivers interested in the effects of singing. Discussion points, links to further reading, and audio and video resources illustrate applications of central concepts.

Kay Norton is Associate Professor of Musicology at Arizona State University.

SINGING AND WELLBEING

Ancient Wisdom, Modern Proof

Kay Norton

Routledge
Taylor & Francis Group

NEW YORK AND LONDON

First published 2016
by Routledge
711 Third Avenue, New York, NY 10017

and by Routledge
2 Park Square, Milton Park, Abingdon, Oxon, OX14 4RN

Routledge is an imprint of the Taylor & Francis Group, an informa business

Library of Congress Cataloging in Publication Data
Norton, Kay, author.
    Singing and wellbeing : ancient wisdom, modern proof / Kay Norton.
      pages cm
    Includes bibliographical references and index.
    1. Singing—Therapeutic use. 2. Singing—History. 3. Singing—
    Physiological aspects. 4. Singing—Social aspects. 5. Singing—
    Psychological aspects. 6. Singing—Religious aspects. 7. Music
    therapy. I. Title.
    ML3920.N678 2016
    783—dc23
                                                    2015000799

ISBN: 978-1-138-82531-4 (hbk)
ISBN: 978-1-138-82532-1 (pbk)
ISBN: 978-1-315-74006-5 (ebk)

Typeset in Bembo
by Keystroke, Station Road, Codsall, Wolverhampton

For all who sing and all who heal.

CONTENTS

FIGURES

CONTRIBUTORS

Robin Rio, MA, MT-BC, is Associate Professor and Music Therapy Clinic Director at Arizona State University. She is co-founder of Strength-Based Improvisation Training and author of *Connecting through Music with People with Dementia*. Her research focuses on music making among clients, therapists, and caregivers to bring support through community engagement and enhance quality of life. She has recorded two CDs of original vocal music with the Daughters of Harriet and has published in *Music Therapy Perspectives*, the *Arts in Psychotherapy*, and the *Nordic Journal of Music Therapy*.

Annamaria Oliverio, PhD, is Lecturer in the School of Social Transformation at Arizona State University. She also works as a music therapist with teenage, adult, and elderly populations. Currently, her research is focusing on hegemony and social control via an examination of the state, music in society, and social constructions of disability.

Jan Dougherty, MS, RN, is Family and Community Services Director at Banner Alzheimer's Institute in Phoenix, Arizona. She is responsible for setting a new standard of care for dementia patients and their families through development and implementation of innovative programs—including early stage programming, arts, and dementia—and an array of caregiver education programs.

PREFACE

"The Therapeutic Capsule"

> The voice brings music into a space of potential meaning, even when actual meaning is left hanging.
>
> *Lawrence Kramer (2002, 54)*

Singing, chanting, and orating exert a power over our species that is documented in every culture's mythology and history. Sirens lured sailors to rocky shipwrecks in Greek myths, Confucius wrote of singers with great respect, and the authors of ancient Sumerian, Egyptian, and Sanskrit texts included songs in their chronicles. The biblical King David was an influential singer, and traditional healing ceremonies throughout the world feature chanting. Songs have marked births, teenage years, courtships, weddings, and funerals.

Nor is singing less influential in the modern age. In 2007, National Public Radio broadcast an excerpt of Luciano Pavarotti performing "Nessun dorma" from Puccini's *Turandot* and asked listeners to describe the singing as a phenomenon distinct from the meaning of the words. "The universe vibrating inside your body," responded one listener. For another, the aria's climax sounded like "humanity taking a victory lap," and another person thought Pavarotti's exultant performance resembled "A newborn baby's first taste of air" (Mai et al. 2007). These metaphors—oneness with the universe, the triumph of our species, a new life—hint at the powerful mysteries to be addressed

FIGURE P.1 Old engraved illustration of Siren statue on the marbles of Athens. Larive and Fleury, *Dictionary of Words and Things (Dictionnaire français illustré des mots et des choses)*, Paris, 1895. Morphart Creation/Shutterstock.

in this book. How has the dynamic combination of air and human anatomy resulted in such a meaningful force?

Why I Wrote This Book

Singing and Wellbeing: Ancient Wisdom, Modern Proof attempts to answer that question. It aims to persuade you that the "inflected voice" remains a largely untapped resource in our quest for optimum health and wellbeing.[1] We naturally use our melodious voices in speaking or singing to infants. But when our family members face serious health challenges, most people forget that the warm, melodious tones we take for granted while soothing a fussy baby might also help the feelings of a disoriented Alzheimer's sufferer or a pre-operative surgery patient. Its capacity to "go up and down" in pitch and its distinctive timbre somehow give the voice surprising power. And although singing or speaking in an inflected voice cannot cure cancer or reverse Alzheimer's disease, a kind voice can ease a patient's journey, regardless of whether restored health is an achievable goal, the patient must contend with chronic pain, or the illness is terminal. Songs—those little packages of vocal artistry found the world over—also double as unifiers in divisive times, vehicles of hope in despair, and even roadmaps to help navigate the ravaged brains of dementia patients. Best of all, singing lifts the moods of the singing and listener alike. Once understood only anecdotally, the healthful properties of melodious speech and song are closer than ever to being quantified by advances in neuroscience and psychology.

The centrality of the inflected voice in human existence will be examined through the lenses of anthropological, evolutionary, historical, musicological, philosophical, and emerging medical evidence.[2] This book contributes to the interdisciplinary bridge-building already underway among musicians, music therapists, medical researchers, healthcare professionals, and caregivers interested in the effects of singing. Though I am well qualified to be a builder on the musical shore, my background is not sufficient to interpret clinical results as a scientist might. My citations and discussions of medical research are therefore invitations: to look further, to participate in cautious and deliberate speculation, and to consult a music therapist or medical professional if these suggestions seem to promise help. Just as medical scholars might feel that I have not addressed the whole picture, so do I feel that physicians and scientists have failed fully to address the meaning of singing in human experience. This book is therefore my best attempt to address the research lacunae arising from the daunting task of synthesizing musical and medical research.

Organization

The opening three chapters comprise Part I, Singing in History, Cognition, and Parenting. They provide underpinnings for my conviction that the inflected voice is central to human experience. Part II, Singing for the Group, the Self, and the Soul, offers three real-life scenarios in which singing affects positive change. At the end of each chapter, I suggest musical and film applications of my central concepts and several Discussion Points suitable for the higher education classroom. The book closes with an annotated timeline noting vocal milestones from mythology and history. Chapter 1, The First Musical Instrument, looks at vocal development in human evolution and offers several reasons that histories of ancient vocal music must remain speculative. Theories about the voice as marker of identity introduce a discussion of its physical apparatus. To close, one of America's most enduring speeches becomes a case in point for vocal influence.

Chapter 2, Neural Mapping and Brain Chemistry: How Singing Is Good for You, reviews selected advances in brain science, music therapy, and other published research that can be used to quantify singing's benefits for the average person. That discussion covers a few details of the brain's structure and explores some of the differences in brain activity while singing and speaking. I examine three newer directions in brain research with implications for singing—neuroplasticity, the mirror neuron hypothesis, and the brain hormone oxytocin.

In Chapter 3, "Womb to Tomb": Singing, Science, and the Mother's Voice, mammalian birth begins a discussion of the lifelong influence of the maternal voice. After a requisite nod to the French post-structuralists, human evolution initiates the chapter's primary argument.[3] Although medical studies show that most babies are familiar with the voices of both parents at birth, humans inhabit the same body as the mother, hear her vocal cadences beginning in the third trimester, and are therefore most attuned to her auditory signature. A brief look at mothering, infant-directed speech, a return to oxytocin, and the remarkable report of one child's responses to his mother's voice—while in a near-death state—substantiate these claims.

Part II, Singing for the Group, the Self, and the Soul, offers three snapshots of human experience in which the good effects of singing and chanting are readily observable. Chapter 4, Singing Our Songs: Damon of Athens, the Blues, and Group Psychology, shows how singing binds people together and helps them persist in the face of persistent hardship. The theories of a fifth-century BCE music philosopher provide a starting point. Commentators on his writings believe Damon was the first to claim that musical modes or "styles," initially named for regional groups, could influence behavior and morality. In other words, hearing music that reflected the way Athenians spoke could influence the listeners to behave like Athenians. I argue that downhome blues, a subset of the wider American blues phenomenon arising around the turn into the twentieth century, is a modern manifestation of Damon's ethos theory. At the end of Chapter 4, I summarize recent research on the positive effects of singing in groups.

Chapter 5, The Loss of Brain Function: How Singing Helps, covers just one of many ways that singing offers improved quality of life to the sick. Dementia is the name for a group of symptoms caused by disorders that affect the brain. While

FIGURE P.2 Head of the singer. Petr Vaclavek/Shutterstock.

the patient is able, the relatively non-invasive experience of singing can help recapture speech or memories, however fragmentary. Reclaiming verbal expression with song allows patients to recapture some small measure of autonomy and self-efficacy—even if the extent of that verbalization is "Twinkle, twinkle, little star, how I wonder what you are." This chapter concludes with case-study reports written by professional music therapists who have utilized singing in life-changing therapies for people suffering from brain traumas or dementia.

Belief systems and spiritual groups the world over utilize the voice to accompany and intensify religious experience. Chapter 6, Singing and Religion, turns attention to singing and chanting in esoteric and indigenous religions, and five exoteric belief systems of the world: Hinduism, Buddhism, Judaism, Christianity, and Islam. Singing in meditation and worship helps to silence the outside world and realign the inner spirit with transcendent principles. As it does in other realms of experience, religious and spiritual singing helps cope with difficulty, establish identity, create a sense of unity and belonging, and foster change and growth.

The Selected Timeline of Vocal Healing Milestones from Mythology and History that closes this book is drawn from many sources, including the website of the History of Medicine Division at the National Library of Medicine, *Music as*

Medicine: The History of Music Therapy since Antiquity edited by Peregrine Horden, Edward Lippmann's work on musical philosophies and aesthetics, Ruth Boxberger's foundational history of music therapy, numerous musicological resources within the *Grove Music Dictionaries*, including "Philosophies of Music" by F.A. Sparshott, Lydia Goehr, and others, scholarly commentaries on religious texts, and fieldwork reports by ethnomusicologists such as Pat Moffitt Cook, Alison Arnold, and Scott Marcus. With no claims of comprehensiveness, I nevertheless present this timeline in an effort to remind readers that we are a singing species and we would be wise to insure a central place for that crucial activity for present and future generations.

To Students, Educators, and Healthcare Professionals

For more than fifteen years, the wellness component of our love affair with music has guided my research, teaching, and community activity. Hundreds of graduate and undergraduate music majors, church choir members, and senior citizens, in addition to esteemed researchers, have joined me in that pursuit. Increasingly, I became convinced that all roads lead to the voice, our original instrument. For students like mine, as well as for pre-med, bioethics, and medical humanities students—to name a few populations—this book introduces the types of ongoing research that connect brain function and the musical voice. For these and the general reader alike, this book synthesizes medical findings with Western music history, musical ethics, aesthetics, and ethnomusicology. Practitioners, specialists, and teachers of music therapy, music education, theology, and the humanities will find that my avenues of inquiry can spark insights and motivate further research into the ways our inflected voices have shaped human experience. The voice is so ubiquitous that we can and do overlook its tremendous power to improve wellness. Evidence appears all around, once we are alerted to this possibility.

Singing and Wellbeing: Ancient Wisdom, Modern Proof is also intended to supplement the medical humanities, a field that requires some introduction. Medical practice is historically defined both as a science and as an art, but today's training of healthcare professionals is dominated by scientific training. As the medical professions respond to ever more sophisticated technology, the "arts" portion is increasingly sidelined. This situation was examined at a conference called by the Rockefeller Foundation in 1976. One result of that meeting was an increase in programs dedicated to the medical humanities within medical schools worldwide. These programs aim much further than the standard undergraduate literature or arts appreciation courses. They directly lead healthcare educators and students to consider the ways the humanities can illuminate aspects of the human condition and inform medical practice. Leaders in the medical humanities discipline include Rita Charon, who founded the Program in Narrative Medicine at Columbia University,[4] and Felice Aull, creator of New York University's online Medical Humanities Database. The NYU database offers information about medical humanities programs in forty-three states, in Canada, and in Africa, Australia, Europe, and the Middle East.[5]

In medical humanities curricula to date, music is the least often represented of the arts; courses that help healthcare professionals understand the value of literature and visual art for healer and patient alike are more common. With this book, physicians, nurses, researchers, and caregivers can learn about the roles the human voice can play in wellness, therapy, and palliative care. Armed with that information, they can consider the ways their own voices can express empathy, soften the delivery of bad news, and simply communicate more effectively with peers. In addition, this study of the musical voice can help healthcare professionals maintain their own emotional wellness, one prerequisite of optimal patient care. Modalities featuring an inflected voice can help an empathetic physician recover from the daily onslaught of patient suffering and help a nurse creatively express thoughts and feelings in time-honored vocal ways such as group singing.

This book provides several models that might be developed and extended by students and healthcare professionals who wish to maximize the positive effects of singing in life and practice.

Notes

1 "Inflected voice" and "therapeutic capsule" are borrowed from George Rousseau.
2 While the literature and practice of music therapy contribute many findings to this book, I am not a music therapist, but a music historian and interpreter of the humanities. Music therapy is an intervention system comprising assessment, treatment, and evaluation involving a board-certified music therapist.
3 Jacques Lacan and his circle problematized the mother's voice as marker of our first identity crisis.
4 Charon is Professor of Clinical Medicine at the College of Physicians and Surgeons of Columbia University and Executive Director of the Program in Narrative Medicine.
5 Felice Aull, a faculty member in the Department of Physiology and Neuroscience at NYU's School of Medicine, founded the Literature, Arts, and Medicine Database in 1993. Lucy Bruell is currently editor-in-chief of the database.

References

Boxberger, R. 1962. "Historical Bases for the Use of Music in Therapy." In *Music Therapy 1961: Eleventh Book of Proceedings of the National Association for Music Therapy, Inc.*, eds. Erwin H. Schneider, Ruth Boxberger, and William W. Sears, 125–66. Lawrence, KS: National Association of Music Therapy.
History of Medicine Division, National Library of Medicine. 2014. National Institutes of Health, www.nlm.nih.gov/hmd/index.html, accessed 2 December 2014.
Horden, P., ed. 2000. *Music as Medicine: The History of Music Therapy since Antiquity.* Aldershot: Ashgate.
Kramer, L. 2002. "Beyond Words and Music: An Essay on Songfulness." In *Musical Meaning: Toward a Critical History.* Berkeley: University of California Press.
Lippmann, E. 1967. *Musical Thought in Ancient Greece.* New York: Columbia University Press.
———. 1986–90. *Musical Aesthetics: A Historical Reader.* 3 vols. New York: Pendragon.

Literature, Arts, and Medicine Database. 2014. Division of Medical Humanities, Department of Medicine at New York University, http://litmed.med.nyu.edu, accessed 26 December 2014.

Mai, L., B. Niblock, and J. Carlson, respectively. 2007. National Public Radio, "Vocal Impressions: Hearing Voices," Round 4, 30 April, www.npr.org, accessed 19 December 2013.

Pavarotti, L. 1973. "Nessun dorma," Act III of G. Puccini's *Turandot* (1926). London Philharmonic with the John Alldis Choir. London: Decca, released 1985.

Program in Narrative Medicine. 2014. Columbia University, www.narrativemedicine.org/leadership.html, accessed 26 December 2014.

Rockefeller Foundation. 1978. *Working Papers: The Healing Role of the Arts*. New York: Rockefeller Foundation.

Rousseau, G. 2000. "The Inflected Voice: Attraction and Curative Properties." In *Musical Healing in Cultural Contexts*, ed. Penelope Gouk, 92–112. Aldershot: Ashgate.

ACKNOWLEDGMENTS

In many ways, *Singing and Wellbeing* summarizes my thinking over the past eighteen years. In 1996, I was introduced to the medical humanities by the late Marjorie Sirridge MD, and Loretta Loftus MD, leaders of the original medical humanities and the arts teaching faculty at the School of Medicine, University of Missouri-Kansas City. I thank them for giving me a topic under which to categorize my thoughts about singing and health. In Arizona, those associated with the Innovations in Medical Education Events and the Bright Idea Network, University of Arizona College of Medicine, gave my work helpful attention. Likewise, I was honored to present my research at the Mayo Clinic/Arizona State University Research Symposia, Best Practices of Medical Educators Series.

Whether or not they realize it, colleagues at the University of Missouri-Kansas City Conservatory of Music and the School of Music and Herberger Institute for Design and the Arts at Arizona State University contributed important concepts to my work. I extend special thanks to William Everett, Lynda Payne, Jennifer Martin, Wanda Lathom-Radocy, and Anne DeLaunay at UMKC. At the ASU School of Music, I'm indebted to faculty music therapists Robin Rio, Barbara J. Crowe, and Julie Hoffer. ASU voice colleagues were excellent sources of crucial information; they include Jerry Doan, Carole FitzPatrick, Judy May, Dale Dreyfoos, William Reber, Robert Barefield, and Anne Kopta. Ethnomusicologists Ted Solis, the late Mark Sunkett, and Richard Haefer contributed important insights about non-Western ways of healing. Musicologists Robert Oldani, Richard Mook, Catherine Saucier, and Sabine Feisst offered continuing interest and support, for which I am most grateful. Through their assistance, administrators Heather Landes, Steven Tepper, and Wayne Bailey made it much easier to accomplish this work.

Colleagues outside the School of Music also made a tremendous impact on the ways I presented this material. They include music therapists Annamaria Oliverio, Kymla Eubanks, and Scott Tonkinson, and musicologists Sara Haefeli and Petra Meyer Frasier. Music librarians Laura Gayle Green, Kathy Abromeit, and Linda Elsasser helped me answer many questions.

The American Music Research Center at the College of Music, University of Colorado, Boulder, under the direction of Thomas Riis, sponsored conferences in 2007 and 2013 that allowed me to share my work with a broader audience. At those meetings, I was especially inspired by the life-changing community sings led by Ysaye Barnwell and Pat Moffitt Cook's beautiful accounts of fieldwork with shamans and healers.

In 2008, a team of which I was a member received a seed grant from ASU's Institute for Humanities Research, which ultimately allowed me to spend a weekend trading ideas with Stephen Mithen, Walter Freeman, Joanne Loewy, Töres Theorell, and Claudius Conrad. I am forever grateful for that opportunity and the thoughts it engendered. The IHR also supported this book with a publication subvention.

I am deeply indebted to Routledge's anonymous reviewers whose comments significantly improved this manuscript. In the late stages of manuscript preparation, I was also gratified to receive advice from internationally respected scholars Ingo Titze, Calixto Machado, István Molnar-Szakacs, Richard Freund, and Thomas Geissmann. Lauren A. Pace was tremendously helpful to me as I planned my medical illustrations.

Adrienne Ashford-Thorpe, Ryan T. Vaughan, Ryan Downey, and Kerry Ginger generously read chapters during the preparation of this book. Their critical commentaries led me to significant improvements. I am fortunate to have many other friends, among them Kim Holmes, Chloe Webb, and Jeannie Dawson, who offered unquestioning support along the way. I share many research interests related to this field with another steadfast advocate, my husband Gary W. Hill. I am blessed, indeed, to have such an intellectually curious and well-informed partner with whom to share ideas, music, family, and life.

I am deeply grateful for having the opportunity to teach about this topic. If it were possible, I would name each of the students who have motivated and cheered me on as I contemplated and wrote this monograph. Their inquisitiveness and passion for interdisciplinary learning challenged me in the most helpful ways. Inspiring students in whose health-related Doctor of Musical Arts degree projects I have participated include Kevin Hanrahan, Stefanie Harger Gardner, Joshua T. Gardner, Jennifer Allen, Allison Dromgold Adams, Susan Hurley, and Mario Vazquez-Morillas. One student, Abby Lloyd, deserves special mention. As my research assistant, she became my third hand in the late-stage preparation of this manuscript. She devoted tremendous energy and insight to the creation of the Timeline, often following her own intuitions in addition to my directions. Any remaining glitches are my responsibility alone.

I was fortunate to grow up in a singing family and community. I am awed by the consoling presence of songs at times of illness and death and have celebrated with song during my joyous times, and especially during my parenting journey to date with sons Brandon and Charlie.

Finally, I am deeply indebted to Constance Ditzel, music acquisitions editor at Routledge, for her creative input and supportive advocacy of this book.

Kay Norton, Phoenix, AZ, December 2014

PART I
Singing in History, Cognition, and Parenting

1

THE FIRST MUSICAL INSTRUMENT

The melodious range of the voice contains the therapeutic capsule.
George Rousseau (2000, 108)

This chapter begins with a look into human evolution and several theories about singing behaviors in our pre-human ancestors. Next, I explain why we have a clearer idea about the evolution of musical instruments than we do about the development of vocal music. The chapter ends with an exploration of the anatomical source of the voice: a physical apparatus activated by the breath. As important as basic anatomy is to vocal production and its powers over humans, the ways song, chant, and lyrical speech are individualized with inflection, pitch range, and language are equally central to the moving power of the voice. The writings of philosophers, poets, and an iconic civil rights leader provide evidence that the voice is an expressive tool—a musical instrument—whose power over humans may be traced to its roles in identity, communication, and persuasion.

Singing in Pre-human Ancestors

Music, including the inflected vocal utterance we call "song," appears in all human cultures and is therefore essential to an understanding of our evolution. As with other persisting behaviors, the concept that music was a fitness advantage in evolution must be considered; otherwise, song would have arisen and disappeared over millennia of development. Just how far back does song extend in the ancestry of Homo sapiens? Though we no longer can study living, early-stage humanoids, we can study living non-human species whose partial evolutionary trajectory we share. In addition, evolutionary biologists actively study song characteristics of unrelated species such as birds to understand which contexts may apply to human singing behavior (Lipkind et al. 2013). In these ways, a view of singing's global value materializes.

In this discussion I adopt W.H. Thorpe's definition of song relevant to songbirds: "What is usually understood by the term song is a series of notes, generally of more than one type, uttered in succession and so related as to form a recognizable sequence or pattern in time" (Thorpe 1961, 15).[1] From Thorpe's perspective, the world is full of non-human songs. Surely all this singing behavior is somehow connected; anthropology offers various ways to discover those connections. Nils L. Wallin was a researcher committed to understanding music in its entire terrestrial sense. He coined the term biomusicology to describe a field in which the origins of music are considered crucial to the study of human origins (Wallin 2000, 5). Music and language were considered close relatives in prior evolution studies, but, before the 1990s, scientific interest centered mainly on the place of language in human evolution. Wallin and co-editors Björn Merker and Steven Brown presented research by twenty-five other scientists and musicologists in the 2000 book *The Origins of Music*. These authors contributed important biomusicological perspectives on music making; works devoted to song are especially enlightening.

Despite differences among the sound-producing mechanisms of, for example, the great whale, Old World monkeys, and the western meadowlark, ongoing

Classification	Earliest appearance in millions (MA) or thousands (Ka) of years	Contained Forms
Species sapiens	200 Ka	Modern humans
[Species neanderthalensis]	[200–30 Ka]	[Neanderthals]
Genus Homo	2.5–2.0 MA	Modern and archaic humans
[Subfamily Homininae]	[8–4 MA]	[Humans, Chimpanzees, Gorillas, Bonobos]
Family Hominidae	7–6 MA	Great Apes (bipedal): Humans and Chimpanzees, Gorillas, Orangutans, Bonobos
Superfamily Hominoidea	34–23 MA	Great And Lesser Apes: (Including Gibbons)
Infraorder Simiiformes	45 MA	Humans, Apes, and Monkeys
Suborder Haplorrhini	55 MA	Humans, Apes, Monkeys, and Tarsiers
Order Primates (Beginning of speciation that will lead to humans.)	85–65 MA	Humans, Apes, Monkeys, Tarsiers, Lemurs, and Lorises

FIGURE 1.1 General dating of bifurcation events in the primate phylogeny.

Note: Dating estimates based on DNA evidence, fossil records, generation times, and other methods are not always compatible. Dates in this chart are therefore general.

research on "vocal" usages among animals presents behavior analogous to that of modern humans in developed societies (Tobias and Seddon 2009). And while singing behavior among primates is quite rare, it has been found in the evolution of four distantly related, non-human primate species: gibbons, orangutans, gorillas, and chimpanzees (see Figure 1.1). The chimpanzee, our closest non-human relative, shares with humans a larynx that repositions during the first two years of life to a spot between the pharynx and the lungs.[2] Our common ancestors also had this feature, a precursor of speech, as long ago as seven million years.

Thomas Geissmann proposes several potential fitness advantages of singing in gibbons and among other apes. Male orangutans utilize lengthy calls partly because they can be heard over long distances, and their calls may mediate inter-individual spacing. In other words, a male may emit these calls to help advertise his territory and intimidate competitors (Geissmann 2000, 115, 119). Gorilla "hoot" series seem to serve long-range group communication, and other vocalizations may provide long-range alarm systems. Loud calls of other primate species may also help locate specific individuals and food sources. Finally, loud calls may strengthen intergroup cohesion. Geissmann suggests the possibility that

> early homonid singing shared many characteristics with loud calls of modern Old World Monkeys and especially apes, such as loudness (for long-distance communication), pure tonal quality of notes, stereotyped phrases, biphasic notes (making sound on the in-breath and the out-breath), accelerando (increasing in speed), possible slow-down near the end of a phrase, locomotor display, and a strong inherited component.
>
> *Geissmann (2000, 118)*

Geissmann then proposes the obvious: "It makes sense to assume that . . . loud calls of early hominids may have been the substrate from which human singing and, ultimately, music evolved" (Geissmann 2000, 118). Hypothetical though it may be, that statement is worth contemplating further. Could singing behavior, which carried with it several fitness advantages, partially explain the evolution of Homo sapiens sapiens into the most powerful and cognitively advanced species on the planet? How might singing have advantaged our evolutionary line to develop a cognitive potential greater than that of hominid substrates such as Old World monkeys?

One way that humans surpassed our primate ancestors musically was in developing a steady pulse or beat.[3] Geissmann suggests that regularly pulsed group participation and coordination may be considered a fitness advantage; a co-ordinated display may be impressive to interlopers and a steady beat signals group cohesiveness to competing groups (Geissmann 2000, 119). It therefore seems reasonable to imagine that early human survival and success in competition evolved into a preference for a rhythmically coordinated vocal display. Humans in groups survive better than loners; highly vocal groups cohere (aided by, among other things, a steady beat) and therefore survive better than less vocal or less vocally cohesive ones. Geissmann's hypothesis, that the best fitness advantage was evolutionarily associated with the most vocal, coordinated human groups, seems plausible given the persistence of singing in our species.[4]

Charles Darwin (1809–82) believed that music and singing evolved as part of courtship displays and that, as with coloration in birds, the male evolved to be most expressive in order to attract the best mates. In "Evolution of Human Music through Sexual Selection," Miller updates Darwin's courtship hypothesis to help explain the persistence of music in human evolution. Restating the truth that music-making could *not* have persisted simply because it is a vehicle of self-expression, he notes that "most animal signal systems have been successfully analyzed as adaptations that manipulate the signal receiver's behavior to the signaler's benefit" (Miller 2000, 336).[5] If, as Miller argues, most of what an animal does is aimed at influencing the behavior of another animal, why has music become so specialized in humans?

Calling upon the work of another predecessor, Miller recounts R.A. Fisher's 1930 theory of runaway sexual selection, to wit: female preference for lowest-sounding male mating calls would eventually result in offspring that both *preferred* low-sounding male voices and had capacities to *make* low sounds (Fischer 1930). Although widely disputed, the idea of a fitness advantage linking female preference for low-voiced males and pubescent male vocal change is fascinating to consider. Fitch and Giedd call the descent of the larynx in pubescent human males "a sexually dimorphic . . . adaptation to give adult males a more imposing and resonant voice relative to females or prepubescent males" (Fitch and Giedd 1999, 1517). It "might represent a . . . means of exaggerating vocally projected body size, and its restriction to males suggests that it is . . . the acoustic equivalent of . . . secondary sexual characteristics seen in males of many other species," such as lions' manes, bisons' humps, and orangutans' cheek pads (Fitch and Giedd 1999, 1520).

To summarize, Miller writes: "Music is what happens when a smart, group-living, anthropoid ape stumbles into the evolutionary wonderland of runaway sexual selection for complex acoustic displays" (Miller 2000, 349). He believes that, even though humans engage in music in groups, the persistence of vocalizing in human evolution is not group oriented. Instead, Miller believes group vocal engagement among humans is valuable for its mood-calibrating purposes and as another facet of sexual selection. Performing in a group under prehistoric conditions meant one was part of a successful band that shared health, energy, capacity to coexist, and a common language (Miller 2000, 353).

Other contributors to *The Origins of Music*—Peter Marler ("Origins of Music and Speech: Insights from Animals"), Peter J.B. Slater ("Birdsong Repertoires: Their Origins and Use"), Harry Jerison ("Paleoneurology and the Biology of Music")—help underscore the relevance of animal singing behavior when parsing the evolution of human music. Evolutionary musicology—like anthropology—proceeds from incomplete, surviving knowledge and posits theoretical models from those key factors, and as *The Origins of Music* editors write, "There is no a priori way of *excluding* the possibility . . . that our distant forebears might have been singing homonids before they became talking humans" (Wallin 2000, 7, emphasis mine). The following section elucidates the reasons anthropologists must rely on speculation in order to construct a history of human singing.

The Elusive Documentation of Vocal Music

Although some might argue that purposefully striking sticks or rocks together pre-dated the first musical sounds from the voice in human evolution, this book rests on the reasonable assumption that singing was our first musical expression. As with any ephemeral product of culture, music history begins with mythology.[6] The Greek god Orpheus, both instrumentalist and singer, wielded power over the living and the dead, human and divine.

> While he sang . . . to the sound of his sweet lyre, the bloodless ghosts themselves were weeping, and the anxious Tantalus stopped clutching at return-flow of the wave, Ixion's twisting wheel stood wonder-bound; and Tityus' liver for a while escaped the vultures, and the listening Belides forgot their sieve-like bowls and even you, O Sisyphus! sat idly on your rock! Then Fame declared that conquered by the song of Orpheus, for the first and only time the hard cheeks of the fierce Eumenides were wet with tears: nor could the royal queen, nor he who rules the lower world deny the prayer of Orpheus.[7]
>
> *Ovid in More (1922)*

Without doubt, ancient people sang, but because the soft tissues of hominid vocal mechanisms almost never survived to be studied by archeologists, evolution of the vocal mechanism has remained unclear. Singing neither required an external device, nor left an artifact; for documented origins of singing, we must be satisfied with the oldest notated song. In 1974, cuneiform expert and philology professor Anne Draffkorn Kilmer reported that the oldest notated song to date was found on a tablet of "Hurrian cult songs from the ancient Levantine city of Ugarit (modern Ras Shamra), dating to the middle of the second millenium BCE," almost 1,000 years prior to the earliest Greek musical notation (Kilmer 1974, 69). Even older—dating to as early as the middle of the third millennium BCE—are "early Dynastic lists of professions ('Early Dynastic Lu') which provide us with the core of the musicological terms for singers and instrumentalists" (Kilmer 1971, 148).[8] But how long did people sing before they felt the necessity to write songs down?

The history of musical instruments is somewhat of a different story, though the earliest stories are also mythological. "Pan is credited with the invention of the pan-pipes," wrote Curt Sachs, "and Mercury is supposed to have devised the lyre when one day he found a dried-out tortoise on the banks of the Nile" (Sachs 1940,

25).[9] Archeologists have uncovered surviving instruments dating to the twelfth century BCE—clay flutes, stone chimes, bronze bells—in the royal tombs of China's northern Henan province. Extant Egyptian instruments include clappers dating from around the twenty-eighth century BCE; evidence of Egyptian lyres and harps from the sixteenth to twelfth centuries BCE indicates they were Asiatic imports.[10] Ancient Mesopotamian cuneiform tablets, dating as far back as the 3rd millennium BCE, offer copious details about musical instruments, the people who played them and where, and associated texts (see Figure 1.2).[11] Without question, though, musical instruments—like purposeful singing—existed much earlier than iconographic or archeological evidence can document, and each new discovery has the potential to revise entire disciplines. The discovery in 2004 of a 30,000-year-old mammoth bone flute caused fresh speculation on the genealogy of that instrument and instrumental music in general (Schneider 2004). That finding notwithstanding, species Homo sapiens first lived in Ethiopia 160,000 years ago, which leaves a sizable gap between the origins of our species and the earliest surviving musical instrument.

Musical instruments themselves supply evidence of singing, since many instruments were created to extend the power of the voice.[12] So-called "talking drums"

FIGURE 1.2 Detail, "Peace Panel," Standard of Ur, ca. 2550 BCE. Detail, Lyrist and possible singer. © The Trustees of the British Museum.

(the Ghanaian hourglass pressure drum, for example) communicate over longer distances than a voice alone. In other cultures, wood, clay, or bone flutes punctuated and intensified vocal requests to the gods. Ling Lun—the legendary founder of music in China—developed the flute to emulate not human, but bird songs. Imitation of vocal beauty may thus have been his primary motivator. Multi-stringed instruments such as the lyre of Orpheus enriched singing—made it more persuasive, perhaps—with sustained accompaniment. Animal horn, conch shell, or gourd trumpets, widespread markers of status and social power, may have originated to mimic the intimidating roar of a lion, elephant, or bear. Metal descendants of these horns had evolved by the fifteenth century to include slides, which multiplied the instrument's available notes. These more "vocal" sackbuts (early trombones) easily supported or substituted for voices in Renaissance cathedral performances— a watershed practice which marks the rise of "classical" instrumental music in the Western world. The greatest builders of Cremona, Italy—the Amati (ca. 1530), Stradivari (ca. 1666), and Guarneri (ca. 1690) families—strove to perfect string instruments that could sob, soar, or exult as effectively as their stated model, the human voice.

The history of the melodious voice is therefore a collage of logical assumptions threaded with contextual interpretation and sparse documentation. We know that vocal inflection precedes instrumental music in each life.[13] Only moments after we take a first breath, we improvise vocally, and that initial performance is far from monotonous. Neither is vocal expression culture-dependent. Regardless of culturally distinct pitch-range variations—here meaning the distance between the highest and lowest common speaking pitches—no human society fails to utilize the voice's pitch variability.[14] All human societies make inflected vocal sound and communicate with the vocal apparatus. Vocal anatomy now ushers in a consideration of its expressive potential.

The Physiological Voice

A human baby normally makes his first vocal sound with a cry at birth. Infants randomly explore the voice through six to eight weeks of age, make vowel noises by three months, babble tunefully (use gibberish or "baby talk") by nine months, and employ short patterns of speech between twelve and twenty-four months. By then, the process of vocal individuation has begun. Vocal pathologies, speech delays, or silence related to conditions such as hearing loss or autism spectrum disorders surely affect some individuals, but even hearing-impaired children show strong biases to communicate in language-like ways that are not affected by parental communication structures (Goldin-Meadow and Mylander, 1984).

Simply stated, vocal sound is generated when air passes through the vocal folds. That sound is modified by multiple points between the folds and the teeth, including palates, tongue, nasal cavity, uvula, and jaw (see Figure 1.3).[15] Ingo Titze, voice professor at University of Iowa and director of the University of Utah's

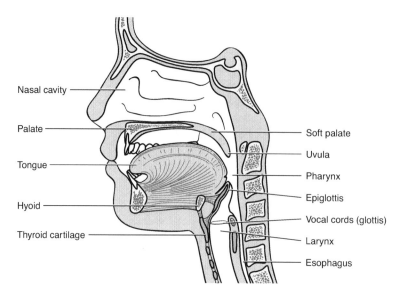

Nasal cavity

Palate

Tongue

Hyoid

Thyroid cartilage

Soft palate

Uvula

Pharynx

Epiglottis

Vocal cords (glottis)

Larynx

Esophagus

FIGURE 1.3 Vocal tract. Art by Jane Whitney, BSc, AAM.

National Center for Voice and Speech, offers an outwardly simple formula. Voice quality equals vocal tract configuration (comprising the several anatomical points beginning with the glottis and ending with the teeth); plus laryngeal anatomy; plus learned component (Titze 2010). With this equation, all the vocal variety humans can produce is explained (Titze 2008).

Vocal tract configuration and laryngeal anatomy are hereditary. Degrees to which the third, learned component counter-balances or "customizes" inheritance are completely individualized. A biological daughter might replicate her mother's high-pitched speaking voice because they share the same genetic vocal tract shape, while a second daughter may *learn* to imitate Mom's voice, even if the younger sister's vocal tract is more similar to Dad's or Grandpa's. A third daughter might imitate Dad's baritone voice, even though she inherited Mom's vocal tract configuration. Thus, the learned component can override genetic predisposition, a situation Titze sees most often when a trained singer, actor, or "pitch man" exhibits his impressive "bag of tricks." Actors such as Bill "Froggy" Laughlin of 1940s *Our Gang* fame or Tom Kenny, who voices the Nickelodeon network's *SpongeBob SquarePants*, build their personas around extreme vocal manipulations.

Sometimes, our highly flexible vocal instruments lead us into dangerous vocal territory. Even young children may require speech therapy to re-learn phonation if they habitually abuse their vocal folds. Expressing anger or frustration through clasped-together vocal folds, yelling, and even explosive coughing can result in a chronically hoarse, raspy voice and potentially debilitating vocal nodules.[16] "Vocal fry" is a term currently used to describe the perpetual hoarseness of many show-business personalities. Some, especially females, began with a desire to sound stereotypically "sexy" and ended with vocal damage. Others, TV chef Rachel Ray, for example, developed a benign cyst due to unconscious vocal tension, which required surgery and therapy (Chitale 2012). On the opposite end of the vocalist spectrum are the singers, ventriloquists, actors, and other "small-muscle athletes" who maximize laryngeal agility and resilience through safe training and conditioning. The stereotypical opera singer who wraps the throat in winter and vocalizes carefully each day reflects the important ways humans can optimize the potential of their inherited vocal equipment, the better to produce great art.

The Meaningful Voice

The voice is meaningful both for what it represents and for what that representation can do. Most fundamentally, the voice is a marker of individuality; it must have been a crucial identifier in pre-literate societies. Even now, when so much communication is typed and delivered in a visual format, we continue to liken important social or cultural phenomena to the voice. When a creator reaches maturity, she has "found her voice." A political result is "the voice of the people," and entire nations or movements are symbolized by the voices of their leaders.

Mid-twentieth-century French essayist and critic Roland Barthes wrote: "We understand music as the embodied voice, produced directly from a human throat or by instrumental proxy" (Barthes 1977). In Barthes's view, "voice" is both inseparable from identity and synonymous with the body that created it.[17] Voice "means" a person just as a flag stands for a country. Thus, the recorded voices of Frank Sinatra, Whitney Houston, or Adolf Hitler evoke the body, mind, and personality of each speaker/singer. Barthes coined the term "grain of the voice" to capture that individualistic thread—"the body in the voice as it sings" (Barthes 1977, 188).

The voice's distinctiveness is a commodity traded in the modern marketplace by politicians, clergy, comedians, musicians, and poets. An actor lends his natural speech patterns to an orange juice or insurance advertisement and, reinforced by multiple repetitions in commercial media, the voice becomes synonymous with the product. And while good basic musicianship is a sine qua non in the pop music world, a vocal artist's most marketable attribute is uniqueness, that particular combination of nasality, breathiness, "gravel," and resonance, to name a few attributes.[18] In our highly commercialized world, each day reinforces the fact that its capacity to identify makes the voice a powerful tool of communication and expression.

Humans have built-in safeguards to ensure that normally hearing babies are born with up to three months' exposure to one important voice.[19] Most of us recall what it felt like in childhood when father spoke in anger or laughed at a joke. These most obvious functions barely scratch the surface of our vocal potential, however. In addressing the many manifestations of the term "voice," cultural historian George Rousseau challenged music therapists to devise "a therapeutic practice that would teach patients (of all melancholic types broadly construed and especially those ... who do not respond to traditional therapies) how to come closer to the 'voices' of those they love" (Rousseau 2000, 92, 108). Whether this proximity is metaphorical (i.e., achieved by remembering the feelings evoked by the voice of a love one) or literal (i.e., achieved by being in the presence of the loved one whose voice was fundamental), Rousseau recognizes power in the variety and potential embodied by the human voice. For him, then, "the melodious range of the voice contains the therapeutic capsule." Given its emotional and communicative significance, it is worth asking what sort of "capsule" or "therapy" the voice can deliver.

Crucial to what Rousseau calls the "inflected" voice is an understanding of the voice as a behavioral tool. We naturally put our voices to a surprisingly wide array of linguistic and non-linguistic uses. In the first category, the voice relays information ("I live on 34th Street and Main"), expresses feelings ("I'm lonely"), or verbalizes an idea in a soliloquy, monologue, speech, or sermon. Even without words, we call upon the voice's infinite variety of pitch, timbre, rhythm, and resonance to soothe a fussy baby, imitate drum solos in a rock song, encourage flagging sportsmen, or express disappointment. Additionally, the musical voice delivers songs, and even in "classical" vocal music words are optional. The "Aria (Cantilena)" from Villa-Lobos's *Bachianas Brasileras Number 5* (1938–45) for soprano and orchestra of cellos is an evocative example of non-linguistic music that features singing. And of course, sung linguistic content can become memorable art.

Ted Gioia rightly calls music a change agent; both musical and verbal utterances take part in that potential to transform (Gioia 2006, 36). The above discussion addressed many of the vocal tract's physical elements, but the vocal apparatus is enlivened by breath, a component that has its own metaphorical implications. Physically sharing breath, as in traditional mouth-to-mouth resuscitation, means transferring two crucial elements of the life force: body heat and air (oxygen and carbon dioxide). The breath can also be a poetic evocation of intimacy. For Shakespeare, it embodied seasonal change ("O, how shall summer's honey breath hold out / Against the wreckful siege of battering days," Sonnet 65, LXV), Caesar's power ("Tell him from his all-obeying breath I hear / The doom of Egypt," *Antony and Cleopatra* III, iii), and the power of Desdemona's kiss ("Ah balmy breath, that dost almost persuade / Justice to break her sword!" *Othello* V, ii). The power of breath is also central in religion and spirituality. For Hindus, prana (vitality) is manifested through the breath among other things; Muslims recite each verse of Salat on a fresh breath; Jews equate the term ruach with breath, wind, or spirit; in Chinese philosophy, qi is synonymous with spirit; and for Christians, the Latin "spiritus" is not "spirit" but "breath."

Individuality and Community

Breath, genetics, and the learned component have offered limitless variety to human voices throughout our history. We are a species of individuals. However, living in groups, where communication and expression are crucial, forces most of us to mediate that individuality. The capacity to articulate an impressive array of vocal sounds over the course of human evolution led to vocally expressive systems (songs and languages) that are differentiated according to geography or region. But while our social natures may have limited our individuality, vocal variety maintained a formidable presence. In fact, the human voice is crucial to group formation, since phonation and articulation help humans communicate, remember, identify, and cohere.

Vocal persuasion in public speaking, "rhetoric," is an ancient art first documented in the fifth century BCE. However, the persuasive use of the human voice must be older than that. Perhaps one reason that vocalization was retained throughout our evolutionary journey was its power to influence people. Gideon Burton stated a fundamental principle of the human voice when he wrote that "a basic premise for rhetoric is the indivisibility of means from meaning; *how* one says something conveys meaning as much as *what* one says" (Burton 1997). Rhetorical devices such as allegory are familiar tools of everyday language.

Rhetoric provides a convenient way to approach the expressive range of the voice. Consider Martin Luther King, Jr.'s "I Have a Dream" speech, delivered at the Lincoln Memorial on 28 August 1963. Early on, King uses a rhetorical device—a metaphor—to explain the purpose of the March on Washington.

> In a sense we have come to our nation's capital to cash a check. When the architects of our republic wrote the magnificent words of the Constitution and the Declaration of Independence, they were signing a promissory note to which every American was to fall heir. This note was a promise that all men, yes, black men as well as white men, would be guaranteed the unalienable rights of life, liberty, and the pursuit of happiness. It is obvious today that America has defaulted on this promissory note insofar as her citizens of color are concerned. Instead of honoring this sacred obligation, America has given the Negro people a bad check, a check which has come back marked "insufficient funds."
>
> *King (1963)*

Even read silently, the words are powerful, but King, a passionate orator, minister, and Civil Rights leader, also capitalized on the "how" of rhetoric in this passage. In so doing, he created a definitive and enduring vocal artifact. Since it currently plays on a continuous loop in an exhibit beneath the Lincoln Memorial in Washington, DC, it literally underscores one of our most iconic national symbols.

King's rhetorical voice is filled with musical qualities. Against a relatively stable baseline of volume, musical pitch, speed, and pronunciation, King punctuates some words with higher pitches ("In a sense we have come to our nation's capital," "come back marked"), elongation ("ALL men"), and dramatic pauses (after "liberty" and "insufficient funds"). As the speech nears its conclusion, King speeds up his word frequency and his baseline pitch rises. He "trumpets" and elongates key words for emphasis. His mounting fervor both feeds and feeds upon that of the audience.

> And when this happens, when we allow freedom to ring, when we let it ring from every village and every hamlet, from every state and every city, we will be able to speed up that day when all of God's children, black men and white men, Jews and Gentiles, Protestants and Catholics, will be able to join hands and sing in the words of the old Negro spiritual, "Free at last! free at last! thank God Almighty, we are free at last!"
>
> *King (1963)*

With his voice and his words, Martin Luther King, Jr., persuaded others to share his own emotional state—they resonated with him on that day and many continue to do so today. In vocal science, resonance can refer to the ways sympathetic vibrations enrich the sound originated by vibrating vocal folds. And in society as well, people sometimes identify with or feel sympathetic to—resonate with—a master speaker or virtuoso vocalist.

Conclusion

New scientific studies on brain function have been on the upswing since about 1990, and the vocal instrument has received welcome attention. Our intuitions about why humans sing, both alone and together, are increasingly supported by scientific findings. In the past couple of decades, researchers have come ever closer to resolving disputes over the evolutionary "fitness advantage" of group vocalization among our hominid ancestors. The voice is at once a physical mechanism, a mark of individuality, and a persuasive tool, and authors such as Roland Barthes and George Rousseau have situated it in their philosophies of personality and wellness. With help from many new resources, the following chapter gives examples of ways an influential voice can play an important role in all stages of life.

Musical Illustration

"Aria (Cantilena)" from Villa-Lobos's *Bachianas Brasileras Number 5* (1938–45).

Rhetorical Illustration

Martin Luther King, Jr.'s "I Have a Dream" speech, www.usconstitution.net/dream.html, 3'33" and following.

Discussion Points

1. Compare and contrast the advantages of solo singing, on the one hand, and group singing, on the other, in human evolution.
2. Speculate on the ways humans might have used the singing voice in the time between the origin of our species (160,000 years ago) and the appearance of our earliest surviving musical instrument (created 30,000 years ago).
3. Analyze a speech, an advertisement, or a song for the ways the inflected voice contributes to persuasion, or effective delivery of linguistic content.

Notes

1   Scientists are divided over the lengths to which Thorpe's description might be applied to animal sounds.
2   Sequencing of the human genome was completed in 2003. That of the chimpanzee was completed in 2005, and the gorilla genome sequence was discovered in 2011.
3   Whether quadrupedal or bipedal, ancestral anatomy provided built-in opportunities to vocalize with the steady beat created, for example, when swaying from side to side. Instruments were not needed to implement a steady beat.
4   Attaching a fitness advantage to vocality is an extremely complex hypothesis and must take into account many factors, one of which is that songbirds, only distantly related to humans, are at least as vocal and as capable of vocal learning as humans are. Current science questions primate-centric evolutionary theory of language development, a research trajectory exemplified by Christopher I. Petkov and Erich D. Jarvis (2012).
5   Also see A.A. Ghazanfar et al. (2007).
6   Chapter 3 reviews several theories about the origins of singing, including that of Steven Mithen.
7   Orphic cults are discussed more fully in Chapter 6.
8   Kilmer, "The Discovery of an Ancient Mesopotamian Theory of Music," *Proceedings of the American Philosophical Society* 115.2 (22 April 1971), 148. See also Janet Smith's 2008 interview with Kilmer, at http://bellaromamusic.com/kilmersmith/kilmerint.html, accessed 20 November 2014.
9   This text addresses impulses and functions that may have created the need for instruments. See also Geiringer (1978) and Engel (1875).
10 *Grove Music Online*, s.v. "China, §III: Musical instruments," by Alan R. Thrasher et al., and s.v., "Egypt, §I: Ancient music," by Robert Anderson et al., accessed 28 December 2014.
11 *Grove Music Online*, s.v. "Mesopotamia," by Anne Kilmer, accessed 28 December 2014.
12 Exceptions include instruments used specifically for dance, such as non-pitched rattles and drums.
13 Vocal exchanges at birth are discussed more fully in Chapter 3.
14 See Schellenberg (2012) for a discussion of tonal languages and music.
15 Discussion of the brain is reserved for Chapter 2.
16 See Johns (2003).
17 My educational cohort, university music majors, often express that their self-images are inseparable from the instruments they play, and that they prefer the sounds of their cellos, pianos, or oboes to those of their physiological voices. Such a perspective may have influenced the early development of musical instruments.
18 A consortium of scientists in Europe and the UK have recently identified the portion of the brain that helps us recognize diverse voices. See von Kriegstein et al. (2012).

19 Chapter 3 elaborates on scientific evidence that babies begin to hear in the third trimester of gestation. Songs sung or stories read to the baby in utero appear to be recognizable to some neonates.

References

Barthes, R. 1977. "The Grain of the Voice." In *Image, Music, Text: Essays Selected and Translated by Stephen Heath*. London: Fontana/HarperCollins.

Burton, G. 1997. "What Is Rhetoric." *Silva Rhetoricae: The Forest of Rhetoric*, http://rhetoric. byu.edu/, accessed 28 December 2014.

Chitale, R. 2012. "Rachel Ray's Vocal Cords on the Mend." ABC News Medical Unit, http://abcnews.go.com/Health/Recipes/rachael-ray-remains-vocal-surgery/story?id= 8594826#.T-ONxL-3I-g, accessed 28 December 2014.

Engel, C. 1875. *Musical Instruments*. London: Chapman and Hall. Updated in 2004 as *Musical Instruments of the World* by Arum Joshi. Jaipur: ABD Publishers.

Fischer, R.A. 1930. *Genetical Theory of Natural Selection*. Oxford: Clarendon Press.

Fitch, W.T., and J. Giedd. 1999. "Morphology and Development of the Human Vocal Tract." *Journal of the Acoustic Society of America* 106.3: 1511–22.

Geiringer, K. 1978. *Instruments in the History of Western Music*. New York: Oxford University Press.

Geissmann, T. 2000. "Gibbon Songs and Human Music from an Evolutionary Perspective." In *The Origins of Music*, eds. N.L. Wallin, B. Merker, and S. Brown, 103–23. Cambridge, MA: MIT Press.

Ghazanfar, A.A., H.K. Turesson, J.X. Maier, R. van Dinther, R.D. Patterson, and N.K. Logothetis. 2007. "Vocal-Tract Resonances as Indexical Cues in Rhesus Monkeys." *Current Biology* 17.5: 425–30.

Gioia, T. 2006. *Healing Songs*. Durham, NC: Duke University Press.

Goldin-Meadow, S., and C. Mylander. 1984. "Gestural Communication in Deaf Children: The Effects and Non-effects of Parental Input on Early Language Development." *Monographs of the Society for Research in Child Development* 49.3–4: 1–151.

Johns, M.M. 2003. "Update on the Etiology, Diagnosis, and Treatment of Vocal Fold Nodules, Polyps, and Cysts." *Current Opinion in Otolaryngology and Head and Neck Surgery* 11.6: 456–61.

Kilmer, A.D. 1971. "The Discovery of an Ancient Mesopotamian Theory of Music." *Proceedings of the American Philosophical Society* 115.2: 148.

———. 1974. "The Cult Song with Music from Ancient Ugarit: Another Interpretation." *Revue d'Assyriologie et d'Archologie Orientale* 68.1: 69–82.

King, Jr., Martin Luther. 1963. "I Have a Dream." 3'33" and following, www.usconstitution. net/dream.html, accessed 28 December 2014.

Kriegstein, K. von, D.R.R. Smith, R.D. Patterson, S.J. Kiebel, and T.D. Griffiths. 2010. "How the Human Brain Recognizes Speech in the Context of Changing Speakers." *Journal of Neuroscience* 30.2: 629–38.

Lipkind, D., G.F. Marcus, D.K. Bemis, K. Sasahara, N. Jacoby, M. Takahasi, K. Suzuki, O. Feher, P. Ravbar, K. Okanoya, and O. Tchernichovski. 2013. Letter: "Stepwise Acquisition of Vocal Combinatorial Capacity in Songbirds and Human Infants." *Nature* 498: 104–8.

Miller, G. 2000. "Evolution of Human Music through Sexual Selection." In *The Origins of Music*, eds. N.L. Wallin, B. Merker, and S. Brown, 329–60. Cambridge, MA: MIT Press.

Ovid. *Metamorphoses*, Book 10 (1st century CE). 1922. Translated by Brookes More. Boston, MA: Cornhill. *Theoi Greek Mythology*, www.theoi.com/Text/OvidMetamorphoses10. html, accessed 28 December 2014.

Petkov, C.I., and E.D. Jarvis. 2012. "Birds, Primates, and Spoken Language Origins: Behavioral Phenotypes and Neurobiological Substrates." *Frontiers in Evolutionary Neuroscience* 4.12. DOI: 10.3389/fnevo.2012.00012, accessed 28 December 2014.

Rousseau, G. 2000. "The Inflected Voice: Attraction and Curative Properties." In *Musical Healing in Cultural Contexts*, ed. Penelope Gouk, 92–112. Aldershot: Ashgate.

Sachs, C. 1940. *The History of Musical Instruments*. New York: W.W. Norton.

Schellenberg, M. 2012. "Does Language Determine Music in Tone Languages?" *Ethnomusicology* 56.2: 266–78.

Schneider, A. "Ice-Age Musicians Fashioned Ivory Flute: A 30,000-Year-Old Instrument Is Uncovered in Germany." *Nature*, online 17 December 2004, www.nature.com/news/2004/041217/full/news041213-14.html, accessed 28 December 2014.

Thorpe, W.H. 1961. *Bird-Song: The Biology of Vocal Communication and Expression in Birds*. Cambridge, UK: Cambridge University Press.

Titze, I. 2008. "The Human Instrument." *Scientific American* 8.1: 94–101.

———. 2010. "Voice and Speech." *National Center for Voice and Speech*, www.ncvs.org/ncvs/tutorials/voiceprod/tutorial/quality.html, accessed 28 December 2014.

Tobias, J.A., and N. Seddon. 2009. "Signal Jamming Mediates Sexual Conflict in a Duetting Bird." *Current Biology* 19: 577–82.

Wallin, N.L. 2000. "An Introduction to Evolutionary Musicology." In *The Origins of Music*, eds. N.L. Wallin, B. Merker, and S. Brown, 3–24. Cambridge, MA: MIT Press.

2

NEURAL MAPPING AND BRAIN CHEMISTRY

How Singing Is Good for You

> Irrespective of the exact nature of the information being the attention's focus, voice stimuli are proposed to recruit processes not activated by other, non-vocal sounds. In other words, voices are "special" for the brain.
>
> *Belin et al. (2011, 712–13)*

The idea that singing is good for you might qualify as a "so what" thesis—those who sing know the benefits and can offer first-hand evidence that singing enriches life. Though the human brain is vastly complex, psychologists and therapists have known for ages that singing works in some therapies when other therapeutic methods do not. In chapters 4, 5, and 6, I spend considerable time on behaviors and mental operations—psychological aspects—associated with singing's role in group bonding, in helping dementia sufferers, and in supporting religious experience, respectively. Those chapters rely on the work of psychologists who have negotiated the complex area of evaluating human motivations and rewards in order to assess the value placed on singing experiences. Psychology and its related musical discipline, music therapy, revolve around understanding the meanings associated with singing.

This chapter focuses, instead, on a scientific area that is a relative newcomer to singing studies. Increasingly with new technologies, neuroscientists are able to observe many of the physiological brain changes produced by singing and listening to voices.[1] Perhaps separately from the good feelings it produces, singing initiates neural activity that can positively affect brain function. These neurological findings are especially important because they have helped validate behavioral interventions like music therapy, the successes of which were rarely respected by the medical community. Clinical findings since 1990 have elevated the status of musical therapy and reinforced the many behavioral and physiological benefits of singing. Chapter 1 of this book summarized the mechanism of phonation—the several points between the glottis and the teeth utilized in singing—the breath, and the voice's roles in human experience. This chapter describes three areas of imaging and neurochemistry relating to the driving aspect of vocal perception and production, the brain.

As stated in the Preface, I am a musical professional and, therefore, my perspective is that of a medical "outsider" making every effort to understand the general implications of burgeoning research that is clearly relevant to my area of expertise. With that caveat in mind, this chapter is but a sampling of newer neuroscientific evidence that addresses benefits of singing. To conclude, I review a few ways that singing's good effect has been used to address modern problems. As it has throughout human history, singing helps us respond creatively to a challenging world.

Antecedents and Milestones in Neurological Research

Descriptions of musical disturbances linked to brain damage date back to the nineteenth century; a brief summary of landmarks is appropriate here (Zatorre 1998, Zatorre and Baum 2012). Though historic findings in neuroscience rarely specified singing as the research target, the field would eventually provide insights about singing and cognition. Jean-Baptiste Bouillaud (1796–1881) published discoveries that helped locate musical centers of the brain in 1865. Well into the twentieth century, descriptions of the brain's complicated landscape were based on post-mortem study of disease- or trauma-induced brain lesions. Pioneering researchers such as Paul Broca (1824–80), who connected loss of speech with damage to the left frontal cortex, necessarily waited for their patients to die in order to gather conclusive evidence. In 1920, Salmon E. Henschen (1847–1930) contributed important findings on amusia (absence or loss of music perception) (Bouillaud 1865 and Henschen 1920). The development of antiseptics by Joseph Lister (1827–1912) and others would ultimately facilitate safer surgical exposure of the brain. These advances allowed neurologists to stimulate specific cortical regions and thus continue the mapping process using living subjects.

Post-surgical patient observation has also contributed a crucial body of research to our understanding of brain functions. British cognitive specialist Brenda Milner (b. 1918) pioneered the field of behavioral neuroscience. Early in her career, Milner received an unusual invitation to be the psychologist for neurosurgeon Wilder Penfield (1891–1976) at Montréal Neurological Institute. In that position, Milner studied patients pre- and post-operatively (Xia 2006). She published the first report on musical deficits after brain surgery in 1962 (Milner 1962). Behavioral findings were still considered marginal in the search to understand brain functions, however.

"During the second half of the 20th century", writes Savoy, "a collection of relatively non-invasive tools for assessing and localizing human brain function in healthy volunteers . . . led to an explosion of research in what is now termed 'Brain Mapping'" (Savoy 2001). When asked in 2006 how she might integrate her life's work into a system, Milner first addressed the lesion method and functional brain imaging.

You need both. With the lesion approach, you have someone who has had a permanent effect of this specific lesion . . . and you can know that the damaged structures were in some way critical to this kind of ability. With brain imaging, you can say that when this person is doing some kind of task, these areas light up. But you don't know which of these areas are really critical to the performance of the task and which are simply incidental. So you really need both approaches.

Quoted in Xia (2006, 171)

Milner's perspective is an important reminder that progressive technology rarely supplants older observation methods entirely.[2]

Physiological brain research continued with non-invasive imaging technologies such as trans-cranial magnetic stimulation, first used successfully in 1985. Modern brain mapping relies on electromagnetic recording and hemodynamic responses to neural activity: PET (1973) or CAT scan (Nobel prize, 1979), MRI (1970s), functional fMRI (1990s), or multi-modal neural imagery (e.g., combining MRI and EEG, 2000s). Each of these methods has spawned elaborate networks of applications. A summary of fMRI neuroimaging methods, for example, may be found in an article by Peter A. Bandettini, chief of the Section on Functional Imaging Methods at the National Institute of Mental Health (Bandettini 2009).

Today, especially because of groundwork laid by Milner and others, physiological and psychological researchers cooperate to an unprecedented extent. The foremost center for interdisciplinary research on music and the brain in North America, if not the world, is located in Montréal. Isabelle Peretz, professor of psychology and chair of the University of Montréal's International Laboratory for Brain, Music, and Sound Research, and Robert Zatorre, professor of neurology and neurosurgery based at the Montréal Neurological Institute and co-director of McGill University's International Laboratory for Brain, Music, and Sound Research, are international leaders and collaborators (Peretz and Zatorre 2003).[3] Their independent and collaborative research exemplifies the benefits of multidisciplinary approaches in fully understanding the ways the brain processes music.

In the final decades of the twentieth century, few outside the scientific community knew about neuroscientific breakthroughs unless an illness or pathology required a brain scan. Oliver Sacks (b. 1933) was among the first neurologists to report connections between neuroscience and music, in language understandable to the general reader.[4] In *A Leg to Stand On* (1984), Sacks described the aftermath of a traumatic leg injury he sustained while hiking in Norway. Alone and with a broken leg, Sacks recalled that, after several false starts, "melody, rhythm, and music" came to his aid, gave him an internal cadence, and helped him to travel down a mountain trail with a shattered leg.

Before crossing the stream, I had *muscled* myself along—moving by main force, with my very strong arms. Now, so to speak, I was *musicked* along. I did not contrive this. It happened to me. I fell into a rhythm, guided by a sort of marching or rowing song, sometimes the Volga Boatmen's Song, sometimes a monotonous chant of my own, accompanied by these words "*Ohne Haste, ohne Rast!*" . . . (Without haste, without rest!). Never had Goethe's words been put to better use! Now, I no longer had to think about going too fast or too slow. I got into the music, got into the swing, and this ensured that my tempo was right. I found myself perfectly coordinated by the rhythm—or perhaps subordinated would be a better term: the musical beat was generated within me, and all my muscles responded obediently—all save those in my left leg which seemed silent—or mute?

Sacks (1984, 13)[5]

So memory provided the music that facilitated his rescue. Elsewhere, Sacks chronicled the experiences of patients for whom music embedded in the brain became torture (Sacks 1970).[6] More recent case studies recount the ways temporal entrainment, for example, allowed music to suggest a gait rhythm for Parkinson's patients (Sacks 2007).

Since 1990, advances in behavioral neuroscience and brain mapping have caused researchers worldwide to think differently about music and singing. Still, the human brain is too complex for scientists to reach complete consensus, a fact illustrated in Figure 2.1. Regarding the area originally defined by Paul Broca, Bruno Dubuc writes: "Though many authors regard Broca's area as consisting of Brodmann areas 44 and 45, other authors say it consists only of area 44, still others only of area 45, and yet others of areas 44, 45, and 47" (Dubuc 2013).[7]

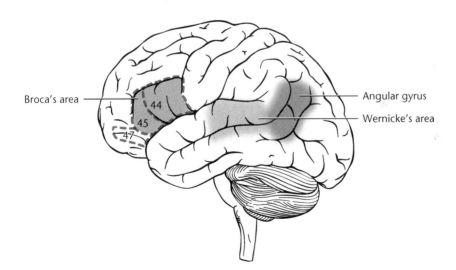

FIGURE 2.1 Broca's and Wernicke's areas of the brain, with several of Brodmann's areas numbered. Art by Jane Whitney, BSc, AAM.

Despite these complexities, the implications of which are not yet fully known even to the scientist, each year brings a wealth of potential evidence to support my thesis that singing wields considerable power over the "human condition" (Grau-Sánchez et al. 2013). Irrefutable evidence of the fact may be obtained from another behavioral discipline, music therapy.

Music Therapy and Medical Environments

The modern profession of music therapy (MT) developed after the First World War, when musicians played in veterans' hospitals, hoping to alleviate patient suffering. Though its purview goes well beyond singing, MT was marginalized in medical hospitals through much of the twentieth century. Still, board-certified music therapists worked in a range of other locations: psychiatric hospitals, rehabilitative facilities, outpatient clinics, day-care treatment centers, agencies serving developmentally disabled persons, community mental health centers, drug and alcohol programs, senior centers, nursing homes, hospice programs, correctional facilities, halfway houses, schools, and private practice. Several factors—the work of countless individual therapists, university MT professors and degree-granting departments, members of burgeoning national and international societies, and increased openness to alternative medicine—have led to greater general awareness of music therapy's benefits. The year 1994 saw the inclusion of music therapy services under the Partial Hospitalization Program in the US, and currently "three states—Michigan, Minnesota, and Indiana—provide Medicaid coverage for the music therapy treatments of children with developmental disabilities" (Xu 2011). Influential hospitals have established music therapy units that offer non-invasive, musical alternatives to standard medical drug therapies.

Noted music therapist Joanne Loewy is director of the Louis Armstrong Center for Music and Medicine at Beth Israel Medical Center in New York and founder, in 1994, of its Department of Music Therapy. That program's clinical research initiatives have improved the lives of patients in neonatal intensive care units and those experiencing chronic obstructive pulmonary disease (COPD), asthma, cardiovascular disease, infusion therapy, and spine surgery (Mount Sinai/Beth Israel 2012). Other noteworthy MT departments associated with children's hospitals in the US are now too numerous to mention.[8] Currently, the American Music Therapy Association's website lists professional MT organizations in Australia, Austria, Brazil, Canada, Denmark, Finland, Germany, Hong Kong, Korea, New Zealand, Switzerland, Taiwan, and the United Kingdom. The World Federation for Music Therapy adds member organizations in Argentina, Chile, Colombia, France, Netherlands, Singapore, and Spain to the total. By all accounts, this is one of the most exciting times to date for the music therapy profession worldwide (American Music Therapy Association 2014).[9]

Music therapists are old hands at utilizing singing to improve quality of life. Their widely documented successes include gains for people living with severe and enduring mental illness, mothers and their preterm infants in neonatal intensive care units, patients with emphysema, and bereaved children (Grocke et al. 2009, Cevasco 2008, Engen 2005, and Roberts 2006, respectively). Familiar as that life-changing work may be to musicians, therapists, and parents, medical professionals are not often trained to appreciate music therapy and its successes. I had a chance to apply what I have learned from this research the day after a moderate, hemorrhagic stroke profoundly affected my mother's movement and speech in 2011. Hospital staff encouraged her to try walking and talking. After a few unsuccessful attempts, she found a gait rhythm from "Onward, Christian Soldiers," which I sang as I held both her hands and walked backward as she took her first steps forward. An hour or so later, she strung her first words together by singing "Happy Birthday" and "Amazing Grace" with me. Intuitive and caring medical professionals in her stroke ICU were singularly unimpressed by the contributions of singing in both cases. Their experiences assured them that her speech and gait would return sooner or later, but for the bewildered post-stroke patient "sooner" was facilitated through song. These experiences are amply documented in behavioral and, increasingly, in clinical research (Schauer and Mauritz 2003).[10] New medical studies point to a sea change in the perception of singing's capacity to ameliorate clinical symptoms. Specifically, singing has joined the therapeutic tool kit for chronic respiratory disease/COPD, combative and/or disoriented dementia patients, irritable bowel syndrome patients, and amnesia, to name a few examples.[11]

Several medical researchers have begun to coordinate tried-and-true music therapy methodologies with brain science. Among them are Hillecke et al. (2005), who offered five general factors that contribute to the success of music therapy. Music can

1. capture attention and thereby distract from symptoms such as pain,
2. change emotional outlook through its effect on the limbic and paralimbic brain regions and help symptoms such as depression,
3. change processes of cognition related to memory and other cognitive function,
4. modify behavior such as walking, and
5. positively affect communication.

Simply put, musical activity engages more areas of the brain than analogous, non-musical activity does. Listening to music, including singing and chanting, activates a greater number of regions than listening to speech, playing a musical instrument is processed in more diverse brain areas than playing cards, and singing has a more widespread effect on the brain than speaking. Does the multifaceted cognition generated by singing give it greater therapeutic potential than speech therapy alone? Apparently so, as one group of researchers affirms: because memory tasks utilizing music and/or singing naturally involve more areas of the brain, those tasks create memories that seem "more resilient to neurological deficits (e.g., dementia or Alzheimer disease) than nonmusical memory" (Thaut et al. 2005, 249).[12]

Measuring brain activation while singing and speaking has attracted several researchers. Among them is music therapist Michael Thaut, professor of music and neuroscience at Colorado State University, and director of the University's Center for Biomedical Research in Music (Thaut 2005). While singing and speaking both stimulate the rhythm and reading centers in the left hemisphere, singing also involves the right hemisphere, where pitch and melodic patterns are processed. And though reading written language and reading music activate regions in the right hemisphere that are near each other, those locations are not identical. Reading music also activates the angular gyrus (see Figure 2.1).[13] Singing's more widespread brain involvement might explain how it can help institute or recapture meaningful speech in an aphasic patient.

In 2006, Callan and colleagues summarized the promises and caveats relating to differences in brain function while speaking and while singing, before reporting on their own experiment (discussed below) (Callan et al. 2006, 1328). They reiterated, for example, that someone who suffers a left-hemisphere stroke might be able to utilize unaffected regions of the right hemisphere, where singing usually resides, to recapture spoken language. But that equation cannot be universally applied, since each stroke is as unique as that patient's brain. Further, lateralization of brain function is related to handedness. So utilizing singing for language rehabilitation after left-hemisphere stroke holds most promise for right-handed individuals. That being said, some right-handed patients with left-hemisphere strokes suffer no aphasia; for others, the damage to the left hemisphere is so extensive that music's capacity to facilitate word production is lost. But singing's greater involvement in brain regions "involved with reward (nucleus accumbens, posterior cingulate, orbital cortex, parahippocampal gyrus) than [those involved] for a speaking task . . . suggests a greater emotional component involved in processing [of singing]" (Callan et al. 2006, 1358).

Emotional engagement in a subject can support learning, as any teacher will attest. An individualized approach is therefore essential when assessing the best therapies for each case of aphasia caused by stroke. Led by the patient's personal history and musical preferences, music therapy has spearheaded the use of therapeutic singing as an accessible, non-invasive option for memory or speech therapies with marked success. In the plainest of terms, it never hurts to try singing.

Several experimental conditions—singing aloud vs. "mental" singing, singing vowels vs. words, singing harmony vs. melody, and brain activation of professional vs. untrained singers—have been compared in clinical research. Callan and colleagues utilized functional magnetic brain imaging (fMRI) to study brain activity while subjects listened to speech, listened to singing, covertly spoke, and covertly sang.[14] They found "a significant difference between singing and speech . . . in the right [inferior frontal gyrus] for the covert production [or 'mental singing'] task; however, no difference was found for the listening task" (Callan et al. 2006, 1339). These findings have important implications for any culture in which passive listening is more prevalent than active musical participation. Where music therapists are unavailable or not covered by health insurance, family or non-musician caregivers need the experience and confidence to try singing in order to "reach" loved ones for whom normal communication has failed. Following is a more detailed look at research on neuroplasticity, the mirror neuron system, and the hormone oxytocin, all of which implicate singing in positive outcomes.

Neuroplasticity

In 1969, a physician named Paul Bach-y-Rita (1934–2006) conducted the first experiments disproving the widely held conviction that the human brain remains unchanged throughout adulthood. In his words:

> My father had made a dramatic recovery from a major stroke with a home program developed by my brother. After my father's death from [another] stroke seven years later . . . the autopsy revealed that recovery had taken place despite very extensive brain damage [from the first stroke].
>
> *Bach-y-Rita (2005, 190)*

Healthy regions of the father's brain had taken over functions once controlled by stroke-damaged areas.

Today, neuroplasticity—the brain's lifelong capacity to reorganize neural pathways based on new experiences—is the well-documented domain of noted researchers, especially Gottfried Schlaug, director of Harvard University's Music Neuroimaging Laboratory and Stroke Recovery Laboratory, and professor of neurology at Beth Israel Deaconess Medical Center and Harvard Medical School (Schlaug 2010). In a 2010 podcast, Schlaug specified one hypothesis that has driven his work: "music-making might potentially change the structure and function of multi-modal integration regions in the brain" (Gaser and Schlaug 2003). Because musicians integrate sophisticated auditory and motor activities, regions in their brains such as the inferior frontal gyrus have rich connections with both the motor and the auditory systems. Across several studies, Schlaug found a difference in this region when comparing adult non-musicians' brains and the brains of adult musicians.

What good is this alteration of brain structure? In a 2011 National Public Radio interview with Richard Knox, Schlaug spoke about melodic intonation therapy (MIT), a singing-based modality that helps aphasics recapture speech after traumas such as stroke or head injury (Schlaug 2011). He recounted the experiences of Laurel Fontaine, who at age eleven had a massive stroke that destroyed 80 percent of the left side of her brain. Standard speech therapy had done little to improve her loss of spoken language, but fifteen weeks of MIT, about a year after the stroke, literally restructured Fontaine's right hemisphere and eventually helped restore her speech (Norton et al. 2009). According to Schlaug, "it is the perfect confirmation [of our hypothesis]—basically, the hardware of the system really changed to support this increased vocal output." And while Fontaine's youth is one factor in her success, Schlaug added that "we know that patients even in their eighties can show plastic changes to their brain—can show adaptations."[15]

Singing has been found beneficial in other studies of brain plasticity as well. In 2005, Thaut, Peterson and McIntosh reported on an experiment that measured the ways music could positively influence memory tasks (Thaut et al. 2005). They posed the question "whether external timing embedded in learning stimuli, via music, can modulate oscillatory synchrony in learning-related neural networks, that is, induce brain plasticity." In their trial, they measured brain activity and memorization success when subjects used verbal memory alone to study word lists and when the same words were studied as lyrics to a song (Thaut et al. 2005, 244, 252). In the first of three trials, Thaut and colleagues found that singing

> contributed an organizational/chunking role of the learning items, and although the left frontal gyrus is associated with cue-based retrieval of words from long-term memory, patients with left frontal damage recruited the right inferior frontal gyrus for the same task.
>
> *Thaut et al. (2005, 247)*[16]

In other words, singing can help break data into memorable portions and access substitute pathways for memory tasks.

The researchers repeated the procedure in a second experiment, but measured the cognition process by analyzing electroencephalographic spectral power during learning and memory retrieval of word lists. Again, they found that "only music facilitation of verbal learning was associated with increased neuronal synchronization" and, further, that singing "induces a statistically higher degree of temporal coherence in coupled neuronal cell assemblies than a spoken stimulus without explicit or implicit regulated temporal structure" (Thaut et al. 2005, 249). Though difficult to conceptualize for laypersons, singing's time-based structure has a beneficial effect on "intrinsic neural time coding of learning-related cell ensembles in the brain." If cognition is imagined as a series of electrical relay switches, then singing helps achieve optimal timing of the relays.

These studies notwithstanding, instrumental music, because it involves other layers of motor activity, and music listening rather than musical participation currently receive a great deal of scientific attention, while brain plasticity experiments involving singing are more abundant among songbird researchers (Janata et al. 2002; Brainard and Doupe 2002). Still, singing-based therapies such as MIT have had substantial success in improving speech and memory.

Mirror Neuron System Theory

In the 1980s and 1990s, a group of neurophysiologists at the University of Parma, Italy, noticed that certain neurons in the premotor and parietal cortex of a macaque fired when it reached for food, but also when this type of monkey observed a person pick up the food (Di Pellegrino et al. 1992). In similar fashion, human infants readily imitate facial expressions, mirror movements, or mimic sounds. Beyond mere parroting, however, "the mirror neuron system has been proposed as a mechanism allowing an individual to understand the *meaning and intention* of a communicative signal by evoking a representation of that signal in the perceiver's own brain" (Molnar-Szakacs and Overy 2006, 235, emphasis mine). Implications for empathy and imitative learning have been proposed. Still, the mirror neuron hypothesis is strenuously debated. Emerging research has launched intriguing theories that have yet to receive unanimous acceptance in the neurological community; nonetheless, mirror neurons may explain several ways singing improves certain disorders or conditions.

Molnar-Szakacs and Overy report several neuroimaging studies showing that the human fronto-parietal mirror neuron system (MNS) is engaged during action observation and imitation (Molnar-Szakacs and Overy 2006, 235). In 2006, they reviewed research findings about the MNS and suggested it might be a central mediator for several aspects of musical experience. They reiterated that human observers recruit their own motor systems when involved in the perception–action work facilitated by the MNS. In other words, we may use the same neural resources to represent and understand the actions of others as when we perform our own actions; this simulation mechanism is automatic and non-conscious. Such a neural system suggests the possibility of neurologically "experiencing" the mind of the other or, as the expression would have it, virtually to "walk in another's shoes" (see Figure 2.2).

What makes music different from any other sound stimulus for the MNS? As illustrated in Figure 2.2, the music we hear activates brain cells dedicated to recognizing purposeful, intentional, and organized stimuli. As expressed by Molnar-Szakacs and Overy, "structural features of the 'motion' information conveyed by the musical signal" are combined with the auditory signal "in the posterior inferior frontal gyrus (Brodmann Area 44) and adjacent premotor cortex." This occurs partially because of a "shared and temporally synchronous recruitment of similar neural mechanisms in the sender and the perceiver of the musical message" (Molnar-Szakacs and Overy 2006, 237). The perceiver's MNS may metaphorically resonate, or vibrate sympathetically, with heard music. In the physical world, sound waves cause a glass goblet to vibrate sympathetically with a singer's voice, or undampened piano strings to resonate with a dog's bark. In the brain, synchronization is less direct, but no less real. Molnar-Szakacs and Overy write:

> The success of music/speech therapy methods such as Melodic Intonation Therapy (MIT) [a highly imitative speech therapy technique based on singing], might thus be due, at least in part, to the fact that their imitative elements involve a direct transfer of sensory information to a motor plan,

leading to a strong recruitment and co-activation of brain regions involved in the perception and production of both music and language.

Molnar-Szakacs and Overy (2006, 237, 238)

Variables such as individual musical training offer multiple avenues for refinement, but some researchers believe that singing clearly activates the mirror neuron system whether we sing along or simply listen to someone else sing. Further, the MNS is perhaps involved with representation of emotions that provide connections with others. Not only do we respond to singing, but we also have the capacity to care about the words we sing or the words sung to us.

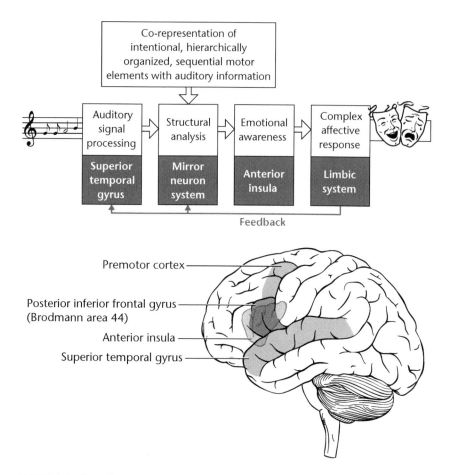

FIGURE 2.2 The mirror neuron system, as proposed by Molnar-Szakacs and Overy. Permission courtesy Istvan Molnar-Szakacs, Katie Overy, and Oxford University Press for *Social Cognitive and Affective Neuroscience* (2006), 237 (adapted). Art by Jane Whitney, BSc, AAM.

Psychologist Stefan Koelsch gave "A Neuroscientific Perspective on Music Therapy" in 2009 that helps the layperson understand the implications of these discoveries in everyday life. In general:

> Perception–action ("mirror") mechanisms are relevant for music therapy, because these mechanisms serve the learning of actions, the understanding of actions, and the prediction of actions of others . . . activation and training of perception–action mechanisms can be used in patients with neurologic disorders.
>
> *Koelsch (2009, 380–1)*

The MNS may also contribute to the successes Broca's aphasia patients experience with melodic intonation therapy (Schlaug et al. 2009).

Singing can help various forms of disrupted speech fluency such as stuttering. England's King George VI, the subject of an Oscar-winning film entitled *The King's Speech*, famously benefited from Lionel Logue's speech therapy, which included singing words the King had trouble speaking (Farndale 2011). Country music singer Mel Tillis exhibits great fluency while singing but significant impairment while speaking, and a host of other celebrities with earlier speech disfluencies— actor Marilyn Monroe, opera singer Robert Merrill, and singer/songwriter Carly Simon, to name a few—rose above those impediments. While researchers in 1976 concluded that "changes in vocalization cannot account for all of the decrease in stuttering that occurs during singing," they were unable to offer a fuller hypothesis to explain singing's benefits (Healey et al. 1976).

Nearly forty years later, the cerebral origins of stuttering still elude neurologists, but several interesting findings have emerged whose benefits are unclear. For example, the misfire located somewhere in the central nervous system which causes stuttering can be temporarily overridden when patients engage in choral speech—speaking in unison with another person. In 2003 and 2004, Saltuklaroglu and colleagues proposed that the MNS is implicated in this phenomenon (Saltuklaroglu et al. 2004, 437). Unfortunately, though choral speaking is the most effective block to stuttering, disfluency returns immediately when choral speaking ends. Choral speaking is impractical for longer-term improvement, so researchers have attempted to delve further into the involvement of the MNS in speech therapy.

Traditional speech therapies, while tremendously effective, sometimes produce an undesirable "therapeutic signature," i.e., slower-than-normal speech that lacks natural inflection. Newer speech therapies stress more prosodic speech because the chances of engaging mirror neurons and ensuring longer-term, stutter-free expression seem to be proportional to the extent of perceptual deviation from normal speech patterns (Saltuklaroglu et al. 2004, 440–1, 445). The continued engagement of mirror neurons appears to be the best means of overriding stuttering, inducing fluent speech in those who stutter, and curbing relapse rates associated with therapeutic interventions. Again, melodic intonation therapy, which capitalizes on neuroplasticity, provides benefits in recapturing language in aphasia and also offers practice in cultivating that more resilient "inflected voice."[17]

The mirror neuron system holds promise for other disabilities as well. The US Centers for Disease Control state that about one in eighty-eight children has been identified to have an autism spectrum disorder (ASD), one of a group of developmental disabilities "characterized by impairments in social interaction and communication and by restricted, repetitive, and stereotyped patterns of behavior" (Centers for Disease Control 2008). Music's capacity to involve the mirror neuron system in improving interactive and communicative issues within ASD makes it a promising avenue for experimentation.[18] Higher-level functions associated with the MNS—imitation and imitation learning, perceiving someone else's intentions, feeling empathy, utilizing language, and representing the self verbally—are deficient in some cases of autism (Molnar-Szakacs et al. 2009). Such deficits have profound effects on childhood and adolescence, where peer cooperation, friendships, and interaction shape daily life. However, many people on the autism spectrum experience a natural attraction to music, and while the abilities of some to judge the feelings of another person may be impaired, Heaton and colleagues showed in 1999 that children with ASD do not differ from neurotypical children in their abilities to perceive happy and sad affect in musical excerpts (Heaton et al. 1999). Molnar-Szakacs and colleagues (2009) explain that the mirror neuron system

> may become sufficiently engaged for children with ASD to move from the appreciation of musical sound patterns to the appreciation of the emotional state of the agent making them; an agent who appears to behave in predictable, familiar ways that are comforting and companionable, rather than confusing. While the social world with its lack of predictability is often confusing and even frightening for the individual with ASD, the predictable patterns typically found in musical stimuli may provide a reassuring and foreseeable avenue for emotion processing . . . Some of the areas of improvement included: increased appropriate social behaviors and decreased inappropriate, stereotypical, and self stimulatory behaviors; increased verbalizations, gestures, and comprehension; and increased communicative acts and engagement with others, among other positive effects.
>
> *Molnar-Szacaks et al. (2009, 92–3)*

Improved socialization is not the only area currently under investigation. Many non-speaking autistic children can sing, and singing has also been shown to elicit speech in children through the use of auditory-motor mapping training (Wan, Demaine et al. 2010, and Wan, Rüber et al. 2010). Researchers mentioned in this section (and others) continue their pursuit of understanding in this area. Molnar-Szakacs and Heaton have reinforced other findings that failed to find emotion recognition deficits in people with ASD. This counters earlier findings that the mirror neuron system in autistic children is "broken"; instead, recruitment of the mirror neuron system allows children with ASD to experience and understand emotional music (Molnar-Szakacs and Heaton 2012).

Oxytocin

Along with neural mapping, relatively recent advances in brain chemistry have better elucidated our love affair with singing. The brain hormone oxytocin (OT) is part of a "suite" of similar compounds, including serotonin and dopamine, that coordinate stress responses and social behaviors (MacDonald and MacDonald 2010). Oxytocin, whose name stems from "quick birth" in Greek, was isolated and synthesized in 1953 by Vincent du Vigneaud (Nobel Prize in Chemistry, 1955). Brain OT plays an important role in the regulation of male and female sexual behavior (Neumann 2008, 860.) Generated in the hypothalamus (see Figure 2.3), it

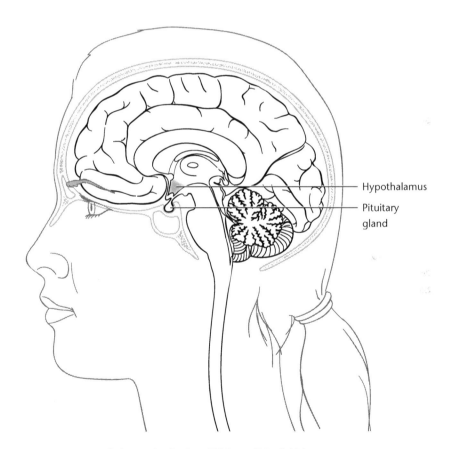

FIGURE 2.3 Hypothalamus. Art by Jane Whitney, BSc, AAM.

acts as a central neurotransmitter/neuromodulator and a peripheral hormone and can affect gene expression and local blood flow, among other things.[19] Evolutionary biologists write that oxytocin has persisted in vertebrates and invertebrates for at least 700 million years, with few modifications. Such longevity suggests essential functions in the human body.

During most of the sixty-odd years since it was isolated, oxytocin was associated only with sexual arousal, pregnancy, birth, lactation, and postpartum mother/child bonding. This neuropeptide also plays an essential role in the "let-down" reflex of lactation (Neville 1998).

According to C. Sue Carter, the association between oxytocin and childbirth "long kept scientists from taking it seriously." She suggests its implications in new experimental conditions measuring economic and financial situations—for example, the way trust is reflected in the brain of a financial investor—made new oxytocin studies "very hot" (quoted in Angier 2009). Oxytocin is expressed after contact with trusted beings of the same species to mitigate the fight/flight response. Macdonald and Macdonald referenced a few studies with male populations in which the administration of intranasal oxytocin biased decision making in consistently prosocial directions; additionally, they noted several studies reporting success using a nasal spray containing OT with post-traumatic stress disorder patients. Fathers of autistic children have also been examined under the effects of intranasal oxytocin (Naber et al. 2013). OT may also help in reading non-verbal social cues including facial expressions, which has led to some research on the future usage of oxytocin with people profoundly affected by autism (Marazziti and Catena Dell'osso 2008). Some theorists regard singing and music as catalysts for the release of this neuropeptide in human evolution. Walter Freeman wrote that as humans created, manipulated, and mastered the effects of various types of music, it became "a human technology for crossing the solipsistic gulf," or a way to reconnect through group experience what increasing individuation had removed from ancient group living (Freeman 2000, 420).

A group led by Christina Grape and Töres Theorell at the Stress Research section of the Karolinska Institute in Stockholm conducted some compelling research in 2002 (Grape et al. 2002). They recorded serum concentrations of OT in two experimental groups—amateur and professional singers—after singing lessons. Both groups showed elevated serum OT levels and both groups self-reported feeling relaxed and energetic after the lessons.[20] Amateurs also self-reported joy and elation, while the "pros" left the lesson feeling less exuberant. Professional singers are likely more self-critical than amateurs.

Grape and colleagues also evaluated heart rate variability (HRV) and found that professional singers were better able to maintain consistent HRV than amateurs were.[21] Researchers also measured several endocrinological/biochemical markers in both groups. Serum cortisol (a stress marker) collected thirty minutes before and thirty minutes after the singing lesson decreased after the lesson in the amateur group, but not in the professional group. Significantly, serum oxytocin increased in both groups after the lesson, and plasma oxytocin also increased for both groups (Grape et al. 2002, 70).

At the same research location, a group conducted a study involving patients with irritable bowel syndrome (IBS) and several markers associated with that stress-related illness (Grape et al. 2009).[22] In a randomized controlled trial measuring serum concentrations of various disease markers, IBS patients were recruited and randomized into a choir singing (n = 28) or a conversation (n = 27) group. Singing experiences took place once a week for a year. About half the subjects finished the study (11–14 subjects in each group). Ultimately, the singing group fared better than the conversation group. In their summary the researchers wrote: "Our findings motivate studies examining the choir singing hypothesis in relation to stress-related conditions," and further:

> After one year the development of gastrointestinal pain tended . . . to have been better in the choir group. The motilin concentration tended to decrease in the choir group and increase in the other group . . . The fibrinogen concentration increased in the information group but not in the choir group . . . Both fibrinogen and VEGF (vascular endothelial growth factor) increased significantly in both groups. There were no significant findings for cholecystokinin.
>
> *Grape et al. (2009, 224)*

In a 2010 report related to the 2009 article, the researchers addressed the IBS study's weakness—a small experimental group and attrition in both groups prior to the twelve month mark—but reiterated their primary finding, "a clear indication that choir singing once a week induces a state of stimulated regeneration during the first half-year in IBS patients" (Grape, Theorell et al. 2010). Choral singing has also been studied at the Center for Lifespan Psychology in the Max Planck Institute for Human Development in Berlin (Müller and Lindenberger 2011).[23]

Conclusion

These medical findings provide a backdrop for understanding why singing "works" in stressful life situations. In *Doing Something Different*, Thorana Nelson offered a collection of stories by solution-focused practitioners of counseling, therapy, training, and life coaching. A handful of the seventy-six stories reference something called "the miracle question." For example, imagine that a miracle will occur tonight and when you arrive at work tomorrow, all your problems with your boss will be solved. What is the first thing you will notice about the atmosphere at work that will indicate the miracle has occurred?

Mark Mitchell's contribution was entitled "A Singing Miracle": "suppose the miracle happened or was starting to happen and you started singing a song the next day. What song would you be singing that would tell you that the miracle was starting to happen?" Mitchell raised this question during a debriefing session with high school students amid the 1991 Los Angeles riots. One student answered, "I would know a miracle happened if we had gotten past this stuff [rioting on campus] and were singing."

Mitchell: "And what would we be singing that would tell us the miracle was starting to happen?"
Student: "We would be singing 'We Shall Overcome.'"

"So," Mitchell writes, "I suggested that we try singing the song. The group responded and sang. It was a very emotional moment in a dramatic situation" (Mitchell 2010, 53–4).

In this hypothetical situation, imagining resolution through singing has the potential to recruit the brain's mirror neuron system so that people can visualize and perhaps even experience a new reality for a while. At the very least, imagin-ing resolution helps reframe the status quo. Such visualization aided by singing might activate the mirror neuron system and motivate creative efforts to keep the oxytocin flowing.

Activists around the world create protest songs to express frustration, grief, opposition, and solidarity—think of John Lennon's "Imagine"—and many invest substantial time and resources to disseminate those songs. John Bell is program director for Search for Common Ground (SFCG), a Washington, DC, and Brussels-based non-governmental organization that "works to transform the way the world deals with conflict—away from adversarial approaches and towards collaborative problem solving" (Bell 2015 "Our Mission"). He describes one of several segments of an SFCG-sponsored documentary series called *The Shape of the Future.* This one explores what an Arab–Israeli peace settlement might be like (Bell 2007). Produced in Hebrew, Arabic, and English-language versions, it was the first program to be shown simultaneously on Israeli, Palestinian, and Arab (Abu Dhabi) television. The documentary's theme song, "In My Heart," was co-written by David Broza and Said Murad, two well-known Israeli and Palestinian musicians. In the lyrics, "our land" equates with the essential elements of life—heart, spirit, blood, and soul. Both simple and profound, these words witness the tremendous devotion to place shared by divergent cultures. The sharing can be grounds for increased understanding. The video of this song ends with a quotation by Yehuda Amichai: "And it is written in the book that we shall not fear. And it is written that we too shall change." Song can be that change agent.

In *Beyond Bullets and Bombs,* Kjell Skyllstad chronicles the compelling story of a song entitled "Zaman el Salaam" (Skyllstad 2007). During an Intifada dem-onstration, Amnon Abutbul, a well-known Israeli singer, was injured by a rock thrown by a Palestinian demonstrator. Abutbul contacted a Palestinian poet, Fatchi Kasem. Together they wrote lyrics for a peace song, "Zaman el Salaam," and for the tune they discovered a melody played by Yair Dalal, a master violinist and oud player who honors both Arabic and Jewish traditions. For a celebration of the Oslo Accords in 1994, Kjell Skyllstad was contacted for music. He recruited 50 Palestinian, 50 Israeli, and 100 Norwegian children who rehearsed "Zaman el Salaam" in their home countries. On 13 September 1994, after a day of unresolved negotiations in both Paris and Oslo, Yassir Arafat and Shimon Peres heard this international children's choir sing in three languages before an audience of 8,000, accompanied by the Oslo Philharmonic and conducted by Zubin Mehta, with Yair Dalal playing on violin.

Stories that move and inspire us are everywhere. Beyond such commonplace phenomena, however, scientists now know that the human mirror neuron system makes it possible for performers and their listeners to share a neurological resonance. That new knowledge intensifies singing's tremendous potential to create better understanding and, perhaps, slightly new solutions to old problems. Add to that potential the capacity of singing to promote brain plasticity— literally, new ways of thinking—and the pro-social effects of oxytocin, and singing, especially in groups, seems worth reconsidering when dealing with interpersonal conflict (MacDonald and MacDonald 2010, Bartz et al. 2011). So although Gaza is still passionately disputed territory and peace seems a naïve hope, this chapter has summarized new knowledge about the ways singing—this powerful agent of change—can thread together ideas that seem unimaginable under other circumstances.

Film Illustration

The King's Speech (2010) directed by Tom Hooper, written by David Seidler, starring Colin Firth and Geoffrey Rush, UK Film Council, See-Saw Films, Bedlam Productions, 2010.

Video Illustrations

"In My Heart" by David Broza and Said Murad, an Arab-Israeli Peace Song sponsored by Search for Common Ground, www.sfcg.org/programmes/cgp/cgp_songs2.html, accessed 29 December 2014.

"Time for Peace" by Fatchi Kasem and Yair Dalal, documentary made in 1995 about the Oslo Accords, with support from UNESCO, www.youtube.com/watch?v=mhZW8vTCVGc, accessed 29 December 2014.

Discussion Points

1. Evaluate the opportunities and limitations associated with two methods of assessing the benefits of singing: neuroscience and music therapy. Brainstorm a model by which these two broad bodies of research might be combined in a single view.

2. In a comprehensive research database, perform a search connecting singing with one of this chapter's three areas of brain research: neuroplasticity, the mirror neuron system, and the hormone oxytocin. Characterize the ways research in that area has progressed since the publication of this book.

3. If singing helps break down barriers among groups and Israeli and Palestinian children sang together at the Oslo Accords in 1994, why is Gaza still disputed territory? Evaluate the benefits of singing in that situation, keeping in mind divergent worldviews, the value of helping versus correcting, and the limitations of social interaction in the contexts of history, culture, and politics.

Notes

1 In their literature review, Callan and colleagues list several areas associated with singing that have drawn research attention, including, but not limited to, perception vs. production of singing, melody vs. song text processing, and differential activations in the brain's reward centers for singing vs. speaking.

2 See Koniari et al. (2012) for retrospective coverage of research on neural involvement in singing and on lesion studies.

3 In 2011, these and other Montréal-based research institutions formed a strategic cluster called the Centre for Research on Brain, Language and Music, of which Peretz and Zatorre are co-directors. See www.crblm.ca, accessed 29 December 2014.

4 See his website, www.oliversacks.com/, accessed 29 December 2014. Sacks's discoveries are not limited to those implicating music.

5 The Goethe text comes from *Zahme Xenien* (Gentle Reminders): "Wie die Gestirn, / Ohne Hast, / Aber ohne Rast / Drehe sich jeder / Um die eigne Last" (As the star, / Without haste, / But without rest / Turn [us] each / To [his] own burden). *Goethes Werke* (Weimar, 1890), III, 247.

6 Because of temporal-lobe seizures, Mrs. O'C heard deafening Irish songs in her head; Mrs. O'M spontaneously heard "Easter Parade," "Glory, Glory, Hallelujah," and "Good Night, Sweet Jesus" in rapid succession as a result of the same sort of epileptic hallucinations or dreams.

7 Korbinian Brodmann (1868–1918) is known for his division of the cerebral cortex into fifty-two regions.

8 See, for examples, programs at Children's Mercy Hospital in Kansas City, MO, www.childrensmercy.org/Content/ChildLife/, and the *Making Music, Making Memories Program* sponsored by Banner Alzheimer's Institute, http://banneralz.org/making-music,-making-memories-program.aspx, both accessed 30 December 2014.

9 American Music Therapy Association website, www.musictherapy.org/about/listserv/, and World Federation of Music Therapy website, www.musictherapyworld.net/WFMT/Membership.html, both accessed 5 July 2012.

10 Importantly, my familiarity with the patient's musical preferences and the fact that my sung rhythm could easily adapt to her successful steps contributed to these phenomena. Music therapists regularly find and apply this "isoprinciple" (mimicking or mirroring even random patient activity in establishing a pattern) as they seek to modify patient activity. See also Hayden et al. (2009).

11 See Chapter 5 for detailed information on music therapy interventions for dementia sufferers. See also Bonilha et al. 2009; Grape et al. 2010; and Haslam and Cook 2002.

12 Learning with music is used here to indicate active involvement, i.e., singing words on a memory list, rather than studying while music plays in the background.

13 Any simple drawing of the human brain reveals little of that organ's vast capacities, or variations among individual brains.

14 "Covert" describes speaking or singing mentally, but making no sound. Daniel Callan, correspondence with author, 22 May 2012.

15 Another melodic intonation therapy success story is former Arizona congresswoman Gabrielle Giffords, who suffered a point-blank gunshot wound to the head at a political event in January 2011.

16 Experiment 1 presented a list of fifteen words in either spoken or sung form. "Chunking" is a short-term memory device apparent, for example, in the subgrouping of phone numbers or mail codes.

17 Recently, scientists at the Max Planck Institute questioned the role singing plays in aphasic speech recovery and posited, instead, that rhythm is the primary cause for improvement in patients with lesions in the basal ganglia. See Stahl et al. (2011).

18 Asperger's syndrome falls on the high-functioning end of the autism spectrum. People with this disorder experience no delay in language or cognitive development and their standardized intelligence quotient scores tend to be above the average scored by neuro-typicals. Both these conditions differentiate typical Asperger's syndrome from classic autism. See Quinton et al. (2011).

19 Gene or genetic expression is a process that takes inherited information (e.g., DNA) and makes a specific functional product from that information. Normal tissue in the body has a particular genetic expression that changes when, for example, that tissue becomes cancerous.

20 Qualitative measures such as self-reporting are informative, especially when wellbeing is one of the conditions measured.

21 HRV is the physiological phenomenon of variation in the time interval between heart-beats. It may reflect changes in body stress, while other physiological parameters are still in "normal" accepted ranges.

22 *Motilin* is a hormone produced from endocrine cells of the duodenal mucosa to help regulate motility of the digestive tract. Motilin has been proposed to initiate the peristaltic reflex in the small intestine and cholecystokinin (CCK) the gastrocolic reflex. VEGF or Vascular Endothelial Growth Factor is an essential regulator of vascular development produced by skin cells. Fibrinogen (which aids in blood clotting) may be elevated in any form of inflammation. Cholecystokinin is a peptide hormone of the gastrointestinal system responsible for stimulating the digestion of fat and protein. Disturbed motilin and CCK release may partly be responsible for the intestinal dysmotility in IBS patients.

23 Not surprisingly, the authors found that respiration became synchronized among eleven singers and a conductor engaged in choir singing. In other words, they breathed together. The complex biomarker heart rate variability (HRV) also synchronized during the singing condition, and coordination of both these responses was higher when singing in unison than when singing pieces with multiple voice parts. While high HRV is usually more positive than a low rate, and HRV changes can be useful in predicting certain conditions and events, Müller and Lindenberger's experiment is only an early investigation of the functional significance of cardiac and respiratory between-person couplings. They make no predictions about the significance of these findings.

References

American Music Therapy Association, http://www.musictherapy.org/about/listserv/, and World Federation of Music Therapy Website, http://www.musictherapyworld.net/WFMT/Membership.html, both accessed 30 December 2014.

Angier, N. 2009. "The Biology behind the Milk of Human Kindness." *New York Times*, 23 November 2009, D2.

Bach-y-Rita, P. 2005. "Emerging Concepts of Brain Function." *Journal of Integrative Neuroscience* 4.2: 183–205.

Bandettini, P. 2009. "What's New in Neuroimaging Methods?" *Annals of the New York Academy of Sciences: The Year in Cognitive Neuroscience* 1156.1: 260–93.

Bartz, J.A., J. Zaki, N. Bolger, and K.N. Ochsner. 2011. "Social Effects of Oxytocin in Humans: Context and Person Matter." *Trends in Cognitive Sciences* 15: 301–9.

Belin, P., P.E.G. Bestelmeyer, M. Latinus, and R. Watson. 2011. "Understanding Voice Perception." *British Journal of Psychology* 102: 712–13.

Bell, J. 2007. "Media and Search for Common Ground in the Middle East." In *Beyond Bullets and Bombs: Grassroots Peacebuilding between Israelis and Palestinians*, ed. Judy Kuriansky, 327–36. Westport, CT: Praeger.

———. 2015. "Our Mission." *Search for Common Ground*, http://www.sfcg.org/, accessed 29 December 2014.

Bonilha, A.G., F. Onofre, M.L. Vieira, M.Y.A. Prado, and J.A. Martinez. 2009. "Effects of Singing Classes on Pulmonary Function and Quality of Life of COPD Patients." *International Journal of Chronic Obstructive Pulmonary Disease* 4: 1–8.

Bouillaud, J.-B. 1865. "Sur la faculté du langage articulé." *Bulletin of the Academie Nationale du Medicin* 30: 752–68.

Brainard, M.S., and A.J. Doupe. 2002. "What Songbirds Teach Us about Learning." *Nature* 417: 351–8.

Callan, D., V. Tsytsarev, T. Hanakawa, A.M. Callan, M. Katsuhara, H. Fukuyama, and R. Turner. 2006. "Song and Speech: Brain Regions Involved with Perception and Covert Production." *NeuroImage* 31: 1327–42.

Centers for Disease Control and Prevention. 2008. "Prevalence of Autism Spectrum Disorders: Autism and Developmental Disabilities Monitoring Network, 14 Sites, United States, Surveillance Summaries." Morbidity and Mortality Weekly Report, http://www.cdc.gov/mmwr/preview/mmwrhtml/ss6103a1.htm?s_cid=ss6103a1_w, accessed 29 December 2014.

Cevasco, A.M. 2008. "The Effects of Mothers' Singing on Full-Term and Preterm Infants and Maternal Emotional Responses." *Journal of Music Therapy* 45.3: 273–306.

Di Pellegrino, G., L. Fadiga, L. Fogassi, V. Gallese, and G. Rizzolatti. 1992. "Understanding Motor Events: A Neurophysiological Study." *Experimental Brain Research* 91: 176–80.

Dubuc, B. 2013. "Broca's Area, Wernicke's Area, and Other Language-Processing Areas in the Brain." *The Brain: From Top to Bottom*, http://thebrain.mcgill.ca/flash/a/a_10/a_10_cr/a_10_cr_lan/a_10_cr_lan.html, accessed 29 December 2014.

Engen, R.L. 2005. "The Singer' Breath: Implications for Treatment of Persons with Emphysema." *Journal of Music Therapy* 42.1: 20–48.

Farndale, N. 2011. "The King's Speech: The Real Story." Culture: Film, *The* [London] *Telegraph*, 5 January 2011, http://www.telegraph.co.uk/culture/film/8223897/The-Kings-Speech-the-real-story.html, accessed 29 December 2014.

Freeman, W. 2000. "A Neurological Role of Music in Social Bonding." In *The Origins of Music*, eds. Nils L. Wallin, Björn Merker, and Steven Brown, 411–24. Cambridge, MA: MIT Press.

Gaser, C., and G. Schlaug. 2003. "Brain Structures Differ between Musicians and Non-musicians." *Journal of Neuroscience* 23.27: 9240–5.

Grape, C., M. Sandgren, L.O. Hansson, M. Ericson, and T. Theorell. 2002. "Does Singing Promote Well-Being?" *Integrative Psychological and Behavioral Science* 38.1: 65–74.

Grape, C., T. Theorell, B.-M. Wikström, and R. Ekman. 2009. "Choir Singing and Fibrinogen, VEGF, Cholecystokinin, and Motilin in IBS patients." *Medical Hypotheses* 72.2: 223–5.

———. 2010. "Letter to the Editor: Comparison between Choir Singing and Group Discussion in Irritable Bowel Syndrome Patients over One Year: Saliva Testosterone Increases in New Choir Singers." *Psychotherapy and Psychosomatics* 79.3: 19–8.

Grape, C., B.M. Wikström, R. Ekman, D. Hasson, and T. Theorell. 2010. "Comparison between Choir Singing and Group Discussion in Irritable Bowel Syndrome Patients over One Year: Saliva Testosterone Increases in New Choir Singers" 2010. *Psychotherapy and Psychosomatics* 79.3: 196–8.

Grau-Sánchez, J., J.L. Amengual, N. Rojo, M. Veciana de Las Heras, J. Montero, F. Rubio, E. Altenmüller, T.F. Münte, A. Rodríguez-Fornells. 2013. "Plasticity in the Sensorimotor Cortex Induced by Music-Supported Therapy in Stroke Patients: A TMS Study." *Frontiers in Human Neuroscience* 7: 494.

Grocke, D., S. Bloch, and D. Castle. 2009. "The Effect of Group Music Therapy on Quality of Life for Participants Living with a Severe and Enduring Mental Illness." *Journal of Music Therapy* 46.2: 90–104.

Haslam, C., and M. Cook. 2002. "Striking a Chord with Amnesic Patients: Evidence that Song Facilitates Memory." *Neurocase* 8: 453–65.

Hayden, R., A.A. Clair, G. Johnson, and D. Otto. 2009. "The Effect of Rhythmic Auditory Stimulation (RAS) on Physical Therapy Outcomes for Patients in Gait Training Following Stroke: A Feasibility Study." *International Journal of Neuroscience* 119.12: 2183–95.

Healey, E.C., A.R. Mallard III, and M.R. Adams. 1976. "Factors Contributing to the Reduction of Stuttering during Singing." *Journal of Speech and Hearing Research* 19.3: 475–80.

Heaton, P., B. Hermelin, and L. Pring. 1999. "Can Children with Autistic Spectrum Disorders Perceive Affect in Music? An Experimental Investigation." *Psychological Medicine* 29.6: 1405–10.

Henschen, S.E. 1920. "On the Function of the Right Hemisphere of the Brain in Relation to the Left in Speech, Music, and Calculation." *Brain* 49: 110–26.

Hillecke, T., A. Nickel, and H.V. Bolay. 2005. "Scientific Perspectives on Music Therapy." *Annals of the New York Academy of Sciences* 1060: 271–82.

Janata, P., B. Tillmann, and J.J. Bharucha. 2002. "Listening to Polyphonic Music Recruits Domain-General Attention and Working Memory Circuits." *Cognitive, Affective, and Behavioral Neuroscience* 2: 121–40.

Koelsch, S. 2009. "A Neuroscientific Perspective on Music Therapy." *The Neurosciences and Music III—Disorders and Plasticity: Annals of the New York Academy of Sciences* 1169: 380–1.

Koniari, D., H. Proios, K. Tsapkini, L.C. Triarhou. 2012. "Singing but Not Speaking: A Retrospect on Music-Language Interrelationships in the Human Brain since Otto Marburg's Zur Frage der Amusie (1919)." In *Advances in Psychology Research* vol. 87, ed. A.M. Columbus, 239–48. Hauppauge, NY: Nova Science Publishers.

Macdonald, K., and T.M. Macdonald. 2010. "The Peptide that Binds: A Systematic Review of Oxytocin and Its Prosocial Effects in Humans." *Harvard Review of Psychiatry* 18.1: 2.

Marazziti, D., and M. Catena Dell'osso. 2008. "The Role of Oxytocin in Neuropsychiatric Disorders." *Current Medical Chemistry* 15.7: 698–704.

Milner, B. 1962. "Laterality Effects in Audition." In *Inter-hemispheric Relations and Cerebral Dominance*, ed. V. Mountcastle, chap. 9. Baltimore, MD: Johns Hopkins Press.

Mitchell, M. 2010. "A Singing Miracle." In *Doing Something Different: Solution-Focused Brief Therapy Practices*, ed. Throrana Strever Nelson, 53–4. New York: Routledge.

Molnar-Szakacs, I., and K. Overy. 2006. "Music and Mirror Neurons: From Motion to 'e'motion." *Social Cognitive and Affective Neuroscience* 1: 235–41.

Molnar-Szakacs, I., M.J. Wang, E.A. Laugeson, K. Overy, W.-L. Wu, and J. Piggot. 2009. Focus Review: "Autism, Emotion Recognition and the Mirror Neuron System: The Case of Music." *McGill Journal of Medicine* 12.2: 87–98.

Molnar-Szakacs, I., and P. Heaton. 2012. "Music: A Unique Window into the World of Autism." *Neurosciences and Music IV: Learning and Memory. Annals of the New York Academy of Sciences* 1252: 318–24.

Mount Sinai/Beth Israel. 2012. The Louis Armstrong Department of Music Therapy, http://www.wehealny.org/services/bi_musictherapy/index.html, accessed 29 December 2014.

Müller, V., and U. Lindenberger. 2011. "Cardiac and Respiratory Patterns Synchronize between Persons during Choir Singing." *Public Library of Science (PLoS) One* 6.9. DOI: 10.1371/journal.pone.0024893, accessed 28 December 2014.

Naber, F.B., I.E. Poslawsky, M.H. van Ijzendoorn, H. van Engeland, and M.J. Bakermans-Kranenburg. 2013. "Brief Report: Oxytocin Enhances Paternal Sensitivity to a Child with Autism: A Double-Blind Within-Subject Experiment with Intranasally Administered Oxytocin." *Journal of Autism and Developmental Disorders* 43.1: 224–9.

Neumann, I.D. 2008. "Brain Oxytocin: A Key Regulator of Emotional and Social Behaviours in Both Females and Males." *Journal of Neuroendocrinology* 20: 858–65.

Neville, M.C. 1998. "Oxytocin and Milk Ejection" and "Biology of the Mammary Gland," National Institutes of Health, http://mammary.nih.gov/reviews/lactation/Neville002/index.html, accessed 29 December 2014.

Norton, A., L. Zipse, S. Marchina, and G. Schlaug. 2009. "Melodic Intonation Therapy: Shared Insights on How It Is Done and Why It Might Help." *Neurosciences and Music III: Disorders and Plasticity, Annals of the New York Academy of Sciences* 1169: 431–6.

Peretz, I., and R. Zatorre, eds. 2003. *The Cognitive Neuroscience of Music.* New York: Oxford University Press.

Quinton, E.-M., A. Bhatara, H. Poissant, E. Fombonne, and D.J. Levitin. 2011. "Emotion Perception in Music in High-Functioning Adolescents with Autism Spectrum Disorders." *Journal of Autism and Developmental Disorders* 41.9: 1240–55.

Roberts, M. 2006. "'I Want to Play and Sing My Story': Home-Based Songwriting for Bereaved Children and Adolescents." *Australian Journal of Music Therapy* 17: 18–34.

Sacks, O. 1970. "Reminiscences." In *The Man Who Mistook His Wife for a Hat*, 132–49. New York: Touchstone.

———. 1984. *A Leg to Stand On.* New York: Touchstone.

———. 2007. *Musicophilia: Tales of Music and the Brain.* New York: Knopf.

Saltuklaroglu, T., J. Kalinowski, and V.K. Guntupalli. 2004. "Towards a Common Neural Substrate in the Immediate and Effective Inhibition of Stuttering." *International Journal of Neuroscience* 114: 435–50.

Savoy, R.L. 2001. "History and Future Directions of Human Brain Mapping and Functional Neuroimaging." *Acta Psychologica* 107.1–3: 9–42.

Schauer, M., and K.H. Mauritz. 2003. "Musical Motor Feedback (MMF) in Walking Hemiparetic Stroke Patients: Randomized Trials of Gait Improvement." *Clinical Rehabilitation* 17.7: 713–22.

Schlaug, G., S. Marchina, and A. Norton. 2009. "Evidence for Plasticity in White Matter Tracts of Chronic Aphasic Patients Undergoing Intense Intonation-Based Speech Therapy." *Neurosciences and Music III—Disorders and Plasticity: Annals of the New York Academy of Sciences* 1169: 385–94.

———. 2010. "Music and the Brain." Interview with Steve Mencher, 29 April. Library of Congress Podcast, http://www.loc.gov/podcasts/musicandthebrain/podcast_schlaug.html, accessed 30 December 2014.

———. 2011. Quoted in Richard Knox. "Singing Therapy Helps Stroke Patients Speak Again." National Public Radio transcript, 26 December, http://m.npr.org/story/144152193?ps=sh_sthdl, accessed 30 December 2014.

Skyllstad, K. 2007. "Salaam Shalom: Singing for Peace between Palestinians and Israelis." In *Beyond Bullets and Bombs: Grassroots Peacebuilding between Israelis and Palestinians*, ed. Judy Kuriansky, 177–81. Westport, CT: Praeger.

Stahl, B., S.A. Kotz, I. Henseler, R. Turner, and S. Geyer. 2011. "Rhythm in Disguise: Why Singing May Not Hold the Key to Recovery from Aphasia." *Brain* 134.10: 3083–93.

Thaut, M. 2005. *Rhythm, Music, and the Brain: Scientific Foundations and Clinical Applications.* New York: Routledge.

Thaut, M., D.A. Peterson, and G.C. McIntosh. 2005. "Temporal Entrainment of Cognitive Functions: Musical Mnemonics Induce Brain Plasticity and Oscillatory Synchrony in Neural Networks Underlying Memory." *Annals of the New York Academy of Sciences* 1060: 243–54.

Wan, C.Y., K. Demaine, L. Sipse, A. Norton, and G. Schlaug. 2010. "From Music Making to Speaking: Engaging the Mirror Neuron System in Autism." *Brain Research Bulletin* 82.3–4: 161–8.

Wan, C.Y., T. Rüber, A. Hohmann, and G. Schlaug. 2010. "The Therapeutic Effects of Singing in Neurological Disorders." *Music Perception* 27.4: 287–95.

Xia, C. 2006. "Understanding the Human Brain: A Lifetime of Dedicated Pursuit, Interview with Brenda Milner." *McGill Journal of Medicine* 9.2: 165–72.

Xu, Lucy. 2011. "Doctor, Can You Prescribe Me Some Mozart?" *Yale Journal of Medicine and Law* 7.3, http://www.yalemedlaw.com/2011/08/doctor-can-you-prescribe-me-some-mozart/, accessed 30 December 2014.

Zatorre, R.J. 1998. "Editorial: Functional Specialization of Human Auditory Cortex for Musical Processing." *Brain* 121.10: 1817.

Zatorre, R., and S. Baum. 2012. "Musical Melody and Speech Intonation: Singing a Different Tune?" *Public Library of Science Biology* 10.7. DOI: 10.1371/journal.pbio.1001372, accessed 29 December 2014.

3

"WOMB TO TOMB"

Singing, Science, and the Mother's Voice

> The universal appeal of music, which used to be considered as a social construct
> that varies from culture to culture, might be better conceived as an adaptive
> response of the organism.
>
> *Isabelle Peretz (2005)[1]*

Scientists confirmed in the 1970s that the average human fetus can hear during
the last trimester of pregnancy (Querleu et al. 1988), and as early as 1994 that the
mother's voice is the most intense acoustical signal in the amniotic environment.
Further:

> Both the newborn and fetus show heart rate decelerations in response to
> speech sounds. This cardiorespiratory attentional response occurs during
> sleep when sensory stimulation is probably influencing perinatal brain devel-
> opment. Early experience with voice has both acute and enduring effects on
> the developing brain. These effects have ramifications for the development
> of the auditory system, as well as for later social and emotional development.
>
> *Fifer and Moon (1994)*

Not surprisingly, babies prefer the mother's voice to that of a similar-sounding
female within a week after birth. When given the choice between a lullaby that
had been read twice a day by the mother during her last five weeks of pregnancy
and a new story, three-day-old newborns prefer the familiar story (Spence and
DeCasper 1982). Infants do not identify the mother on the basis of vision alone
until they are three months old (Burnham 1993).[2] Common sense and all this
data notwithstanding, the possibility that the voice's role in human experience is
intimately involved with survival has not gained much traction in the medical field.
While modern therapists and nurses often utilize the voice to underpin health
goals, vocal delivery is far less likely to be considered a potential tool in physician–patient interaction, to the detriment of patient wellbeing. In this chapter I
summarize evidence supporting the notion that we evolved as voice-driven beings

and that we receive intrinsic rewards when we seek out and find a meaningful, inflected voice.

Caveat: Lacan and French Post-structuralist Thought[3]

Any postmodern discussion of "the maternal" must acknowledge Freud's theories and the many philosophical and psychological works he inspired. In particular, Jacques Lacan (1901–81) contributed to our understanding of infancy when he developed the concept of a "mirror stage" that occurs between six and eighteen months of age. This developmental milestone, in which the child can recognize herself in the mirror and recognize the difference between self and image, marks her entry into the world of symbols and language, and the formation of ego. In the mirror stage, an infant progresses from a seamless perception of her universe into a differentiated relationship with "other" and, most fundamentally, with mother (Scherzinger 1999). The breast, undeniably, is not a part of the self. According to Lacan, the ego is formed from the conflicts that arise in that mirror stage, where joy over the realization that "I'm a person, too" mixes with depression over the truth that "mother is separate and I do not control her." In Lacan's symbolic matrix, father is part of social order, a realization that occurs simultaneously with the child's realization that the mother's body is a separate entity. Summarizing Lacan's system, Martin Scherzinger writes that, in the mirror stage, "access to . . . reality, like access to the mother's body, is no longer direct; the child is plunged into the primary repression of desire. This movement in which fullness of meaning perpetually fades . . . is the unconscious" (Scherzinger 1999, 98). In contrast to Freud's pre-linguistic and instinctual unconscious, Lacan's unconscious is structured symbolically, like language. Again quoting Scherzinger (1999, 98), "[Lacan's unconscious] divides up the fullness one knows in the imaginary, and irrevocably severs the subject from an experience of unmediated reality." The mirror stage is thus a developmental stage marked by loss.

Lacanians have interpreted the sonorous womb, a critical factor in this chapter, in many ways. Lacan believed it functioned as "imaginary primordial enclosure formed by the *imago* of the mother's body" (Lacan 1966).[4] In the same vein, composer Michel Chion wrote:

> In the beginning, in the uterine darkness, was the voice, the Mother's voice. For the child once born, the mother is more an olfactory and vocal continuum than an image. Her voice originates in all points of space, while her form enters and leaves the visual field. We can imagine the voice of the Mother weaving around the child a network of connections it's tempting to call the umbilical web. A rather horrifying expression to be sure, in its evocation of spiders—and in fact, this original vocal connection will remain ambivalent.
>
> *Quoted in Link (2010, 41)*

Guy Rosolato (b. 1924) wrote less pessimistically of "a sonorous womb, a murmuring house, or Music of the Spheres." He casts the mother's voice as "the first model of auditory pleasure" and writes further that "music finds its roots and its nostalgia in [this] original atmosphere" (quoted in Bottge 2005, 189).

Even as I argue that humans are motivated to re-create a sonorous intimacy with an important other, I also acknowledge Lacan's and other crucial perspectives on the mother's voice in human experience. The psychic scar that originated in the mirror stage forever biases some adults against a powerful female voice. For them, the mother's voice might represent the painful second birth of the mirror stage. Further, since a "good mother" cannot be considered a constant in any cultural context, many adults perpetually strive to recover from inattentive, unwilling, or abusive female parents. Yet, in this most fundamental, umbilical connection with another, emerging science repeatedly provides evidence that—whether characterized by joy or misery—the infant's relationship with its gestational parent hinges critically on her inflected, musical voice (see Figure 3.1).[5] In the following pages, I will survey evolutionary and behavioral reasons humans are specifically equipped to live out this paradigm.

FIGURE 3.1 Mother and child. re_bekka/Shutterstock.

Evolution and Mothering

Chapter 1 summarized the work of several researchers who suggest singing became a fitness advantage as humans evolved. I reserved discussion of two crucial roles in human evolution, the gestation and care of offspring, for this chapter. The former function falls exclusively to women and, in most societies, the latter is also a feminine domain.

Ellen Dissanayake is an evolutionary ethologist; that field is concerned with animal behaviors in their natural environments. In her view, the primate propensity not just for sociability but also for relationship or communion became so crucial in human evolution that "special affiliative mechanisms" evolved to enhance and ensure their presence (Dissanayake 2000, 389). One watershed in this evolution occurred around 1.8 million years ago, when quadrupedal ancestors progressed to Homo erectus, the first bipedal hominid. This change in locomotive style initiated physiological changes that would drastically affect gestation and birth (see Figure 3.2). "During hominization," writes Dissanayake, "increasing commitments to bipedal locomotion and expanding brain size affected gestation length" (Dissanayake 2000, 390). Upright posture resulted over time in a narrowing birth canal. Increasing head

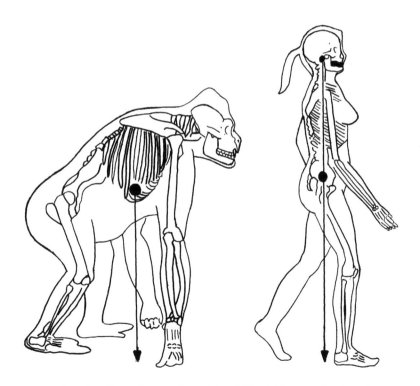

FIGURE 3.2 Drawing illustrating quadrupedal and bipedal locomotion in primates.

(Ma = million years ago; Ka = thousand years ago)

4,000 Ma	Life appeared on Earth
505 Ma	First vertebrates
ca. 365 Ma	First amphibians
300 Ma	First reptiles
256 Ma	Reptiles split from earliest mammal-like creatures
220 Ma	First mammals
65–85 Ma	Beginning of speciation that will lead to primate order
40 Ma	Primates split into wet-nosed and dry-nosed
25 Ma	A type of dry-nosed primate develops into two superfamilies, Old World monkeys and apes
15 Ma	Family Hominidae (great apes) speciate from ancestors of the lesser ape (gibbon); gorillas and orangutans diverged
13 Ma	Homininae ancestors speciate from the ancestors of the orangutan, common ancestor of humans and other great apes
10 Ma	Hominini speciate from the ancestors of the gorilla
7–6 Ma	Hominina speciate from the ancestors of the chimpanzee; both chimpanzees and humans have a larynx that repositions during the first two years of life to a spot between the pharynx and the lungs, indicating that the common ancestors have this feature, a precursor of speech
3.85–2.95 Ma	Australopithecus afarensis left human-like footprints on volcanic ash in Laetoli, Tanzania, providing strong evidence of full-time bipedalism (though it did not walk in the way humans do)
2.5 Ma	Appearance of genus Homo
2 Ma	Humans first arose; subsequent human evolution has been within a single, continuous human species
1.8 Ma	Homo erectus evolved in Africa
1.2 Ma	Homo antecessor is the common genetic ancestor of humans and Neanderthals. At present estimate, humans have approximately 20,000–25,000 genes and share 99% of their DNA with the now extinct Neanderthal and 95–99% of their DNA with their closest living evolutionary relative, chimpanzees. The human variant of the FOXP2 gene (linked to the control of speech) has been found to be identical in Neanderthals. It can therefore be deduced that Homo antecessor would also have had the human FOXP2 gene.
200 Ka	Earliest fossil evidence for archaic Homo sapiens
160 Ka	Species Homo sapiens lived in Ethiopia
50 Ka	Migration to South Asia
40 Ka	Migration to Australia and Europe
95–17 Ka	Species Homo floresiensis dies out, leaving Homo sapiens as the only living species of the genus Homo

FIGURE 3.3 Selected ancestry of humans. Adapted from *Human Evolution Timeline Interactive*, Smithsonian National Museum of Natural History, http://human origins.si.edu/evidence/human-evolution-timeline-interactive; Thomas Geissmann, "Gibbon Songs and Human Music from an Evolutionary Perspective," Figure 7.1 Phylogenetic tree of extant primate families and some subfamilies, in *The Origins of Music*, eds. Nils L. Wallin, Björn Merker, and Steven Brown (Cambridge, MA: MIT Press, 2000), 104.

size led to premature births and, consequently, increasingly dependent infants. Not just birth, but mothering, too, was profoundly affected. Bipedalism "created intense selective pressure for proximate physiological and cognitive mechanisms to ensure longer and better maternal care" (Dissanayake 2000, 390). Figure 3.3 summarizes human ancestry, with particular attention paid to divergence from other hominids, the shift to bipedalism, and evolution of inflected vocal capabilities.

Dissanayake uses the generic term "making special" when discussing artistic activities of pre-Homo sapiens species. "Making special" may be seen as analogous to the "special affiliative mechanisms" she proposes as after-effects of full-time bipedalism (Dissanayake 1992). Her theory of musical origins revolves around parent–offspring interactions: most often, those between mother and infant.

The persistence of inflected vocal interactions, insists Dissanayake, now referring to modern humans, goes beyond lullabies or maternal singing to "ritualized packages of sequential behaviors" between mothers and their infants under six months of age (Dissanayake 2000, 390). This mother–infant vocal interaction can

1. direct and modulate infant's state or level of attention and arousal
2. offer emotional regulation and support, and help the infant achieve equilibrium and self-regulation
3. acquaint with expressive or prosodic features of language
4. expose to prototypical and meaningful sounds and patterns of spoken language
5. develop cognitive abilities for recognizing agency (I can make the ball move), object (I can reach for the ball), goal (I'm crying because my diaper is wet), and instrumentality (Mother uses the spoon to feed me) . . . and lead to intentionality, reciprocity, and expansion beyond the present situation
6. reinforce neural structures for socioemotional functioning
7. introduce cultural norms of appropriate behavior
8. help establish dyadic attunement and reciprocity, enable the pair to anticipate and adjust to each other's individual natures and lay the foundation for later Bowlbian attachment.

Dissanayake (2000, 393)[6]

Cultural patterns of infant–mother interaction vary around the globe and Western world, with middle-class mothers appearing to be the most highly vocal in early infant communication. Nonetheless, ubiquity suggests that vocally inflected human mother–infant bonding behavior is less culturally specific than evolutionarily mandated. Dissanayake cites several studies of contemporary hunter-gatherer societies that report vocally, visually, and physically stimulating caretaker–infant interaction (Konner 1977, Hamilton 1981, Hewlett 1991).

Archaeologist Stephen Mithen also believes that this interaction mechanism, variously dubbed "motherese," "parentese," or "infant-directed speech" (IDS), evolved to ensure a close mother–child bond.

> The general character of [infant-directed speech] is well known to all: a higher overall pitch, a wider range of pitch, longer "hyperarticulated" vowels and pauses, shorter phrases and greater repetition than are found in speech directed to older children and adults. Research using "nonsense" words or non-native language demonstrates that IDS is universally used and understood. This suggests that its foundation pre-dates modern humans' final journey out of Africa.
>
> *Mithen (2006, 69–70)*

Mithen proposes that Neanderthals, completely evolved by 130,000 years ago and extinct by 30,000 years ago, responded to bipedalism and consequently premature infants with infant-directed speech and singing. In short, the Neanderthal mother sang to her infant to confirm she was nearby. As the "gatherer" partner of her hunter-gatherer species, the Neanderthal mother's hands would often have been occupied with work other than the tactile nurturing of her offspring. The voice, Mithen argues, thus became a sort of long-distance caress for Neanderthal infants.

Behavioral studies conducted in the past couple of decades support these evolutionary theories. Psychologist Sandra Trehub's work addresses the role of the mother as primary reinforcer of the human predisposition for music. Trehub found that after birth, and regardless of cultural variation, "Mothers' performances of songs seem to become ritualized, which may facilitate their use as communicative signals to prelinguistic infants" (Trehub 2001, 8). These ritualized interchanges (e.g., covering and uncovering the face repeatedly with an inflected word such as "boo!") comprise infant-directed speech—an example of Dissanayake's "special affiliative mechanisms." In a 2001 article, Trehub wrote:

> Mothers sing regularly to infants, doing so in a distinctive manner marked by high pitch, slow tempo, and emotional expressiveness . . . [infants are] more attentive to maternal singing than to maternal speech.
>
> *Trehub (2001, 1)*

Significantly, Trehub focuses on the development of mother-to-infant singing not as a prelude to speech but as an end in itself. Her work echoes that of Mithen and Dissanayake—"maternal singing could have enhanced infant survival in difficult ancestral conditions." Helpless infants would have "created intense selection pressures for parental commitment, including pressures for infant displays to sustain such commitment" (Trehub 2001, 10–11). Therefore, these displays were mutually reinforced, providing a biological insurance policy for the unwilling or uncomfortable mother. When she provided proximate care, mother was rewarded with a smile or coo, and the baby was rewarded for smiling or cooing by tactile and inflected interaction.

Trehub then turns to singing. "It is likely that singing to infants promotes reciprocal emotional ties . . . Presumably, mothers' growing attachment to infants would lead them to generate increasingly expressive performances" (Trehub 2001, 10–11). In pre-human primates, infants would have needed to demonstrate the value of these performances with the intended response (e.g., arousal or sleepiness) to insure the performances continued. So crucial is inflected IDS that "the healthy and contented offspring of singing mothers would be more likely to pass on their genes than would the offspring of non-singing mothers" (Trehub 2001, 10–11).

In that statement, Trehub theorizes about musical universals—specifically, behaviors observable in all groups under discussion. Debates about cultural relativism characterized twentieth-century anthropology and ethnomusicology, and persist into the present century. In a 2003 issue of *Nature Neuroscience*, Trehub countered relativist criticism with a proposition about modern humans: "The results of several studies imply that infants are universalists in the sense that they are perceptually equipped for the music of any culture" (Trehub 2003, 670). Rather than suggesting that one musical style or expression is the universal song of the human race, Trehub observes that although a newborn has been hearing for some time at birth and strongly prefers the mother's songs, normally hearing newborns have the capacity to develop expertise in any subsequent cultural home. International adoptees who "lose" the mother language in a new country provide ample evidence of this cognitive flexibility. Ultimately, wrote Trehub, musical similarities across cultures are likely to outstrip similarities across languages, especially if the focus is on everyday music rather than art music, and musical functions rather than styles of performance (Trehub 2003, 670). "Indeed, the *music* in speech seems to underlie its attractiveness to prelinguistic infants" (Trehub 2003, 671, n54). Along with Mariève Corbeil and Isabel Peretz, Trehub further refined the definition of "the music in speech" in 2013. In an experiment testing infant responses to "happy-sounding infant-directed speech," hummed lullabies, and happily sung Turkish children's songs, they determined that "happy voice quality rather than vocal mode (speech or singing) was the principal contributor to infant attention, regardless of age" (Corbeil et al. 2013, 372). The music in speech must therefore have something to do with the mood of the speaker. Expressed in reverse, singing is one way to infuse the spoken voice with joyful, melodious contours. Biochemistry has begun to supply another reason that highly musical, infant-directed speech has persisted in human evolution.

Oxytocin and Parenting

So far, this chapter has presented evidence that inflected vocal utterance, singing, and elements of musicality (pure tone quality, stereotyped phrases, accelerando, ritardando) represented general fitness advantages in the development of our primate ancestors. Inflected vocality has been proposed as a mechanism crucial to mother–infant bonding in bipedal species such as Neanderthals. We know by testing newborns and infants that motherese and infant-directed speech have the capacity to organize brain function. This section will return to a topic addressed in the previous chapter, the peptide oxytocin (OT). This neurochemical reward is substantively involved in the persistence of mother–infant vocal interactions. For millennia, oxytocin has infused mammalian births; it is implicated in cervical dilation, uterine contractions, lactation letdown reflex, contractions during the first few weeks of breastfeeding, and bonding. Interwoven in these actions are inflected vocalizations, not just with the mother but also with the father.

Seltzer and colleagues reported in 2010 that "Social vocalizations can release oxytocin in humans" (Seltzer et al. 2010). In an experiment involving sixty-one pre-menarcheal girls (aged seven through twelve) and their mothers, a social stressor was introduced to the children. Mother–daughter dyads were assigned randomly to experience three experimental conditions: complete contact (i.e., full complement of comfort), speech only, and no contact. They found that:

> Children receiving a full complement of comfort including physical, vocal and non-verbal contact showed the highest levels of OT and the swiftest return to baseline of a biological marker of stress (salivary cortisol), but a strikingly similar hormonal profile emerged in children comforted solely by their mother's voice.
>
> *Seltzer et al. (2010, abstract)*

Maternal vocalizations were nearly as important as touch in the regulation of stress among these girls.

Galbally and colleagues performed a meta-analysis of sixty-nine oxytocin studies conducted between 2005 and 2009, each of which focused on mother–infant relations (Galbally et al. 2011). Methodologies varied among the eight studies that remained after inclusion and exclusion criteria were applied. These studies reaffirmed the roles formerly considered to represent the extent of OT's role in sexual and reproductive behavior, and refined understanding of the mechanisms by which OT is expressed in mothering. The primary clinical division in one reported experiment was "secure attachment style" in mothers versus some form of "insecure/avoidant/dismissing style." Not surprisingly, serum OT levels were higher among secure mothers after interacting with their own children (Galbally et al. 2011, 8). MRI scans showed securely attached mothers had OT expression that strongly correlated with activation of the hypothalamus/pituitary region and the ventral striatum when they *saw* smiling and crying photos of their own infant. These regions are active in OT and dopamine-reward centers in the brain. It follows, then, that socially relevant cues (smiling, cooing) may reward certain maternal behaviors, stimulate OT uptake in the mother's brain, and therefore underscore her capacity to offer consistent, nurturing care. Interestingly, OT also facilitates interaction with an unfamiliar child (Galbally et al. 2011, 10). And perhaps most relevant to the present argument, OT production in mothers is maintained after birth, not only by lactation and nursing but also by infant clinging, facial expressions, and vocal calls. These latter three infant behaviors also affect OT expression in fathers (Velandia et al. 2010). Exchanging vocalizations can make the child and both parents feel better.

Both mother and fetus produce oxytocin at birth and OT crosses the placenta; maternal oxytocin thus affects the fetal brain. In planned cesarean births, however, the mother's oxytocin upsurge does not naturally occur. Pitocin, a synthetic oxytocin, is sometimes administered to the mother to minimize uterine blood loss during cesarean births, but high supplemental doses of oxytocin can be harmful to the mother. As a result, alternate ways of encouraging bonding after cesarean births have recently been studied. In a 2010 study, Velandia and colleagues wrote:

> Skin-to-skin contact between infants and parents immediately after planned cesarean section promotes vocal interaction. When placed in skin-to-skin contact and exposed to the parents' speech, the infants initiated communication with soliciting calls with the parents within approximately 15 minutes after birth. These findings give reason to encourage parents to keep the newborn in skin-to-skin contact after cesarean section, to support the early onset of the first vocal communication.
>
> *Velandia et al. (2010, abstract)*

This early communication, "vocal calls," according to the Galbally study, activates post-natal OT uptake and facilitates mother–infant bonding. The voice is thus recruited to stimulate the brain in leveling the "bonding field" between vaginal and cesarean births. The power of inflected vocal interactions surely must not wane after the birth experience.

Conclusion

A group of medical researchers in Cuba led by Calixto Machado has established the fact that the brain sometimes continues to recognize familiar voices even after we are too ill to respond in any other way (Machado et al. 2007). They studied a child who had been in a persistent vegetative state for four years after coming very close to drowning. Using a combination of MRI and EEG technology to record the child's brain responses, researchers employed five different women of the same age as the mother in the experiment. Each of the women and the mother spoke identical expressions that were typical in the patient's daily life. First, they found significant differences in the child's brain activity between baseline conditions and mother talks conditions (see Figure 3.4). These statistical differences were localized in the lateral and posterior regions of the subject's left hemisphere, a brain region involved with language. Despite his vegetative state, the child's brain still could respond to linguistic input: "the results demonstrate recognition of the mother's voice and indicate high-level residual linguistic processing in a patient meeting clinical criteria for the [vegetative state]" (Machado et al. 2007, 126). In a follow-up essay, Machado and colleagues reported that they had assessed

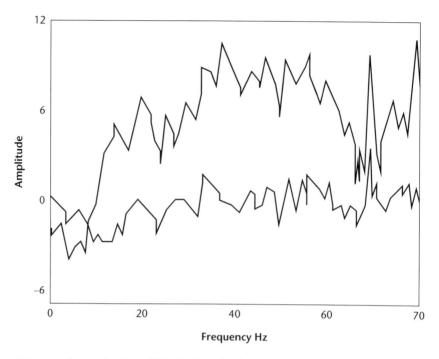

FIGURE 3.4 Reproduction of Machado and others, Figure 1a, 125, "Comparison of mother talks vs. basal record (upper curve) showed significant differences in the EEG spectrum for frequencies from 14 to 58 Hz with a peak at 32.2 Hz. No significant differences were found between unknown women vs. basal conditions (lower curve)." Adapted. Permissions Calixto Machado and SAGE Publications for *Clinical EEG Neuroscience* (2007).

heart-rate variability during the same experiment. While the unfamiliar female voices had elicited "arousal characterized by sympathetic activation, the mother's voice caused an additional, parasympathetic activation, probably related to a shift to a 'positive' emotion during this experimental condition" (Machado et al. 2011, 1059). Apparently, the powerful maternal voice continues not only to stimulate, but to be recognized and to generate some sort of pleasure response, well into near-death states.[7]

This chapter has revealed that hearing humans are well acquainted with the cadences of mother's voice by the time they are born. Even those for whom the term "mother" conjures up the worst feelings might acknowledge the power of that primordial sound. Philosopher and musicologist Lawrence Kramer goes as far as to suggest that any "intimacy [between humans] . . . suggest[s] the young child's envelopment by the face or voice of the mother" (Kramer 2002, 52). Anthropologists and ethologists looking backward into human evolution point out critical junctures that necessitated a strengthening of mother–offspring bonding. In practice, the voice became a third hand in child rearing when the female parent was manually engaged in the other demands of bipedal life. And in modern humans, every new birth is attended by a neuropeptide that rewards the infant for vocal calls, as it rewards both parents in their postnatal crash-course of ways to soothe, interest, and focus the baby's attention. Neither does this fundamental equation disappear when a child can no longer respond with cries of his own or eye contact. Even the brain of a child as close to death as modern medicine can measure can respond to that sound so central to human experience. Not just healthcare, but education, politics, and indeed all of human interaction might be transformed by rethinking the human predisposition to respond to an inflected voice.

Film Illustration

Wit (based on Margaret Edson's 1995 play of the same name), 2001 TV movie directed by Mike Nichols and starring Emma Thompson and Eileen Atkins.

Discussion Points

1. Get permission to observe vocal and singing interactions between a child younger than seven months old and his or her parent. Document examples of "ritualized packages of sequential behaviors" and categorize those behaviors, using Dissanayake's list of eight potential benefits provided in the chapter (e.g., "modulate infant's state of arousal").
2. In many cultures, evolving parental roles have changed biological implications of the mother–child singing bond. Theorize three promising areas of research related to the phenomenon of fathers undertaking increased nurturing responsibilities in some modern cultures.
3. Survey several films or videos in which a mother's singing voice appears to exert power over a son or daughter (e.g., Alfred Hitchcock's *The Man Who Knew Too Much*, 1956). Extrapolate a list of potential cinematic usages for the mother's voice based on these films.

Notes

1   "Womb to tomb" is borrowed from Stephen Sondheim and others, libretto, *West Side Story*, I, ii, 1957.
2   See also DeCasper and Fifer (1980).
3   The present discussion is informed by Bottge (2005) and Van Buren (1993).
4   Lacan gives credit to Swiss-born psychologist Melanie Klein for that perspective. "Imago" is the image (either in the mirror or of the caregiver) with which the infant identifies.
5   "Even hearing-disabled children have shown preference for infant-directed or emotionally heightened sign language in clinical studies." See Trehub (2003, 671). Further: "There are visual, non-vocal analogs of infants' attraction to maternal speech and

singing: hearing as well as deaf infants prefer the gestural patterns of infant-directed sign language to those of conventional sign language. Emotional expressiveness seems to be the common factor in these across-modality preferences." See also Masataka (1998).

6   Edward John Mostyn Bowlby (1907–90) pioneered modern attachment theory related to child development.

7   O'Kelly et al. (2013), as well as other researchers, have found patients to be responsive to recorded music in minimally conscious and vegetative states.

References

Bottge, K.M. 2005. "Brahms's 'Wiegenlied' and the Maternal Voice." *19th-Century Music* 28.3: 185–213.

Burnham, D. 1993. "Visual Recognition of Mother by Young Infants: Facilitation by Speech." *Perception* 22.10: 1135.

Chion, M. 1999. *The Voice in Cinema*, trans. Claudia Gorbman. New York: Columbia University Press, 61. Quoted in Stan Link. 2010. "The Monster and the Music Box." In *Music in the Horror Film: Listening to Fear*, ed. Neil William Lerner, 38–54. New York: Routledge.

Corbeil, M., I. Peretz, and S. Trehub. 2013. "Speech vs. Singing: Infants Choose Happier Sounds." *Frontiers in Psychology* 26.4. DOI: 10.3389/fpsyg.2013.00372, accessed 31 December 2014.

DeCasper, A.J., and W.P. Fifer. 1980. "Of Human Bonding: Newborns Prefer Their Mother's Voices." *Science* 208: 1174–6.

Dissanayake, E. 2000. 1992. *Homo Aestheticus: Where Art Comes From and Why*. New York: Free Press.

———. 2000. "Antecedents of the Temporal Arts in Early Mother–Infant Interaction." In *The Origins of Music*, eds. N.L. Wallin, B. Merker, and S. Brown, 389–410. Cambridge, MA: MIT Press.

Fifer, W.P., and C.M. Moon. 1994. "The Role of Mother's Voice in the Organization of Brain Function in the Newborn." *Acta Paediatrica* Supplement 397: 86–93.

Galbally, M., A.J. Lewis, M. van Ijzendoorn, and M. Permezel. 2011. "The Role of Oxytocin in Mother–Infant Relations: A Systematic Review of Human Studies." *Harvard Review of Psychiatry* 19.1: 1–14.

Hamilton, A. 1981. *Nature and Nurture: Aboriginal Child-Rearing in North-Central Arnhem Land*. Canberra: Australian Institute of Aboriginal Studies.

Hewlett, B.S. 1991. *Intimate Fathers: The Nature and Context of Aka Pygmy Paternal Infant Care*. Ann Arbor: University of Michigan Press.

Konner, M. 1977. "Infancy among the Kalahari Desert San." In *Culture and Infancy*, eds. P.H. Liederman, S.R. Tulkin, and A. Rosenfeld, 287–328. New York: Academic Press.

Kramer, L. 2002. "Beyond Words and Music: An Essay on Songfulness." In *Musical Meaning: Toward a Critical History*, 51–67. Berkeley: University of California Press.

Lacan, J. 1966. *Écrits*. Paris: Éditions du Seuil. Trans. Bruce Fink. New York: Norton, 2006.

Link, S. 2010. "The Monster and the Music Box: Children and the Soundtrack of Horror." In *Music in the Horror Film: Listening to Fear*, ed. Neil William Lerner, 38–54. New York: Routledge.

Machado, C., J. Korein, E. Aubert, J. Bosch, M.A. Alvarez, R. Rodríguez, P. Valdés, L. Portela, M. Garcia, N. Pérez, M. Chinchilla, Y. Machado, and Y. Machado. 2007. "Recognizing a Mother's Voice in the Persistent Vegetative State." *Clinical EEG Neuroscience* 38.3: 124–6.

Machado, C., M. Estévez, J. Gutiérrez, C. Beltrán, Y. Machado, Y. Machado, M. Chinchilla, and J. Pérez-Nellar. 2011. Letter to the Editor: "Recognition of the Mom's Voice with an Emotional Content in a PVS Patient." *Clinical Neurophysiology* 122.5: 1059–60.

Masataka, N. 1998. "Perception of Motherese in Japanese Sign Language by 6-Month-Old Hearing Infants." *Developmental Psychology* 34.2: 241–6.

Mithen, S. 2006. *The Singing Neanderthals: The Origins of Music, Mind, Language, and Body.* Cambridge, MA: Harvard University Press.

O'Kelly, J., L. James, R. Palaniappan, J. Taborin, J. Fachner, and W.L. Magee. 2013. "Neurophysiological and Behavioral Responses to Music Therapy in Vegetative and Minimally Conscious States." *Frontiers in Human Neuroscience* 7.884. DOI: 10.3389/fnhum.2013.00884, accessed 30 December 2014.

Peretz, I. 2005. "The Nature of Music." *International Journal of Music Education* 23.2: 105.

Querleu, D., X. Renard, F. Versyp, L. Paris-Delrue, and G. Crèpin. 1988. "Fetal Hearing." *European Journal of Obstetrics & Gynecology and Reproductive Biology* 29: 191–212.

Rosolato. 1974. "La voix: Entre corps et langage." *Revue française de psychanalyse* 37: 81. Translated and quoted in K.M. Bottge. 2005. "Brahms's 'Wiegenlied' and the Maternal Voice." *19th-Century Music* 28.3: 185–213.

Scherzinger, M. 1999. "When the Music of Psychoanalysis Becomes the Psychoanalysis of Music." *Current Musicology* 66: 95–115. Review essay of D. Schwarz. *Listening Subjects: Music, Psychoanalysis, Culture.* Durham, NC: Duke University Press, 1997.

Seltzer, L.J., T.E. Ziegler, and S.D. Pollak. 2010. "Social Vocalizations Can Release Oxytocin in Humans." *Proceedings of the Royal Society of Biological Sciences* 277.1694: 2661–6.

Spence, M.J., and A.J. DeCasper. 1982. "Human Fetuses Perceive Maternal Speech." Meeting of the International Conference on Infant Studies, Austin, TX.

Trehub, S. 2001. "Musical Predispositions in Infancy." *Annals of the New York Academy of Science* 930: 1–16.

———. 2003. "The Development of Musicality." *Nature Neuroscience* 6.7: 669–73.

Van Buren, J. 1993. "Mother–Infant Semiotics: Intuition and the Development of Human Subjectivity—Klein/Lacan Fantasy and Meaning." *Journal of the American Academy of Psychoanalysis* 21.4: 567–80.

Velandia, M., A. Matthisen, K. Uvnäs-Moberg, and E. Nissen. 2010. "Onset of Vocal Interaction between Parents and Newborns in Skin-to-Skin Contact Immediately after Elective Cesarean Section." *Birth: Issues in Perinatal Care* 37.3: 192–201.

PART II

Singing for the Group, the Self, and the Soul

4

SINGING OUR SONGS

Damon of Athens, the Blues, and Group Psychology

> Blues aren't just about us being sad . . . It's a way to remember . . . The blues talk about black folk, how we lived, the way we were treated. And we're still going on.
>
> *Irene "Mama Rene" Walker (quoted in Cobb 1999)*

One way we recognize people from the same group is by their music; songs can unify and bind groups of like-minded people. Cultures across the world provide examples of this brand of cohesiveness. In the film *The Singing Revolution*, James and Maureen Tusty document that "in the late 1980's, music was . . . used as a unifying force when hundreds of thousands gathered to sing forbidden Estonian songs, demanding their right for self-determination from a brutal Soviet occupier" (Tusty and Tusty 2006). Holocaust victims expressed solidarity with song even as they were herded to gas chambers in Auschwitz, as Ruth Elias recalls:

> We heard singing, very soft at first, then louder and louder. It was the Czech national anthem . . . (Where is my homeland?). Then, much louder, "Hatikvah" (Hope), the Jewish national anthem . . . Our friends were about to be gassed. These songs were their last clear message to the prisoners who were left in the family camp.
>
> *Elias (1998, 117)*

On another continent, singing within the African National Congress articulated a cause and, thus, contributed to greater equity for marginalized black South Africans. Enoch Sontonga's 1897 hymn "Nkosi Sikelel' iAfrika"[1] was incorporated into an anti-apartheid song that would eventually become the current South African national anthem. Not surprisingly, this composite song was featured at memorial services for former South African president Nelson Mandela (1918–2013) (Figure 4.1).[2] These instances reveal the predisposition to sing together when courage or camaraderie is needed most.

FIGURE 4.1 Enoch Sontonga, "Nkosi Sikelel' iAfrika" (public domain).

This chapter is the most speculative in the book. I use the thoughts of fifth-century Pythagoreans as a theoretical point of departure and a subset of the kaleidoscopic genre of blues as a case in point. In the fifth century BCE, Damon reportedly observed that people of the same Greek tribe or regional group made characteristic vocal sounds. Furthermore, these songs could persuade outsiders to adopt characteristics of the originators. In a vastly different time and place, a song style coalesced that would be called blues. This cultural product expressed fundamental truths about a group of people who shared similar experiences relating to one common denominator: a heritage of enslavement in a particular geographical region. If, for the sake of argument, Damon's paradigm can be applied to people so removed by culture, chronology, and experience as 1900s African Americans, then some general truths about all of us might emerge. Downhome blues did become a talisman for its originating society, and, further, blues music was magnetic, even irresistible, to outsiders. As this chapter will show, blues transformed the music of others well beyond its Mississippi delta origins. Damon's musical ethos theory, manifested in such a vastly different environment, is just preparation for my fundamental question. Where does song get the power to bind people within a group and transform people outside that group? This chapter intersperses information on ethos theory and downhome blues with modern scientific evidence of the ways shared singing can accomplish this cultural work.

Ethos and Blues

Ancient Greek philosophers commented often on the connection between music—mousikē, the activities of the nine Muses—and moral character, or ethos. Musical styles as well as people possessed ethos, but as many disagreements as unifying features have been transmitted about this ancient belief. One position was attributed to Damon of Oa (fifth century BCE).

> [We know that music moves the soul]; further, joyful music makes one joyful and vice-versa. A musical effect is utilized in accord with the ethos of each soul. National styles or "modes" are construed as . . . scale systems, whose intervals are generated by ratios characteristic of the personality types and behavior patterns of their users.
>
> *Quoted in Wallace (2004, 257–8)*[3]

Robert Wallace has reconstructed Damon's work based on Plato's testimony. He sums up this point: "In Damon's view (as Plato represents it), musical styles not only 'fit' behavior, they also determine or shape it, both for individuals and for society" (Wallace 2004, 258). In Republic (ca. 380 BCE), Plato attributed great power to musical ethos. He warned his readers about the dangers of new modes: "the modes of music are never disturbed without unsettling of the most fundamental political and social conventions" (translated in Weiss and Taruskin 1984, 8).

Dorians, an ancient Greek ethnic group, may be resurrected to illustrate this perspective. Damon might have said that the Dorians' characteristic musical mode (what might today be considered the Dorians' musical style) reflected identifying qualities of Doric Greek dialect (see Figure 4.2).[4] A logical cycle might emerge: Dorians spoke and acted in specific ways, which were exemplified in Dorian dialectical or musical style. Dorians were considered warlike or bellicose; Ionians, on the other hand, were associated with bacchanals and dance. Further, as Plato's writing above indicates, Dorian style not only *represented* Dorians; hearing the Dorian style persuaded listeners to assume a stereotypically Dorian way of behaving.

The chaos caused by dangerous or incorrect modes is related frequently in Greek and Roman literature. In *On the Doctrines of Hippocrates and Plato* by Galen (131–200 CE) and *On the Marriage of Philology and Mercury* by Martianus Capella (fifth century CE) may be found accounts of

> drunken youths [who] were acting crazy to the Phrygian tune of an aulos player. Damon had the aulete change to a Dorian *harmonia* and the youths were calmed.
>
> *Related in Wallace (2004, 260)*

This theory of music's power to shape morality or behavior was especially crucial in Damon's time, when civic responsibility was extremely important. Nor were

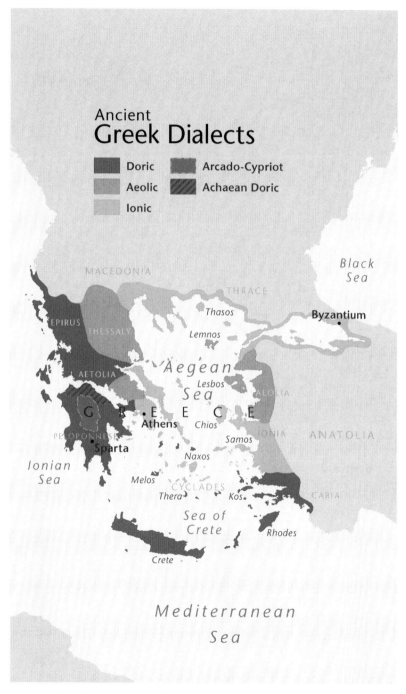

FIGURE 4.2 Distribution of several ancient Greek dialects, ca. fifth through fourth centuries BCE. Dreamline Cartography, 2014.

Western philosophers the only great thinkers to be concerned with music's power over humans. According to the *Analects* of Confucius (Legge 2002), "The Master said, 'It is by the Odes that the mind is aroused. 2. It is by the Rules of Propriety that the character is established. 3. It is from Music that the finish is received.'"

Because it relies on written documentation, history necessarily records the thoughts of the most learned members of a society—members of intellectual elites such as Confucius, Pythagoras, and Damon. Surely, however, the correspondence between a culture's characteristic utterances and its identity was as familiar to the common classes. Chapter 2 presented various ways that even pre-human ancestors utilized coordinated singing for functional purposes like locating group members, food, and territories. Modern humans of Damon's time spoke Greek dialects dependent upon region, as indicated in Figure 4.2. Song dialects, whether documented by the likes of Damon or not, would have been part of societal living. Today, a variety of human groups—teenagers, religious believers, war veterans, citizens, and entire generations—claim shared song styles. Sometimes, those styles are intended to call for and implement social change, as seen in this chapter's opening illustration.

Blues song works well to represent Damon's point, but who constitutes my blues culture? The answer to that question is not straightforward. More than ten million people from as many as forty-five African ethnic groups were displaced to the Americas by the transatlantic slave trade between 1650 and 1900. They brought with them languages and dialects, cultures, and musical practices. In the New World, most underwent the cruel and dehumanizing experience of the slavery system. Slave-owners, especially in what would become the United States, learned quickly that African drums intensified uprisings and riots; in many places percussion instruments were banned from slave quarters.[5] A piece of legislation from colonial Georgia details this situation from the white perspective:

> It is absolutely necessary to the Safety of this Province that all due Care be taken to restrain the Wanderings and Meetings of Negroes and other Slaves at all times and more Especially on Saturday Night, Sundays, and other Holidays and their using and Carrying Wooden Swords and other Mischievous and dangerous Weapons or using or keeping of Drums, Horns, or other loud instruments which may call together or give . . . Notice to one another of their wicked Designs and Purposes.
>
> *Candler, quoted in Broucek (1963, 77)*

Yet, those very instruments had provided the transplanted Africans with a method of communication in the absence of shared languages. They had come from Senegal, Gambia, Sierra Leone, and Angola, might have spent time in South America or the Caribbean, and were eventually thrown together in the British colonies with no regard for culture of origin. When drums were banned in some areas, vocalizations—as well as body percussion—were naturally highlighted as these forced émigrés sought self-expression. Around the turn of the twentieth century, vocal expressions such as these contributed to what is now called blues.[6]

The genealogy of blues is one of the many fascinating journeys that together comprise American musical history; a complete blues history cannot be recounted here in any depth. Blues evolved from the musically rich environments and social contexts of the post-bellum Mississippi River area and its tributaries (Titon 1981, 15ff.). Songs eventually called blues surfaced in 1890s dance venues, where people performed angular, loose-limbed steps such as the shimmy and the black bottom.

These dance songs featured improvised lyrics. Black folk song, including Reconstruction-era (and perhaps older) field hollers of solo people working outdoors, contributed a distinctive vocal timbre and a characteristic melodic shape: a repeated line of text leading to a high note, then a descent. In 1890s dance venues, black folk songs—called blues only in retrospect—were accompanied by instruments such as the Spanish guitar, which entered the US in the late nineteenth century. Violins, mandolins, banjos, and harmonicas also enriched the delivery (Titon 1981, 16).

By 1900, the steady beats, improvised lyrics, and insistent bodily presence bequeathed from the dance hall; melodic structure from folk song; a singing dialect to be detailed later; and accompaniments exploiting strummed, plucked, and blown instruments that could easily imitate vocal sounds had coalesced into the subgenre featured in this chapter, downhome blues. Jeff Todd Titon writes: "in the phrase downhome blues, the word 'blues' indicates both a musical style based on particular sounds and a feeling associated with it, the juxtaposed 'downhome' locates the feeling as a place in the mental landscape of black America" (Titon 1981, xiv, emphasis in original).

Downhome blues disseminated outside its birthplace and acculturated with white tastes, beginning in the second decade of the twentieth century. Titon differentiates between downhome and vaudeville blues, the latter popularized in the 1920s by "blues queens" such as Mamie Smith (1883–1946), Ma Rainey (1886–1939), Bessie Smith (1894–1937), and Ethel Waters (1896–1977). Even if they began their careers in downhome settings, these professional women recorded a blues style that bore witness to white tastes for clear articulation and sweet, mild vocal timbres. Further, blues queens did not accompany themselves; they fronted their own bands and many built international careers.[7] Standardized, acculturated blues also appeared in core repertoires of jazz bands led by W.C. Handy (1873–1958) and Ferdinand "Jelly Roll" Morton (1890–1941).

In contrast, male farmers or drifting seasonal laborers in the Delta entertained their friends with downhome blues. Titon writes: "Some had experience in carnivals, minstrel shows and medicine shows, but most downhome singing was Saturday night parties in crowded juke joints, or outside (Titon 1981, xv)." Mississippi natives like Charley Patton (ca. 1891–1934), Tommy Johnson (1896–1956), and Son House (1902–88) accompanied themselves on guitar, sang with a raspy tone (often in contrast to their spoken voices), and slurred their consonants. Their blues tunes varied in phrase and harmonic content. Though downhome blues were also found in the southeastern US, in New Orleans, and in Midwestern cities, they developed most fully in east Texas and the Mississippi River delta and were well known to entertainers and audiences there by 1903 (Titon 1981, 28).

Downhome blues appeared most frequently where an audience was present. House parties, outdoor picnics, and juke (jook) joints were the most common rural venues. And musicians were never the reason for juke joints; they provided the entertainment background to the "gamblers, pimps, bootleggers, tough guys . . . gangsters," and regular customers casting off the troubles of the working week (Wald 2004, 269, 273). Blues performers played and sang a range of music for blacks and whites: music that included ragtime songs, ballads, popular songs, and even social dance songs such as "Goodnight, Irene," a waltz-meter tune first played by Huddie Ledbetter (Leadbelly, 1885–1949) in 1908.[8]

In contrast to their rural counterparts, town blues musicians performed in cafés and on street corners and sidewalks, bus and rail stations, and in parks. City blues performers shared many of the town venues, but added vaudeville theaters, saloons, and cabarets. Finally, some blues performers joined traveling tent shows, medicine shows, and circuses, while others developed regular circuits of blues venues. Downhome blues were not recorded in quantity until 1926, when the Texan Blind Lemon Jefferson (1897–1929) made his first cut with Paramount. Fortunately for blues historians, however, downhome bluesmen frequently documented their early-twentieth-century experiences in oral and written forms.

Titon writes at length about the philosophical bond between blues and black religious songs such as spirituals. Though the worldviews of these two genres differed, "they preached the same advice: treat people right" (Titon 1981, 33). Blues addressed the most fundamental of human needs and desires—shelter, clothing, food, love, and sex—in ways that challenged black and white religious audiences alike. Nevertheless, downhome blues commented upon and advocated ethical living, an important tenet of Greek ethos. And though blues music has been characterized as the personal lament of a solitary individual, minister and former blues artist Rubin Lacy spoke of its universality: "Sometimes I'd propose [lyrics] as [if] it happened to me in order to hit somebody else, 'cause everything that happened to one person has at some time or other happened to another one. If not, it will" (quoted in Evans 1967, 7).

Titon writes that blues musicians provided a vehicle for societal dissent that was accepted and even supported by the white power structure. Downhome blues men

> ultimately encouraged solidarity within the culture and kept the community together, helping to provide a supportive alternative to white middle-class beliefs. Without the blues, the black experience down home would have been significantly closer to white middle-class behavior, making it infinitely more difficult for black people today to find a separate identity in an Afro-American culture distinct from Anglo-American culture
>
> *Titon (1981, 59)*

Wielding art to bolster the spirit under outrageous circumstance is a hallmark of marginalized people, and nowhere is that maxim more evident than in the experiences of Africans forcibly relocated to the US as part of the slave trade. Blues helped African Americans create an identity separate from the dominant white establishment and, in so doing, forever changed America's musical landscape.

The Downhome Blues Aesthetic and Group Bonding

The language of blues is metaphor; popular-style blues man Willie Dixon famously said, "The blues is the truth." Rev. Arnold "Gatemouth" Moore generalized that "The blues are just situations in life" (Cobb 1999). But for African Americans with enslavement in their genealogies those situations were most often dire. In their study of human behavior and social organization, Cross and Woodruff write: "Music performs a huge array of functions across different cultures, but one very generic feature that they all seem to share is the management of social relationships, particularly in situations of social uncertainty" (Cross and Woodruff [2009] 2014, 2). What about music, and for our purposes song, allows that to happen? First, say Cross and Woodruff, music is a "natural sign." As proven in film scores, music has the capacity to heighten and, sometimes, direct audience perception. This quality is "natural" because music's potential for meaning is naturally understandable to humans.[9] Music has structural similarity to language, it is a temporal art comprising expectation and arrival, and its gestural language is, in some ways, analogous to human movement. Said another way, music's ups and downs, complexities and simplicities, and antecedents and consequents feel like the experience of life. Therefore, "a close relationship can be postulated between the motivational states of listeners and the global motivational structures of musical sound" (Cross and Woodruff [2009] 2014, 6). This reciprocity was conditioned by our biological heritage.

The second factor relates to activities in society and seems quite similar to the first. Music also has power to mean something because musical responses are mediated by and within cultures. The entire experience of music—whether participatory or passive—is culturally contingent. However, even if a listener fails to appreciate the cultural significance of an Indian raga, for example, she can still recognize it as something other than pure speech. This fact has led cultural theorists such as John Blacking to speculate that there must be a "supra-cultural cognitive" resonance that leads different composers, listeners, and musical systems to use the same modes of musical thought. And that resonance, as Cross and Woodruff argue, is seated in the ways music embodies particularly human modes of interaction across cultures. Just as music's meaningfulness is recognizable from human to human, so it is recognizable as music from culture to culture.

The third dimension of musical meaning postulated by Cross and Woodruff relates to music as a cultural product. The authors reference a study by Tomasello and colleagues which explains the human capacity for, and motivation toward, a "shared intentionality" among members of a culture (Tomasello et al. 2005). Shared goals and mutually understood roles for pursuing those goals comprise this shared intentionality. Motivations for gathering together at a downhome blues venue—to commiserate, be seen, reaffirm identity, dance, experience vocal and instrumental music, and socialize—would have been obvious, as well as unspoken.

Simply being present to gamble, eat, dance, and perhaps sing along with songs that represented the group felt good in these blues venues, as in so many other places.[10] Where do those good feelings come from? Today's scientific protocols are far removed from the real experiences to be had in a 1910s juke joint, but more than ever before we have grounds for speculating about the psychological and physical processes at work when people gathered together there. Many studies, a few of which will be referenced below, have studied biomarkers associated with group singing and reported significant positive results.

It goes without saying that the cultural environments experienced by black audiences in 1910s America and German ones a century later are vastly different. Juke joints were notorious havens for alcohol and drug abuse. Yet, variables such as chronic intoxication actually increase the concentration of salivary cortisol both while inebriated and during withdrawal (Adinoff et al. 2003). Further, allostatic load—cumulative psychological burdens associated with adverse living conditions such as poverty, marginalization, hopelessness, or neighborhood violence—reportedly creates increased levels of stress biomarkers such as salivary cortisol in some populations (Worthman and Panter-Brick 2008). So the biomarkers associated with the stresses felt by relatively advantaged populations may, in fact, be far less significant than in those "living on the edge" of the dominant culture. Allostatic load in association with variables of race, class, and gender is the subject of ongoing clinical attention (Geronimus et al. 2006). One especially informative study by Louise Hawkley and colleagues recruited 208 white, Hispanic, and black urban participants between the ages of fifty-one and sixty-nine (Hawkley et al. 2011). Variables such as perceived stress, personality type, hostility, and optimism were studied as mediators in the association between socioeconomic status (SES) and allostatic load (AL). Hawkley and colleagues stated three potentially generalizable findings from their study. First, AL is a good indicator of SES-related wear and tear on the body. Second, none of the stress indicators they measured mediated the relationship between SES and AL, but poor sleep quality and hostility both contributed to that relationship. Finally, "although low SES is typically thought to lead to AL through increased challenge, [they provided] the first evidence that the restorative properties associated with sleep quality play a significant role in explaining the relationship between SES and AL" (Hawkley et al. 2011, 1143).

The research studies referenced here reinforce human complexity and difference, but hopefully will also suggest ideas about the psycho-physiological good received by juke joint aficionados. We will never know all the physical and psychological factors that motivated poor African Americans to create and experience blues together. Yet, as elsewhere in this book, research findings about other groups may suggest reasons that the downhome blues population left these venues feeling relieved and somewhat renewed by their encounters with song.

Human immune function is affected by psychological factors; stress has a profound influence on the immune system and can be a predisposing factor to diseases involving the immune system (Kuhn 2002).[11] Immunoglobulin A (IgA) is secreted in bodily substances such as tears and saliva. It plays important functions in the immune system and is considered the body's first line of defense against bacterial and viral infections of the upper respiratory pathway. The potential for singing to help with stress management becomes clearer as scientists measure salivary IgA (SIgA) in pre- and post-singing experiences.

In 2002, Kuhn compared active and passive music involvement in the production of SIgA. Participants were randomly assigned to one control and two experimental groups. Each participant provided salivary samples pre- and post-musical activity. The active experimental group participated in a thirty-minute music-making session, which included leader/response drumming and singing sessions, as well as short improvisations on tone bars and drums. The passive experimental group listened to live performances of other people singing and playing on piano, flute, and tuba. Participants in the control group were allowed to move around and talk to others, but they were not allowed to listen to music, sing, hum, tap music, or even talk about music during the experiment.[12] SIgA concentrations in the active participant group showed significantly greater increases than those of the control group. Further, active participation created significantly greater concentrations of SIgA than did passive listening.

In a 2004 study, Kreutz and colleagues focused on choir singing versus listening, collected self-reporting data, and assayed pre- and post-choral rehearsal levels of SIgA and cortisol, the latter a hormone whose concentration in saliva increases with increased stress (Kreutz et al. 2004).[13] Using psychological and physiological measures, this study reinforced earlier findings that singing leads to increases in both positive affect and the production of SIgA. Participants in this German study also self-evaluated their affective states with the Positive and Negative Affect Schedule (PANAS) (Watson et al. 1988). Salivary samples were collected and the PANAS was completed before and after two sixty-minute rehearsals, which occurred one week apart. Week one was the singing condition and, in the second week, rehearsal time was spent listening to Mozart's Requiem and hearing articles about eighteenth-century music read aloud. When music was played, participants were instructed to listen as attentively as if they were singing.

This research group found that active singing led to a decrease in negative mood and an increase in positive mood and SIgA, but that singing did not affect cortisol responses. The listening-only group reported increased negative mood after the rehearsal (possibly because they had expected to sing rather than listen only), a decrease in cortisol, and no significant changes in positive mood and SIgA.[14] These findings about stress biomarkers are far removed, but may yet have application to the people who frequented our 1910s juke joint.

In 2011, Müller and Lindenberger reported on another possible reason that downhome blues aficionados may have felt they were part of a cohesive social structure. Respiration, they learned, becomes synchronized among choir singers. They also measured heart rate variability (HRV), the variation in the time interval between heartbeats. A heart rate that is highly variable and responsive to bodily demands is believed to bestow a survival advantage, whereas reduced HRV may be associated with poorer cardiovascular health and outcomes (Routledge et al. 2010). Having a high HRV is thus good for health. Müller and Lindenberger also found that HRV, in addition to respiration, synchronized among group singers. Coordination of both these responses was higher when singing in unison than when singing pieces with multiple voice parts (Müller and Lindenberger 2011).

Finally, entrainment, an effect of rhythm, has received extended attention from musical and neuroscientific researchers such as Michael Thaut, who writes: "Auditory rhythms rapidly entrain motor responses into stable steady synchronization states below and above conscious perception thresholds" (Thaut 2003, abstract). Put simply, music can synchronize organisms to its rhythmic patterning (Thaut 2005, Thaut et al. 2005). This entrainment function underscores dancing, physical exercise and labor, marching, and many other forms of musical activity (Bispham 2006). But in addition to the observable ways we entrain with music (e.g., dancing with the beat), our brains actually entrain with music at levels so minuscule as to be undetectable except with the help of brain imaging technology. Returning to Cross and Woodruff, "music, like language, uses entrainment to coordinate interaction, but in music this serves as a primary function and hence its cues for interaction are more strongly evident" (Cross and Woodruff 2009, 13).

Bonding and Blues Elements

The previous section speculated about ways that simply being in the blues environment and participating in various ways contributed to wellbeing. Elements of the downhome blues genre offer further reasons it works particularly well in social bonding. Elijah Wald lists several relevant definitions of blues, the most limited of which references chord patterns. Twelve-bar blues is most familiar, but that framework may only have been standardized after 1912, when the first blues songs were published. Rural black Americans in the Delta had been employing that chord pattern and many others for more than a decade by that time. Nevertheless, when the average person refers to a standard blues chord progression, they usually mean something like the one pictured in Figure 4.3.

Leader/response procedure is often heard as a dialogue between singer and instrumentalist in blues. In her famous 1925 recording of "St. Louis Blues," Bessie Smith sings during the first two bars of the first phrase (Smith, Armstrong, and Longshaw 1925). Her "call" is followed by two bars of "response" played by Louis Armstrong on cornet. In the informal setting of the juke joint, this procedure

	1 2 3 4	1 2 3 4	1 2 3 4	1 2 3 4
Phrase 1	I	I	I	I
Phrase 2 R	IV	IV	I	I
Phrase 3	V	(IV)	I	I

FIGURE 4.3 Basic twelve-bar blues structure. R=repeat of phrase 1. Chords: I=tonic, IV=subdominant, V=dominant. Leader unshaded, response shaded.

may have invited audience members to improvise responses ("I know that's right," "Sing it,"), as well.

In a 2013 study, Vickhoff and colleagues studied heart rate variability (HRV) vis à vis musical structure (Vickhoff et al. 2013). Reinforcing early work by Müller and Lindenberger, they observed "clear entrainment effect between [group] singers in terms of heart rate acceleration and deceleration [a biomarker distinct from HRV] as soon as they sang a simple structure in unison" (Vickhoff et al. 2013, 12). They extended their findings into a hypothesis about the meanings this entrainment may have had in human evolution, but their statement requires some preliminary explanation. Respiratory sinus arrhythmia (RSA) refers to the naturally occurring variation in HRV during a breathing cycle (e.g., inhale and exhale). RSA is dependent upon respiration rate and is more marked when a complete respiration cycle of inhalation and exhalation takes about ten seconds. Pronounced RSA is a benefit to circulation and improves wellbeing. That is why rosary prayers and chanted yoga mantras have proven to affect HRV and RSA positively.

HRV and RSA also reflect changes in the way the autonomic nervous system is engaged in breathing. RSA inhalation temporarily suppresses the autonomic nervous system (ANS) and heart rate increases. At the exhalation, heart rate decreases and the autonomic nervous system once again engages. Vagal tone describes this process. Vickhoff and colleagues summarize that:

> The vagal effect of breathing is, as pointed out, an ANS reaction. It is hardwired and thus universal. It could therefore be expected that various cultures use this technique wherever people gather to achieve relaxed communicative states. Interestingly, coordinated respiratory activity, irrespective if it is caused by yoga breathing, mantra chanting, praying or singing, is ritually performed in most religions. This is a common factor, more so than the semantic content of beliefs.
>
> *Vickhoff et al. (2013, 13)*

Finally, they wrote: "Choir singing coordinates the neurophysiological activity for timing, motor production of words and melody, respiration and HRV." Doubtless, singing in a choir and feeling the grooves in a downhome blues event are distinct in many ways. Nevertheless, the similarities between choir singing and other synchronized group musical expressions are worth contemplating. Blues phrase structures, especially the stereotypical twelve-bar blues form, incorporate phrase repetition and leader/response possibilities within each phrase that provide opportunities for vagal breathing to create a collective, relaxed state.

In addition to chord progression models, a depressed or melancholy mood is often associated with blues. Evidence of the human desire to lament is as old as documentary history. Melancholia was one of the four temperaments in the Greek system of wellness; managing or balancing that temperament required balancing the humor of black bile.[15] Thrēnos, the ancient Greek lament for a deceased person, was commonly used to help release the strong emotions that accompanied a death. In *Table-Talk* (657a), Plutarch (46–120 CE) observed that "thrēnoidia (threnody) and the epikedeios aulos move the emotions and cause tears to flow, thus little by little consuming and removing distress." Aristides Quintilianus (third century CE, *On Music*, ii.4) noted that music was employed in certain "funeral rites to break off the extreme of passion by means of melody."[16] Professional lamenters in Ancient Greece, often women, sang elegies for funeral rituals of the wealthy. Their songs featured leader/response format and the aulos was considered an appropriate accompaniment. Lamenting in Ireland, called keening, was first referenced in the seventh century and has been documented at least since the seventeenth century.[17] Since the sixteenth century, a sense of melancholy or depression has been called the "blue devils."

Clearly, the melancholy utterances of blues reflect a universal human condition, but the blues lament is distinctive. In 1970, Albert Murray elaborated on the linguistic component of blues:

> When the Negro musician or dancer swings the blues, he is fulfilling the same fundamental existential requirement that determines the mission of the poet, priest, and medicine man ... He is making an affirmative and hence exemplary and heroic response to that which André Malraux describes as 'la condition humaine.' Extemporizing in response to the exigencies of the situation ... he is confronting, acknowledging, and contending with the infernal absurdities and ever-impending frustrations inherent in the nature of all existence by playing with the possibilities that are also there.
>
> *Murray (1970, 58)*

Blues gave its creators an artistic framework for social commentary, best understood by members of the blues community, but widely appreciated outside it.

Commenting on life in such a way has long been part of the musical culture in some parts of Africa. As early as the seventeenth century, French writers used the term "griot" (fem. "griotte") to describe a class of hereditary professional musical and verbal artisans in some regions of Senegambia.[18] *Griot* is a French rendering of local West African terms: Arabic *iggio*; Wolof *gewel*; Fulfulde *gawlo*; Maninka (Malinke)–Xasonke (Kassonke)–Bamana (Bamara) *jeli*; Mandinka *jali*; and Soninke

Won't you iron my jumper	starch my overalls
I'm gon' find my woman said she's	in this world somewhere
Well it's good to you mama	sure lord killin' me
Well it's good to you mama	sure lord killin' poor me
Well it's good to you mama says it's	sure lord killin' me
I wonder do my	rider think of me
I wonder do my	rider think of poor me
Cryin' if she did she would	sure lord feel my care
I woke this mornin'	said my mornin' prayer
I woke up this mornin' I	said my mornin' prayer
I woke this mornin' babe I	said my mornin' prayer
I ain't got no woman	speak in my behalf
I ain't got no woman now	speak in my behalf
I ain't got no woman to	speak in my behalf
Won't you iron my jumper	starch my overalls
Won't you iron my jumper	starch my overalls
I'm goin' find my woman said she's	in this world somewhere
She don't like me to holler	tried to murmur low

FIGURE 4.4 Text transcription by Jeff Todd Titon of Tommy Johnson, "Lonesome Blues" lyrics, take 1, Victor 45463-1, Memphis, TN, 31 August 1928. From Jeff Todd Titon, *Early Downhome Blues: A Musical and Cultural Analysis*, 2nd ed. Copyright © 1995 by the University of North Carolina Press. Used by permission of the publisher.

jaare. Griots are found primarily in Senegal, the Gambia, Guinea, and Mali and belong to a limited number of lineages with probable roots in ancient Ghana or Mali. Griots soliloquized on life and, at other times, relayed current news to the general population as balladeers did in other cultures. In downhome blues, Delta blues griots expressed the facts of life with distinctive irony, imagery, double entendre, and humor (see Figure 4.4).

Rhythm may be the most powerful group adhesive in any song's toolbox. Wald's third element of blues involves West African tonal (e.g., "blue notes") and rhythmic practices (e.g., playing "behind" the beat).[19] Blue notes will be described momentarily; blues rhythm is a complex interplay between improvised vocalization and steady beat. All music embellishes expected rhythmic structures; downhome blues music displays virtuoso improvisation on rhythmic expectations. Blues performance style requires the appearance of ease in the execution of often daunting rhythmic complexity.

In a 2009 study, Large and Snyder studied periodicity in music.[20] In most popular songs, we hear a steady beat or recurring pulse. We may tap our feet to this beat; it also provides a framework for much popular dancing. Remarkably, either through inheritance or nurture, most humans can discern a recurring beat when one exists and the music is culturally relevant for the listener.

The steady beat becomes periodic when some beats are stressed. These emphasized beats organize the music into recurring patterns, most commonly, of two, three, or four beats.[21] Meter is the term that describes the perceived grouping of steady beats by emphasis on certain beats. Being able to identify musical meter takes more experience than perceiving the long string of steady beats. Nevertheless, the very students who have trouble differentiating a waltz, which has triple meter, from a standard blues tune, which usually has a four-beat organization, do not usually have trouble responding to those meters with the body. In other words, though we may not be able to categorize them, we often do sense metrical organization in music.

In many popular music forms, drummers often play on all four beats of a four-meter song. In his introduction to rock history, John Covach provides an example of a basic drum set pattern for a rock song in four-meter (Covach 2006, 216).

Meter:	1	&	2	&	3	&	4	&
High-Hat (cymbals):	x	x	x	x	x	x	x	x
Snare:			x				x	
Bass drum:	x				x	x		

The rock drummer utilizes both hands and feet to play this lightly stylized underlay of pulse. The bass drum defines the accented beats in the bar, and the snare emphasizes the back beats. The high-hat insures a sense of moving forward. Pulses or beats we feel when we are dancing, marching, or swaying with music are not necessarily as audible as they appear to be in this example, however. Even in rock, drummers weave complex counter-rhythms, add pick-ups to signal a change from verse to chorus, or insert breathtaking solos around steady beat patterns like the one seen above.

Meter, phrase structure, and sections like verses and choruses are some of the periodicities evident in music. Our brains respond to these regularities in music with periodic activities of their own. Large and Snyder write that our

> perception of pulse and meter result from rhythmic bursts of high-frequency neural activity in response to musical rhythms. High-frequency bursts of activity may enable communication between neural areas, such as auditory and motor cortices, during rhythm perception and production.
>
> *Large and Snyder (2009, abstract)*

Our brains somehow translate musical, rhythmic periodicities into bursts of cerebral activity that allow us to perceive those periodicities. And why should our brains do that? "One possible function of such a transformation is to enable synchronization between individuals through perception of a common abstract temporal structure (e.g., during music performance)." Our perceptive network for musical periodicity helps synchronize our brain function with that of others when in a group. The downhome blues audience would have had one more way to synchronize.

Blue notes may be traces of African indigenous musical languages that feature microtones, that is, musical intervals smaller than the half steps of the European piano (see Figures 4.5 and 4.6). For many listeners, blue notes give the genre its distinctive flavor. Returning to the 1925 recording of "St. Louis Blues," Bessie Smith bends almost every pitch in the opening line, "I hate to see the eve'ning sun go down." She sustains an especially poignant blue note on the rhythmically

Pitch slightly higher than notated, but insufficiently high to be properly notated by the next higher chromatic step.

Pitch slightly lower than notated, but insufficiently low to be properly notated by the next lower chromatic step.

♩ = ____ (initial)   Metronome marking for initial stanza in quarter-note equivalents per minute.

Slurs from and to definite pitches.

FIGURE 4.5 Key to melodic transcription in Figure 4.6. From Jeff Todd Titon, *Early Downhome Blues: A Musical and Cultural Analysis*, 2nd ed. Copyright © 1995 by the University of North Carolina Press. Used by permission of the publisher.

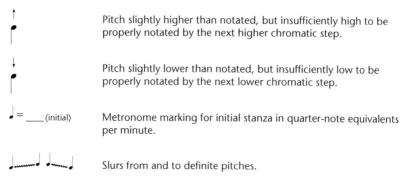

FIGURE 4.6 Melodic transcription by Jeff Todd Titon of Tommy Johnson, "Lonesome Blues," take 1, Victor 45463-1, Memphis, TN, 31 August 1928. From Jeff Todd Titon, *Early Downhome Blues: A Musical and Cultural Analysis*, 2nd ed. Copyright © 1995 by the University of North Carolina Press. Used by permission of the publisher.

elongated word "sun." Blue notes have received a wealth of scholarly attention, much of it controversial. Gerhard Kubik cautions against trying to fit blue notes into a Western tonal system and instead argues that a blues melody is an autonomous whole (Kubik 2008, 17). The best blues research strategy, in his mind, acknowledges that blues vocal lines are integrated entities within which no tones have particular status. In other words, it may be best to recognize Smith's version of "St. Louis Blues" as an entire cognitive system that displays parts of other musical styles, but is not governed by rules of other styles.

Significantly, Kubik places the voice at the center of blues; he writes: "the majority of blues guitarists . . . developed non-Western guitar styles and techniques. But this seems to have happened *in response to* and *imitation of* the patterns of the voice" (Kubik 2008, 17–18, emphasis mine). And blue notes may simply reflect the musical dialect of our latter-day Dorians, downhome blues folk. Kubik even references the guitar's importation into blues in vocal terms:

> When foreign instruments are adopted in a culture, the original heritage tends to "retreat" to the human voice as a primary instrument. For this reason, it can be expected that in the blues the non-Western traits must be particularly concentrated in the lines and timbre-melodic patterns produced by the human voice, which in turn is imitated or commented on by the guitar.
>
> *Kubik (2008, 18)*

Perhaps the most identifiable blues characteristic is the timbre of the black blues artist. This coarsely grained, even gravelly, vocal sound would inspire as many subsequent artists as would any other element of blues. Growls, cries, and slides add seasoning to downhome blues, and these elements survived to inspire subsequent generations of popular singers.

To summarize this discussion of blues elements, along with a complex address of rhythm, what are commonly called blue notes create a flexible and colorful vocal style that helped externalize emotions ranging from simple despair, to poetic resignation, to ironic disbelief. Twelve-bar blues progression was Western Europe's contribution, honed and made characteristic by Mississippi guitarists. Finally, blues texts combined the expressive work of balladeers and griots with metaphorical languages. Repression of freedoms engendered linguistic coding in songs. In these ways, formerly enslaved people from many nations and cultures, whose forced immigration followed divergent routes, collectively created a vocally expressive form that represented shared experiences within the New World slavery and postbellum societies. Sharing experiences and perspectives musically is a way to be known by others. Blues also facilitated catharsis through humor or commiseration, and, in a gloss on Nietzche's famous statement, blues made art out of tragedy.

Singing Our Songs

So far in this chapter, I have pinpointed a specific group and musical genre. Like the members of all cohesive groups, downhome blues people shared heritage, experiences, and feelings that were culturally contingent. The rest of this section presents further research about the therapeutic and affirming aspects of group singing. Psychologists, especially, have studied the connection between group singing and wellbeing, and others have found that singing together results in cooperation, shared perspectives, and joint intentions (Bailey and Davidson 2003).[22] Singing together presumes breathing and rendering pitch and rhythm in coordinated fashion. When we sing together, we also may give voice to a set of words that is deeply meaningful. Words articulated with our tongues have a way of insinuating into our hearts. The reasons Damon's paradigm remains relevant today are deeply seated in human behavior and biology.

Diverse groups have been subjects of group singing studies, but as one researcher wrote: "Wellbeing is a complex construct and difficult to measure quantitatively" (Cohen 2009, 59). Independently and as a team, Betty Bailey and Jane Davidson have contributed an important body of research to date on the benefits of singing in specific populations (Bailey and Davidson 2002, 2003, 2005). In a 2002 study, the authors gathered interview data from seven members of a choir for once-homeless men in francophone Montréal. By the time of the study, each of the seven had secured permanent housing, but each still sang with the group. Four themes emerged. In their semi-structured interviews, some noted that singing alleviated depression and enhanced emotional and physical wellbeing. In addition, the choir gave participants a supportive context in which they could develop social skills and achieve collective goals. Several felt that performing for an audience encouraged a sense of personal worth and provided a way to re-engage with wider social networks. Finally, singing in a group provided a mental challenge that required concentration and learning new material. This concentration helped turn the focus away from internal problems. For these members of the choir, singing was an agent for change.

In 2005, Bailey and Davidson turned their attention to class differences. They compared their 2002 results with new data collected from a far more impoverished group of homeless men in an economically disadvantaged area of anglophone Nova Scotia. Researchers noted a robust similarity in the reports from both choirs; singing created energy, positive emotional experiences, and relaxation. Additionally, the socially advantaged singers (2002) listed the benefits of developing musical knowledge and skill, meeting the challenges of the classical choir repertoire, and a sense of achievement. In contrast, the more marginalized participants (2005) noted the positive benefits of stimulation, concentration, and ordering of inner mental space. The less challenging life is, perhaps, the more singers can appreciate musical challenges.

In a 2010 study, Clift and Hancox surveyed 1,124 choral singers drawn from twenty-one choral societies and choirs in England (N=633), Germany (N=325) and Australia (N=166).

The average age of choristers was relatively high (M = 57 years, SD = 15) with a third aged 60–69 and a fifth aged 70 and above. Women substantially outnumbered men (72 vs 28 per cent). Choristers reported engagement with choral singing for a mean of 27 years (SD = 11 years); 42 per cent reported having had singing lessons; 62 per cent played a musical instrument and only 6 per cent were told as children that they could not sing.

Clift and Hancox (2010, 85)

The researchers were particularly interested in the responses of participants who strongly endorsed singing but who described themselves as having enduring challenges to psychological wellbeing such as clinical depression and panic disorders, significant family and relationship challenges, physical health problems and/or disability, and recent bereavement. That subgroup reported benefits such as *positive affect or mood* ("when you sing, you cannot be sad for long," "[choir] means you are in a team"); *focused attention* ("puts troubles on hold," "[allows me to] switch off everyday concerns"); *controlled deep breathing* ("helps with signs of anxiety, like yoga or walking to relieve stress"); *social support* ("[choir is an] intrinsically social activity); *social cooperation and coordination* ("helps make friends," "People from all walks of life, coming together to make a unified impact"); *cognitive stimulation*; and requires regular *commitment and practice* ("Making the effort to attend choir practice on wet, cold evenings instead of watching TV must be better for health") (Clift and Hancox 2010, 90–1, emphasis mine).

These benefits might just as easily result from other group activities. Group singing, however, has the power to engage physiological processes unaddressed by participation in comparable social groups. Still, everyone participating in the Bailey and Davidson studies, as well as in the one by Clift and Hancox, chose to be in a choir that later became central to a study. Because they do not assess people who have no interest in choirs, these findings cannot be generalized for a broad population.

Quantitative and nominal data from Cohen's study comparing the wellbeing responses of choir groups including inmates in a nine-month substance abuse treatment community and a separate, minimum-security facility suggested that choral singing may enhance inmate singers' wellbeing (Cohen 2009, 60). Cohen's two experiments involved: (1) comparisons between a ten-member choir which only performed inside the prison and a ten-member group of inmates who did not sing in a choir, and (2) a study of a forty-eight-member choir comprising prison inmates and volunteers who performed in a concert outside the facility. Some participants in experiment two had also participated in experiment one. Choir groups in experiment one participated in nine weekly, ninety-minute rehearsals that blended rote learning and musical score reading. In the second experiment, choirs rehearsed twice per week. The Friedman Well-Being Scale (FWBS), a twenty-item semantic differential scale, measured composite wellbeing and five subscales: (a) emotional stability, (b) sociability, (c) joviality, (d) self-esteem, and (e) happiness (Friedman 1994). Results indicated no significant differences between experimental and control groups in composite wellbeing scores in both experiments. "However, in experiment one, there was a significant increase between pre- and post-composite well-being scores for both groups" (Cohen 2009, 56).

Also for experiment one, members of the choir group were asked weekly to write a response to the question "How are you feeling today?" Researchers were interested to learn whether or not responses would be related to the choir experience. The query yielded responses such as these: "For the last hour I have been looking forward to rehearsal tonight" and "Hopeful and looking forward to our performances." Non-choir-related, but still positive, were responses including "I'm content" and "I feel peaceful, joyous within myself. I have thirty-four days left until my release." The one negative choir-related response related to an inmate's insecurity about how his scar from nose surgery would look during the performance, and examples of negative non-choir responses included "Concern. Worry about my family" and "Stressed, overwhelmed" (Cohen 2009, 58).

When questioned about the performance experience as a whole after the concert, the singing group in experiment one expressed elements of autonomous functioning: "After Sunday's concert I feel so different. I feel that I can be successful out in society," and "The reward of the performances and the satisfaction of achieving a goal such as this are all positives that I will carry with me for the rest of my life" (Cohen 2009, 58). Similar responses reflected examples of positive relationships with others.

Cohen's second experiment evaluated a choir comprising the two groups from experiment one, a third group of male general population inmate singers, and male volunteer singers from the surrounding community. For the participants who did not participate in the first experiment, the setting was a different minimum-security unit. All four groups did not perform together until the day of the concert. The social element of the public concert appeared to play a crucial role in the inmates' feelings of wellbeing.

After the concert, the inmates received accolades from audience members while standing in a reception line.

> The evening concluded with inmates and volunteers sharing a home-cooked meal. These social experiences contrasted dramatically with daily interactions between inmates and correctional staff at the facility. Moreover, the simple fact that the inmates left their prison facilities to perform in public may have played a role in the increased well-being scores.
>
> *Cohen (2009, 61)*

Inmates also expressed appreciation for the social interaction:

> "It was fun singing with all my brothers," and "Words cannot explain how much I enjoyed that day" . . . "I had a swell time," and "This is how I felt about the concert: ecstatic, elated, excited, joyful, grateful."
>
> *Cohen (2009, 61)*

As with many studies involving qualitative data (self-reporting), these experiments raise as many questions as they provide answers. To what extent did singing together, separate from performing outside the prison, affect wellbeing positively? For behavioral scientists, the search will continue to find the best sorts of protocols to evaluate the benefits of group singing. For those of us in the humanities, these studies provide more reasons to give group singing a try in various types of settings.

Social Identity

Songs can contribute fundamentally to the ways members perceive their group. Peter Rentfrow and Samuel Gosling queried the personality correlates of music preferences in a relatively homogeneous population—1,383 undergraduate students at the University of Texas at Austin (Rentfrow and Gosling 2003). Their findings indicate that people shape social and physical environments, sometimes with music, to reinforce their own dispositions and self-views. In other words, people may choose music in order to appear "hip," sustain a melancholy mood, or represent deeply held beliefs. Musical choices are individualistic and preference can be linked to personality, degree to which the listener enjoys or avoids physiological arousal, and social identity. In an earlier study, North and Hargreaves found that people use music as a "badge" to communicate their values, attitudes, and self-views (North and Hargreaves 1999).

Through three experiments carried out in 2011, Boer and colleagues demonstrated that "music can create interpersonal bonds between young people because music preferences can be cues for similar or dissimilar value orientations, with similarity in values then contributing to social attraction" (Boer et al. 2011, abstract).[23] Value similarity, they write, is the missing link in explaining the musical bonding phenomenon, a fact that seems to hold for Western and non-Western samples and in experimental and natural settings (see Figure 4.7).[24] Individuals who like similar music show higher social attraction toward each other than those who do not favor similar music.[25] Value similarity is one driving cue for interpersonal attraction.

Boer and colleagues carried out three studies. For study 1, they recruited 338 German youth fans of rock, metal, hip-hop, and electronic music (electro) through Internet sites. They found that "shared music preferences can generate social attraction, which likely is induced by assumed value similarities" (Boer et al. 2011, 1161). Study 2, involving a smaller cohort of sixty-seven German fans of only two musical styles—metal and hip-hop—showed that shared music preferences can increase social attraction (compared to situations in which no information about music preferences is known). Musical bonding thus can be explained, in part, by value similarity, which in turn is indicated by shared music preferences. In contrast to the Western participant groups in the first two experiments, study 3 involved forty-seven pairs of same-sex, randomly assigned roommates in the Chinese cultural context of a Hong Kong university (Boer et al. 2011, 1164). Again, perceived similarity in musical taste was strongly associated with social attraction.

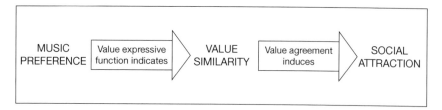

FIGURE 4.7 Proposed musical bonding model, from Diana Boer, Ronald Fischer, Micha Strack, Michael H. Bone, Eva Lo, and Jason Lam, "How Shared Preferences in Music Create Bonds between People: Values as the Missing Link," *Personality and Social Psychology Bulletin* 37.9 (2011): 1161. Used with permission.

One group of researchers investigated the effects of vocal content in music on physiological arousal. Loui and colleagues presented their subjects with excerpts from two versions of songs that were well known to them and identical except for the presence or absence of vocal content. Songs included Whitney Houston's version of "I Will Always Love You," "Last Dance" featuring Donna Summer, and "Every Breath You Take" by The Police. Participants made continuous, as well as discrete, ratings of perceived arousal, as well as familiarity ratings, for each version of each song.[26] Here, arousal is a measure of perceived energy level, ranging from low (calming) to high (exciting). The researchers found that music incorporating voice was better recognized than all other instrumental versions, a finding supported elsewhere (Weiss et al. 2012), and discovered a highly significant main effect of vocals on arousal (Loui et al. 2013, 4). Further, female participants rated their arousal levels higher, and the positive effect of vocals on arousal ratings was stronger for females than for males. One possible explanation for the gender effect, they write,

> is that the need to detect emotional signals rapidly may be more evolutionarily advantageous for women. Supporting evidence along this possible evolutionary basis of gender-bias in selecting for emotion in vocal content comes from electrophysiological literature showing that the dishabituation [a way of responding to old stimuli as if it were new] of emotional voice content is more robust in females, and is furthermore regulated by estrogen levels.
>
> *Loui and others (2013, 4)*

Among other findings in the study by Loui and colleagues is the fact that females' arousal increased with age, which led the researchers to call for more studies about the generational ways that listeners identify with music.

Conclusion

By the early years of the twentieth century, the universal human urge to sing out feelings had surfaced in the Mississippi delta region of the American South (see Figure 4.8). Blues is a badge of identity claimed by many groups of people, one of which was the focus of this chapter. But blues is not only "for" a limited group of people; singing and listening to blues awaken sympathetic feelings in people of highly diverse groups. Pythagoras, Damon, and Plato would not have been surprised to learn that downhome blues soon expanded and proliferated far beyond the juke joints, tent shows, and dance parties of its origins. In the United States alone, where British and European folk song, dances, musical theater, and sacred song had held sway in the nineteenth century, blues and its cousin, jazz, forever changed the very building blocks of American popular music. The Great Migration (1910–70) widened the reach of the blues world to northern and eastern urban centers such as Chicago and New York.

Folk forms such as downhome blues are incredibly sticky phenomena that, in their proliferation, naturally accumulate souvenirs of their travels. Initially marketed by sheet music publishers and white recording producers to a black

FIGURE 4.8 *Two Youths with Guitar*, ca. 1905, by William White. Traditional print from White's original glass negative by Roy Ward, 1980s. Reproduced with permission of Roy Ward.

audience as "race records," blues absorbed other elements: boogie-woogie style piano, sharply emphasized back beats, the Kansas City "shout" style of vocal delivery, and electric guitar, bass drums, electric organ from the black urban gospel movement. This evolved cultural product would be renamed "rhythm and blues" in 1949, again by white recording entrepreneurs. With its swing rhythms, saxophones that imitated the voice with honking and screaming effects, and blues-ballad singing style, R&B swept America's dance parties, first those of young African Americans in the 1950s. The transformation of blues sentiments such as Billy Ward's "I rock 'em and roll 'em all night long, I'm your sixty minute man"—into "we're gonna rock around the clock tonight"—facilitated the spread of R&B to a young white audience in the 1960s.[27] In 1956, Mississippi native Elvis Presley reflected his admiration for bluesmen like Arthur "Big Boy" Crudup—whose 1946 "That's All Right" inspired Presley's first recording. "Down in Tupelo, Mississippi, I used to hear old Arthur Crudup . . . and I said if I ever got to the place I could feel all old Arthur felt, I'd be a music man like nobody ever saw" (quoted in Wald 2004, 207). Blues genealogy persisted in the hybrid of R&B and gospel of Ray Charles, and its message transformed into ideals of ethnic essence and pride in the soul music of Otis Redding and Aretha Franklin, whose 1967 Atlantic recording of Redding's "Respect" became a rallying call for African Americans during the Civil Rights Movement. The Beatles ("I'm Down," 1965), the Jimi Hendrix Experience ("Red House," 1966), the Rolling Stones ("Honky Tonk Woman," 1969), and numerous other pivotal acts freely infused their 1960s rock music with blues. Fascination with blues continues through performers such as Bonnie Raitt ("Love Me Like a Man," 1972) and blues artists/advocates such as Shemekia Copeland ("Sounds Like the Devil," 2009).

What accounts for the tremendous influence of blues in the US and abroad? Balancing a celebration of love and sex with dark humor and wry commentary on loss, mistreatment, corruption, and poverty, blues music captures essential truths about the human condition. Hearing a blues tune can make someone feel known and understood. Writing and singing a blues song can give voice to emotions ranging from deepest sorrow to bitter disappointment to spirited celebration of the high life. Still, blues has been just the case in point to illustrate the many ways that any shared song repertoire, from blues to grand opera, can bind together, organize, identify, and uplift the people who enjoy it. Songs can encourage solidarity, help distinguish one group from another, and reinforce defining principles of what is important in life. Especially in times of social uncertainty, shared songs can manage social relationships.

Singing together and, to a lesser extent, experiencing but not singing songs of one's group can support immune function, decrease negative mood, increase positive mood. Being bound by songs coordinates interaction and synchronizes individuals as they experience common abstract structures such as twelve-bar blues. Singing together is a mood changer that distracts, relieves stress through entrained breathing, and boosts self-esteem. Because it feels so good, singing in a group lends structure and goals to the lives of the disaffected and marginalized. Shared song can be a badge of identity and belonging that communicates value similarity. People tend to be more open to people who actually do enjoy the same songs, or even to people we perceive to enjoy the same songs. And while music without singing can also accomplish all these things, vocal music is recognized more easily than its non-vocal counterpart. The very presence of the human voice in music leads to enhanced cognitive arousal among its listeners (Loui et al. 2013, 4).

Several researchers have found that women are more likely to report strong benefits associated with choir singing than men. Further, women's perceptions of the benefits of singing are substantially independent of general psychological well-being (Clift and Hancox 2010, 92). In the study of English, German, and Australian choir members by Clift and Hancox, no significant, parallel correlation emerged for the men. This fact is especially intriguing because downhome blues singers were overwhelmingly male. Perhaps the benefits derived from singing in that population are highly correlated with solo, rather than group, singing. Certainly, despite all the constraints felt by African Americans in the first decades of the twentieth century, males were freer to pursue downhome blues performance than women in the Delta of the turn of the century. Wald relates that women went crazy over bluesman B.B. King in the 1940s and 1950s. Wald's informants explained that male downhome blues consumers generally followed the tastes of the female population. Still, institutions such as the notorious Angola prison (Louisiana State Penitentiary) and Parchman Farm (Mississippi State Penitentiary) became repositories of male blues traditions. Leadbelly (Huddie Leadbetter, 1885–1949), a bluesman who commanded more than 500 songs, was sentenced to Angola in 1930 on a murder charge and was discovered there in 1933 by folklorist John A. Lomax. Ironically, the incarceration of an influential black singer contributed to the preservation of downhome blues and other black folk-song traditions. Would Leadbelly have self-selected choral singing in another culture, place, and time? These thoughts about highly divergent singers and environments underscore the need for further research about contributions of gender, class, and culture to the positive effects of group singing.

Cross and Woodruff summarize many of this chapter's points:

> In the context of collective musical behaviours, processes of *entrainment* are likely to endow the communal activity with a powerful sense of joint and coordinated action, allowing the emergence of a sense that aims are shared and enhancing the likelihood that participants will experience each others' states and intentions as mutually manifest. Hence entrainment processes in music provide a potent means of promoting a sense of joint affiliation that helps maintain the collective integrity of a musical act even though music's floating intentionality affords each participant the possibility of interpreting its significance quite differently. Music's semantic indeterminacy . . . together with its affiliative powers (rooted in processes of entrainment and in its

exploitation of motivational-structural principles) render it effective as a communicative medium that is optimised for the management of situations of social uncertainty.

Cross and Woodruff (2009, 9)

In times of social uncertainty—from prehistoric through modern enslavement, and from plague to AIDS to Ebola epidemics—as well as in less stressful environments, singing together is both manifesto and antidote that continues to improve the lives of all the world's people.

Musical Illustrations

"Song of Sorrow," *Bulu Songs from the Cameroons*, Folkways FW04451.

"Field Hollers, Calls, and Cries," *Negro Folk Music of Alabama*, various artists (Folkways Records, 1951).

Thomas J. Marshall, "Arwhoolie" (Cornfield Holler), *Negro Work Songs and Calls*, Library of Congress Archive of Folk Culture, Rounder CD 1517.

Vera Hall, "Another Man Done Gone," 1940, www.encyclopediaofalabama.org, accessed 28 December 2014.

"There's a Meeting Here Tonight," William Francis Allen, Charles Pickard Ware, and Lucy McKim Garrison, 1842–77, *Slave Songs of the United States*. New York: A. Simpson & Co., 1867.

Film Illustrations

As It Is in Heaven (2004), feature film directed by Kay Pollak. For a Swedish church choir, singing changes community identity.

The Choir (2007), documentary by Michael Davie about the redemptive power of choral singing in a South African prison.

The Shawshank Redemption (1994), feature film written and directed by Frank Darabont. It depicts the arresting power of recorded operatic singing in a maximum security prison.

Discussion Points

1. Brainstorm about good topics for future scientific studies. Come up with ideas for experimental conditions and experimental/participant groups, where the findings might shed new light on the value of group singing.
2. Which other groups seem to exemplify Damon's musical ethos theory?
3. Study the folk song of a culture not addressed in this chapter. When those songs are sung in indigenous groups of people, is the cultural work of the song repertoire similar to that discussed here?

Notes

1 "Sontonga, a member of the Mpinga clan in the Xhosa nation, wrote the original melody with first verse and chorus of this song in 1897, and it has since taken on more verses and been arranged numerous ways. It has been the closing anthem of the African National Congress as well as the national anthem of several African countries over its lifetime." Jeffrey Snedeker, "N'kosi Sikelel' iAfrika," *Horn Call* 40.1 (October 2009): 79. For a thorough discussion of the current anthem's components, see Owen Dean, "An Anthem to Ignorance: South Africa's Case of 'Nkosi Sikelel' iAfrika,'" *The Anton Mostert Chair of Intellectual Property* blog, 18 June 2012, http://blogs.sun.ac.za/iplaw/news-3/from-ipstell/page/4/, accessed 13 December 2014.

2 "God Bless Africa, let its [Africa's] horn be raised, Listen also to our prayers, Lord bless us, we are the family of it [Africa], Lord bless our nation, Stop wars and sufferings, Save, save our nation, The nation of South Africa—South Africa. From the blue of our heavens, From the depths of our seas, Over our everlasting mountains, Where the cliffs give answer." That powerful song was the official anthem for the African National Congress beginning in 1925 and during the apartheid era, and became part of the South African national anthem in 1994.

3 Wallace points out that Damon appears not to have left written work, and that the sources for Damon are "marked by an extraordinary contamination of Damon's theories with later philosophical materials, in particular from neo-Platonist and neo-Pythagorean traditions." Whether or not Damon documented this thought himself, it serves a useful purpose here.

4 The spoken language of the Dorian Greeks is a matter of speculation. Einar Haugen elaborates: "there was in the classical period no unified Greek norm, only a group of closely related norms. While these 'dialects' bore the names of various Greek regions, they were not spoken but written varieties of Greek, each one specialized for certain literary uses, e.g., Ionic for history, Doric for the choral lyric, and Attic for tragedy. In this period the language called 'Greek' was therefore a group of distinct, but related written norms known as 'dialects.' It is usually assumed that the written dialects were ultimately based on spoken dialects of the regions whose names they bore." "Dialect, Language, Nation." *American Anthropologist* 68.4 (August 1966): 923.

5 Slaveholders in the United States "worked harder" to destroy African culture than did their counterparts in the Caribbean and South America.

6 See *Negro Folk Music of Alabama*, Volume 1, Folkways Records, 1951, www.folkways.si.edu/negro-folk-music-of-alabama-vol-1-secular-music/african-american/album/ Smithsonian, accessed 27 December 2014.

7 Waters, especially, would find great success on Broadway beginning in the 1930s and in films such as *Cabin in the Sky* (1943) and *A Member of the Wedding* (1952).

8 Though some argue that blues singers performed non-blues music primarily for the white audience, Elijah Wald (2004, 68) affirms that even in small Delta towns "there have always been plenty of black dancers who wanted to hear the latest hit sounds . . . and plenty of white folks who demanded the rawest, raunchiest, most primitive blues."

9 Being naturally recognizable as music does not negate the fact that music is a highly constructed cultural product.

10 It is unlikely that consumers of downhome blues listened or even danced in silence. Western European notions of "performer" and "audience," though present in some form, would not have precluded vocal affirmations and singing along, improvised by audience members at blues venues. Whether they joined in on a boozy chorus of "Goodnight Irene" or danced without singing, however, downhome blues aficionados would have shared intentionality of place, culture, and identity.

11 Small study size (N=33), mixed vocal and instrumental experiences in the active group, musical choices, time of year (i.e., "flu season"), and age range of participants

(an average of twenty years) were some of the variables that require further research in order to generalize the benefits suggested by Kuhn's findings.

12 As this control indicates, performing music mentally affects biomarkers such as SIg-A.

13 As in the Kuhn study, the number of participants was relatively small and the subjects were members of a pre-existing choir.

14 Limitations of this study include the sample size, the fact that the researchers employed only one musical work, the Mozart Requiem in both groups, and the study did not control for greater physical activity associated with singing as opposed to listening. Physical activity is known to influence mucosal immune system responses (Kreutz et al. 2004, 632).

15 Maimonides' prescription for balancing the humor of black bile is discussed in Chapter 6.

16 *Grove Music Online*, s.v. "thrēnos," by G. Chew and T. Matthieson, accessed 28 December 2014.

17 *Grove Music Online*, s.v. "lament," by J. Porter, accessed 28 December 2014.

18 *Grove Music Online*, s.v. "griot," by E. Charry, accessed 28 December 2014.

19 Wald's fourth definition, a combination of the other three, witnesses the widespread relevance of blues outside its originating group. Blues, he writes, is "whatever listeners, performers, and marketers have understood to be part of the genre . . . whatever a substantial audience understood the word to mean in any particular period or region." *Grove Dictionary of American Music*, s.v. "blues," by E. Wald, accessed 31 December 2014.

20 Other periodicities in human experience include the wake/sleep cycle, the seasons, and the monthly menstrual cycle.

21 Folk music featuring five, seven, and other meters is also common.

22 Bailey and Davidson's 2003 study addressed three methods of musical engagement: active (in this case, singing in a choir), passively listening to music with others, and passively listening to music alone. Their questionnaire evaluated the perceived holistic health effects of music in these three modalities. Singing reportedly improved mood, left participants feeling exhilarated, fostered a sense of achievement, provided a creative experience, and created a "kind of high." On a majority of questions, group singing was reported to be more beneficial than either isolated listening or social listening. However, some responses indicated that listening to music alone had its benefits—reducing stress, releasing suppressed emotions, relaxing the participants, and releasing tension.

23 Their experimental group formation was led by the fact that music may provide a particularly salient bonding context for young (college-age) people because of their high commitment to music.

24 The research team worked in international settings: Boer in National Taiwan University in Taipei, Fischer in Victoria University of Wellington, New Zealand; Strack in Georg-August-University, Göttingen, Germany; Bond at Hong Kong Polytechnic University; Lo and Lam at Chinese University of Hong Kong.

25 Boer and colleagues provide an exhaustive review of literature on music, personality traits, and value orientation.

26 This study combines psychological perspectives with biomarkers such as estrogen production and hence is discussed here.

27 Billy Ward and the Dominoes recorded "Sixty Minute Man," which quickly topped the R&B and popular charts in 1951; "Shake, Rattle, and Roll" was first recorded by Joe Turner in February 1954 and then by Bill Haley and His Comets in June of 1954.

References

Adinoff, B., K. Ruether, S. Krebaum, A. Iranmanesh, and M.J. Williams. 2003. "Increased Salivary Cortisol Concentrations during Chronic Alcohol Intoxication in a Naturalistic Clinical Sample of Men." *Alcoholism, Clinical and Experimental Research* 27.9: 1420–7.

Bailey, B., and J. Davidson. 2002. "Adaptive Characteristics of Group Singing: Perceptions from Members of a Choir for Homeless Men." *Musicae Scientiae* 6.2: 221–56

———. 2003. "Perceived Holistic Health Effects of Three Levels of Music Participation." In *Proceedings of the 5th Triennial ESCOM (European Society for the Cognitive Sciences of Music) Conference*, eds. R. Kopiez, A.C. Lehmann, I. Wolther, and C. Wolf, 220–3.

———. 2005. "Effects of Group Singing and Performance for Marginalized and Middle-Class Singers." *Psychology of Music* 33.3: 269–303.

Bispham, J. 2006. "Rhythm in Music: What Is It? Who Has It? and Why?" *Music Perception* 24.2: 125–34.

Boer, D., R. Fischer, M. Strack, M.H. Bone, E. Lo, and J. Lam. 2011. "How Shared Preferences in Music Create Bonds between People: Values as the Missing Link." *Personality and Social Psychology Bulletin* 37.9: 1159–71.

Candler, A.D., ed. 1908. *The Colonial Records of the State of Georgia* 18, 130, Atlanta: Franklin Printing and Publishing. Quoted in J.W. Broucek. 1963. "Eighteenth Century Music in Savannah, Georgia." EdD diss., Florida State University.

Clift, S., and G. Hancox. 2010. "The Significance of Choral Singing for Sustaining Psychological Wellbeing: Findings from a Survey of Choristers in England, Australia and Germany." *Music Performance Research* 3.1: 79–96.

Cobb, C.E., Jr. 1999. "Traveling the Blues Highway." *National Geographic Magazine* April: 42–69.

Cohen, M.L. 2009. "Choral Singing and Prison Inmates: Influences of Performing in a Prison Choir." *Journal of Correctional Education* 60.1: 52–65.

Covach, J. 2006. *What's That Sound? An Introduction to Rock and Its History*. New York: W.W. Norton.

Cross, I., and G.E. Woodruff. 2009. "Music as a Communicative Medium." In *The Prehistory of Language* I, eds. R. Botha and C. Knight, 113–44. Oxford: Oxford University Press. Reprinted 2014, The College Music Society, 1–21, www.music.org/pdf/summit/2014medium.pdf, accessed 27 December 2014.

Elias, R. 1998. *Triumph of Hope: From Theresienstadt and Auschwitz to Israel*, trans. Margot Bettauer Dembo. New York: John Wiley and Sons.

Evans, D. 1967. "Rev. Rubin Lacy." *Blues Unlimited* 44, June–July.

Friedman, P. 1994. *Friedman Well-Being Scale and Professional Manual*. Redwood City, CA: Mind Garden.

Geronimus, A.T., M. Hicken, D. Keene, and J. Bound. 2006. "'Weathering' and Age Patterns of Allostatic Load Scores among Blacks and Whites in the United States." *Journal of Public Health* 95.6: 826–33.

Hawkley, L.C., L.A. Lavelle, G.G. Berntson, and J.T. Cacioppo. 2011. "Mediators of the Relationship between Socioeconomic Status and Allostatic Load in the Chicago Health, Aging, and Social Relations Study (CHASRS)." *Psychophysiology* 48: 1134–45.

Kreutz, G., S. Bongard, S. Rohrmann, V. Hodapp, and D. Greve. 2004. "Effects of Choir Singing or Listening on Secretory Immunoglobulin A, Cortisol, and Emotional State." *Journal of Behavioral Medicine* 27/6: 623–35.

Kubik, G. 2008. "Bourdon, Blue Notes, and Pentatonism in the Blues: An Africanist Perspective." In *Ramblin' on My Mind: New Perspectives on the Blues*, ed. David Evans, 11–48. Urbana: University of Illinois Press.

Kuhn, D. 2002. "The Effects of Active and Passive Participation in Musical Activity on the Immune System as Measured by Salivary Immunoglobulin A (SIgA)." *Journal of Music Therapy* 39.1: 30–9.

Large, E.W., and J.S. Snyder. 2009. "Pulse and Meter as Neural Resonance." *Annals of the New York Academy of Science* 1169: 46–57.

Legge, J. 2002. *The Analects of Confucius (from the Chinese Classics) by Confucius.* Project Gutenberg, www.gutenberg.org/cache/epub/3330/pg3330.html, accessed 27 December 2014.

Loui, P., J.P. Bachorik, H.C. Li, G. Schlaug. 2013. "Effects of Voice on Emotional Arousal." *Frontiers in Psychology* 4.675: 1–6. DOI: 10.3389/fpsyg.2013.00675, accessed 28 December 2014.

Müller, V., and U. Lindenberger. 2011. "Cardiac and Respiratory Patterns Synchronize between Persons during Choir Singing." *Public Library of Science (PLoS) One* 6.9. DOI: 10.1371/journal.pone.0024893, accessed 28 December 2014.

Murray, A. 1970. *The Omni-Americans: Black Experience and American Culture.* New York: Da Capo.

North, A.C., and D.J. Hargreaves. 1999. "Music and Adolescent Identity." *Music Education Research* 1: 75–92.

Plato. *Republic* 424 b–c. 1984. Translated in Pierro Weiss and Richard Taruskin. *Music in the Western World: A History in Documents.* New York: Schirmer/Macmillan.

Rentfrow, P.J., and S.D. Gosling. 2003. "The Do Re Mi's of Everyday Life: The Structure and Personality Correlates of Music Preferences." *Journal of Personality and Social Psychology* 84.6: 1236–56.

Routledge, F.S., T.S. Campbell, J.A. McFetridge-Durdle, and S.L. Bacon. 2010. "Improvements in Heart Rate Variability with Exercise Therapy." *Canadian Journal of Cardiology* 26.6: 303–12.

Smith, B. 1925. With L. Armstrong, cornet, and F. Longshaw, harmonium. "St. Louis Blues" by W.C. Handy. Columbia 14064-D.

Thaut, M. 2003. "Neural Basis of Rhythmic Timing Networks in the Brain." *Annals of the New York Academy of Sciences* 999 (The Neurosciences and Music): 364–73.

————. 2005. *Rhythm, Music, and the Brain: Scientific Foundations and Clinical Applications* (Studies on New Music Research). New York: Routledge.

Thaut, M., D.A. Peterson, and G.C. McIntosh. 2005. "Temporal Entrainment of Cognitive Functions: Musical Mnemonics Induce Brain Plasticity and Oscillatory Synchrony in Neural Networks Underlying Memory." *Annals of the New York Academy of Sciences* 1060: 243–54.

Titon, J.T. 1981. *Downhome Blues Lyrics: An Anthology from the Post-World War II Era.* Boston, MA: Twayne/G.K. Hall.

Tomasello, M., M. Carpenter, J. Call, T. Behne, and H. Moll. 2005. "Understanding and Sharing Intentions: The Origins of Cultural Cognition." *Behavioral and Brain Sciences* 28.5: 675–91.

Tusty, James, and Maureen Tusty. 2006. "The Music." *The Singing Revolution: A Documentary Film.* www.singingrevolution.com, accessed 27 December 2014.

Vickhoff, B., H. Malmgren, R. Åström, G. Nyberg, S.-R. Ekström, M. Engwall, J. Snygg, M. Nilsson, and R. Jörnsten. 2013. "Music Structure Determines Heart Rate Variability of Singers." *Frontiers in Psychology* 4.334: 1–16.

Wald, E. 2004. *Escaping the Delta: Robert Johnson and the Invention of the Blues.* New York: Amistad/HarperCollins.

Wallace, R.W. 2004. "Damon of Oa: A Music Theorist Ostracized?" In *Music and the Muses: The Culture of 'Mousikē' in the Classical Athenian City-State*, eds. P. Murray and P. Wilson, 249–68. New York: Oxford.

Watson, D., L.A. Clark, and A. Tellegen. 1988. "Development and Validation of Brief Measures of Positive and Negative Affect: The PANAS Scales." *Journal of Personality and Social Psychology* 54.6: 1063–70.

Weiss, M.W., S.E. Trehub, and E.G. Schellenberg. 2012. "Something in the Way She Sings: Enhanced Memory for Vocal Melodies." *Psychological Science* 23: 1074–8. DOI: 10.1177/0956797612442552, accessed 28 December 2014.

Worthman, C.M., and C. Panter-Brick. 2008. "Homeless Street Children in Nepal: Use of Allostatic Load to Assess the Burden of Childhood Adversity." *Development and Psychopathology* 20.1: 233–55.

5

THE LOSS OF BRAIN FUNCTION

How Singing Helps

> If I want to change the behavior of a dementia patient immediately, I introduce chocolate, music, or prayer.
>
> *Jan Dougherty, RN, MS, Director of Family and Community Services,*
> *Banner Alzheimer's Institute, Phoenix, AZ (to author, February 2010)*

What happens to a lifetime of song when a person develops dementia? Losses of mobility, memory, independence, self-control, identity, preferences, and agency are accompanied too often by a loss of the "sound track of life" that included singing. Prior to the onset of the disease, this mental sound track was recorded and re-inforced in the brain's memory centers. Baseball fans could count on voicing their enjoyment of "Take Me Out to the Ballgame" in the seventh inning. Worshippers reinforced a sense of belonging with hymns or chants. Birthdays were incomplete without song. Songs accompanied courtships, weddings, military service, television programs, graduations, road trips, and movies—they represent the vocal music of preference, but also, to borrow John Zorn's phrase, "the music of our subconscious" (Zorn 1990). In too many cases, as dementia takes its toll on everyday experience, the patient has fewer opportunities to experience this "song-track" of life. Without purposive intervention, the songs all but disappear, long before actual death.

The good news is that singing can trigger small flashes of familiarity in the bewildering fog of dementia. However, documenting these improvements in medical and behavioral studies requires extra care. For that reason, the first pages of this chapter address the specific research challenges posed by dementia and the ethical ways they are addressed. The next section examines how the positive effects of singing can ameliorate symptoms of dementia and other losses of brain function, and improve quality of life for those already suffering from these afflictions. Case study reports by music therapists and professors Robin Rio and Annamaria Oliverio, and Director of Family and Community Services at Banner Alzheimer's Institute in Phoenix, Jan Dougherty, will punctuate this discussion. Finally, the chapter will suggest some guidelines to help non-professionals offer relatively non-invasive singing experiences to those with dementia.

Guiding this chapter is the fact that, in the overwhelming majority of situations, it never hurts to try singing in an attempt to have a connected moment with a dementia sufferer. While fleeting, these experiences can bolster a sense of autonomy for the patient. A patient's personhood can be affirmed when he remembers and sings a song from childhood, even though he cannot remember how to tie his shoes. Singing can also facilitate meaningful interaction, for example between a grandchild and grandparent. In short, relatively risk-free singing can help dementia patients feel better connected with their worlds.

General Considerations about Research and Dementia

According to the American Alzheimer's Association: "Dementia is not a specific disease. It's an overall term that describes a wide range of symptoms associated with a decline in memory or other thinking skills severe enough to reduce a person's ability to perform everyday activities." Further, "at this time, there is no treatment to cure, delay, or stop the progression of Alzheimer's disease" (Alzheimer's Association 2014). Alzheimer's disease and vascular events such as stroke are responsible for approximately 80 percent and 10 percent of dementias, respectively. Other causes of dementia include brain trauma, Parkinson's disease, and drug abuse, to name a few.

Dementias are usually progressive. In the beginning, no impairment is noticeable. Next comes mild cognitive impairment; the individual has increasing trouble recalling names and the words for common objects, and may have difficulty completing social or work-related tasks. In moderate cognitive decline, the dementia sufferer cannot perform mental arithmetic, such as counting backward from 100 by sevens, or remember her own personal history. She becomes moody and withdrawn in socially or mentally challenging situations. Choosing seasonally appropriate clothes and remembering the day and date are increasingly difficult. Often, the patient is aware that he is missing important parts of everyday experience, but is powerless to restore the patterns of his former life. Sometimes, the patient works very hard to hide his cognitive losses. Consequently, he can suffer agitation, anxiety, depression, and confusion. These symptoms may worsen in the evenings—a phenomenon known as sundowner's syndrome. Next comes severe cognitive decline, in which a person is increasingly challenged in taking care of personal needs such as dressing and toileting, in personality and sleep patterns, and in remembering the usages for hygienic staples such as toothpaste. Restless wandering, combativeness, and loss of appetite frequently accompany mid-stage dementia. Finally, late-stage or severe dementia renders an individual incapable of independent management of her daily personal care. Late-stage patients may also lose the ability to smile, sit without support, and hold up the head. Reflexes become abnormal, muscles grow rigid, and swallowing is impaired (Alzheimer's Association 2014).

The greatest risk of developing Alzheimer's is associated with age, and the world's population is aging. In a 2010 issue of *Scientific American*, Gary Stix predicted that the "numbers of people diagnosed with Alzheimer's will increase by nearly fifty percent during the next twenty years" (Stix 2010, 52). Although a cure continues to elude researchers, the medical profession pursues its vigorous search for ways to predict, prevent, and reverse the effects of Alzheimer's and other dementias. Presently, the US National Institute on Aging funds twenty-three separate Alzheimer's Disease Research Centers at major medical institutions across the US. The Alzheimer's Prevention Initiative, a $100 million-dollar project sponsored by the Banner Alzheimer's Institute in Phoenix, AZ, exemplifies innovative research directions worldwide. These projects target people in many countries whose ages and genetic backgrounds place them at the highest imminent risk for developing Alzheimer's disease symptoms (Banner Alzheimer's Institute 2014).

Another form of dementia research and care involves the development of new protocols to address the symptoms of these illnesses. Logsdon and colleagues write that the search for new treatments for individuals with Alzheimer's disease and related dementias (ADRD) proliferated in the 1990s. These treatments addressed "a variety of goals, including improving cognitive status, delaying the onset of more severe symptoms, maximizing day-to-day functioning, and reducing behavioral problems such as depression and agitation" (Logsdon et al. 2002). Since then, new and effective treatments have been developed.

> One class of drugs, called cholinesterase inhibitors, includes donepezil, rivastigmine, and galantamine. These drugs can temporarily improve or stabilize memory and thinking skills in some people by increasing the activity of the cholinergic brain network. The drug memantine is in another class of medications called NMDA receptor agonists, which prevent declines in learning and memory.
>
> *National Institute of Neurological Disorders and Stroke (2014)*

When administered in early stage dementia, these drugs can slow disease progression for some people.

While these initiatives continue, other researchers investigate the quality of life (QOL) and wellbeing of those already suffering from dementia. These less tangible areas are difficult to quantify, but the promises they offer dementia patients and their caregivers make the struggle for documentation worthwhile. The term "wellbeing" is often used in describing goals for the dementia patient.

> Traditionally, health-related quality of life has been linked to patient outcomes, and has generally focused on deficits in functioning (e.g., pain, negative affect). In contrast, wellbeing focuses on assets in functioning, including positive emotions and psychological resources (e.g., positive affect, autonomy, mastery) as key components.
>
> *Centers for Disease Control and Prevention (2014)*

Wellbeing is integrated into general definitions of health; the World Health Organization (WHO) defines health as "A state of complete physical, mental, and social wellbeing, not merely the absence of disease." Niyi Awofeso juxtaposes that statement with newer, culturally influenced definitions that address personal responsibility, human rights and equality, and spiritual wellbeing (Awofeso 2005).

Dementia is not the only pathology concerned with these areas. The concept of wellbeing has led researchers, practitioners, and caregivers to question the extent to which any intervention improves a patient's quality of life. Therefore, remission of an illness is not the only goal of clinical intervention. Chemotherapy is one potential cure for cancer that may negatively affect QOL; treatment-associated toxicities can negatively affect QOL. For example, a breast cancer patient treated with some forms of chemotherapy may develop mouth sores. Even in the presence of such odious side effects, however, QOL is difficult to assess because it is highly personal. One chemotherapy patient may consider mouth sores a small price to pay for the opportunity to survive breast cancer, while another may find that, even when appropriately treated, oral skin lesions disrupt quality of life too profoundly to justify the primary cancer treatment. Another research area addressing quality of life is palliative care, which focuses on preventing or alleviating patient suffering (Kumar 2012). Palliation, which is strongly implicated in hospice care during terminal illness, addresses issues such as pain, shortness of breath, fatigue, constipation, nausea, loss of appetite, and sleep problems.

Who should evaluate a dementia patient's quality of life? The observations of physicians, caregivers, behavioral specialists, and family members can partially answer that question. But to learn how a patient feels, one must ask in a comprehensible way that allows the patient every reasonable opportunity to respond. Self-reporting, a qualitative research tool, is thus central to the assessment of quality of life.[1] Qualitative research may not be considered "hard" science by some observers, but those concerned with patient feelings and comfort levels rely on regular queries such as "how are you today?" or "does the wound on your heel hurt today?" (Kitwood and Bredin 1994).[2] To derive the most from self-reporting, healthcare professionals and other caregivers must be well acquainted with the individual, especially when dementia is present. Dementia research relies heavily on qualitative data; therefore, this chapter will present a fair amount of that research type. Quantitative studies, surveyed here too, also provide crucial information for dementia researchers and caregivers (Crowe 2009).

Reporting on Dementia Patients' Quality of Life in Singing Interventions

Determining the benefits, efficacy, and risks associated with QOL interventions for cognitively impaired older adults poses unique challenges. For example, embedded in many statements about quality of life is the presumption that the person with dementia has adequate cognitive abilities to assess her own feelings (Logsdon et al.

2002, 511). In fact, many individuals, even in mid-stage dementia, cannot recognize or communicate basic needs such as hunger and thirst, sleepiness, or need for the restroom. They may misidentify feelings of anxiety as back pain simply because they can remember the words to express back pain. "Varying deficits of memory, attention, judgment, insight, and communication," write Logsdon and colleagues, "influence the ability of individuals with cognitive impairment to comprehend questions or communicate their own subjective states" (Logsdon et al. 2002, 511). In a singing study, Davidson and Fedele noted the mismatch between this population of patients and standard quantitative research methodology.

> The lack of outcomes from the standardized measures indicates that these types of measures are either not sufficiently fine-grained or appropriate to the context of the short-term singing program to account for the changes that are otherwise captured in the qualitative measures.
>
> *Davidson and Fedele (2011)*

In addition, even if the person with dementia can self-report, conditions such as depression, agitation, or psychosis may impact QOL ratings. Further, judgments about what is important to QOL may change as the disease progresses or the living situation changes. Cuddy and Duffin observe that:

> Current tests and procedures in music perception and cognition—those that have been employed with brain damaged patients—require fairly intact memory and cognitive processing skills to follow test instructions. They seem not suited to the testing of dementia.
>
> *Cuddy and Duffin (2005, 230)*

How, then, can any statement be made with confidence concerning QOL for dementia sufferers? Cuddy and Duffin suggest that "musical recognition and memory may be reliably assessed with existing tests if behavioral observation is employed to overcome the problem of verbal or written communication" (Cuddy and Duffin 2005, 230).

Helping dementia patients express their own quality of life has received sustained research attention. While a full review is beyond the scope of this chapter, the report by Logsdon and colleagues offers one set of protocols for evaluating quality of life among this population. They set out to test the validity and reliability of a new measurement scale they developed, the QOL-AD (Quality of Life in Alzheimer's Disease). And although they do not address singing specifically, their study introduces the critical variables and evaluative tools required for any valid, ethical study involving people with dementia. A closer look at this study is an important preparation for the discussion about singing to come.

While some people with dementia can evaluate their own QOL, proxy reports made by the primary caregiver or close relative may substantiate self-reporting

(Logsdon et al. 2002, 518–19). Proxy reports are also informative when the patient is unable to self-evaluate. When the individual with dementia is able, she and her caregiver can each rate the patient's physical health, energy, mood, and memory, among other variables, using a simple scale: poor, fair, good, or excellent. A third source for QOL data is direct observation of predefined behaviors such as smiling or moving in time to music. Especially in this final method of data gathering, the observer or rater must be sensitive to subtle nuances of affect and behavior. Logsdon and colleagues gathered data using the first two methods, self- and proxy reporting, in their 2002 study.

Subjects included 177 patient/caregiver pairs who met the inclusion criterion of "probable" or "possible" Alzheimer's disease based on a comprehensive diagnostic evaluation. To be included in the study, participants had to reside outside a group living center (i.e., at home or with relatives), they had to be ambulatory, and they had to have an actively involved caregiver who lived with them or spent every day with them.[3] Ninety-four percent of the patient/caregiver dyads lived together and the remaining 6 percent saw each other every day. As with all scientific research, this study was limited to certain types of patients with dementia and their caregivers.[4]

Is it possible to know whether a patient will be able to assess herself before she is asked to do so? The mini mental state exam (MMSE, or Folstein test) is commonly used to evaluate cognitive impairment.[5] Typical items in this ten-minute assessment direct the patient to draw a clock face with numerals, identify the date and year, say as many words as possible beginning with the same letter, or spell a word such as "world" forward and backward. The MMSE is scored from 0 to 30; according to the Alzheimer's Association, a score of 20 to 24 suggests mild dementia, 13 to 20 suggests moderate dementia, and less than 12 indicates severe dementia. Participants in the Logsdon study expressed a mean MMSE score of 16.4 (standard deviation of 7.3). Twenty-two individuals were unable to understand the evaluative measures sufficiently to provide meaningful responses. The mean score for patients who were unable to complete the MMSE was 4.1 (SD = 3.2) (Logsdon et al. 2002, 513).

Researchers gathered four types of information from each patient and caregiver: perceived QOL, behavioral competence, psychological status, and interpersonal environment. For each of the domains other than perceived QOL, specific measurement scales with proven validity were utilized.[6] Behavioral competence was measured by activities of daily living such as bathing and dressing, as well as shopping and home management. Memory, depression, and disruption were also evaluated since each can affect behavioral competence. Psychological status was measured with a Geriatric Depression Scale, a self-reporting measure that all except twenty-two dyads were able to complete. Consistency between caregiver and patient reports was only "good," as opposed to a more robust level. An additional tool, the Pleasant Events Schedule-AD Short Form, helped scale patients' enjoyment of twenty activities and frequency of engagement with each activity.

Physical functioning—related to mobility and the impact of physical disability on an individual's ability to walk, climb stairs, and lift objects—was evaluated alongside the individual's ability to carry out normal daily activities. Importantly, most subjects in the Logsdon study resided at home and the caregivers were family members. Therefore, the interpersonal environment was evaluated in this experiment. Caregiver burden and depression are important factors when family members undertake primary responsibility for a dementia patient, and these factors were evaluated with individual scales.

The Logsdon experiment ultimately found that the new instrument, the QOL-AD, was reliable and valid for individuals whose MMSE scores are greater than 10. It showed that individuals with mild to moderate dementia "can rate their own life quality well into the progression of the disease. Further, the study results suggest that caregiver ratings do not substitute for patient ratings" (Logsdon et al. 2002, 516–18). The researchers saw the greatest correlation of caregiver and patient QOL assessments in middle-stage dementia cases, but caregiver/patient assessments were never identical. In other scientific studies, incongruous reports might indicate that the experimental design was flawed. However, as the researchers write:

> Because there is no "gold standard" for QOL and it is widely agreed that QOL assessment involves subjective perceptions, the correlation between patient and caregiver reports likely reflects a real difference in the way they perceive the patient's QOL rather than a lack of reliability of the measure itself.
>
> *Logsdon et al. (2002, 518)*

For example, an empathetic caregiver might believe his loved one's QOL is less positive than the patient himself perceives it to be, or vice versa.

This section has addressed several components of dementia research: that dementia has no cure though the search in that field continues, and that other research addresses prevention, cognitive improvement, and quality of life, among other areas. I summarized one set of results, which indicated that quality of life can be measured and is highly personal and contextual. Some dementia patients can, and others cannot, evaluate their own QOL. The next section will briefly address ethical considerations when designing research protocols for a dementia patient population.

Singing with Dementia Patients: Special Considerations and Benefits

Like all human subjects in industrialized nations, dementia sufferers are protected from inhumane treatment, and for good reason. No benefit comes of an experiment that causes a person with dementia to experience additional frustration and failure, lowered self-esteem, or increased depression. Members of this population should be screened as early as possible and their personal histories recorded so that procedures involving saliva swabs, for example, will not inadvertently awaken frightening memories. Since the Nuremberg Code of 1947, all human subjects have been guaranteed the power to refuse participation, to drop out mid-experiment, and to refuse any portion of a protocol without a specified reason. Researchers must insure that no harm or suffering occurs in connection with the experiment.

Even when consent is given by either the patient or her proxy, it can be difficult to collect data from a person with dementia. Levels of confusion or misunderstanding can vary widely day to day. Just because the subject gave consent on one day does not guarantee that he remembers that decision a few days later. Additionally, the cognitive abilities of individuals with dementia regress over time, so "improvement over time" measures may be altogether invalid. Each case of dementia affects a specific life, together with its unique conceptual landscape. Two individuals may have exactly the same sort of stroke in nearly identical areas of the brain, which causes roughly the same level of disability. Yet, one individual may not have completed high school but grew up singing popular songs in the family, singing in church, synagogue, or mosque throughout adulthood, and singing along daily with the radio. The other stroke patient may have grown up in a family whose enjoyment of singing was profound, but passive; they attended choir concerts and sometimes played recorded vocal music on the radio but rarely, if ever, sang themselves. What is retained in post-stroke dementia and what is lost for these two individuals? Cuddy and Duffin write that "the diffuse location of specific brain pathology and the multiple domains of cognitive deficit make it difficult to predict and account for patterns of loss and sparing of function" (Cuddy and Duffin 2005, 230). As a result, findings in dementia research may not contribute knowledge that can be generalized to a broad segment of the dementia population. Nevertheless, a host of researchers remain committed to creating ways of evaluating and expressing the good that can come from singing with dementia patients.

Singing can take a variety of forms. At the outset of this section, several types of encounters that involve singing with dementia sufferers must be differentiated. Music therapy (MT), involving a professionally certified music therapist, can of course include singing and is addressed most directly in the case histories to follow this section. Like that of any professional therapist, the work of a music therapist would take volumes to describe in full. Only brief generalization is possible here. The music therapist records personal background on each new patient, creates a relationship with him that includes specific goals, and plans interactions that will help him achieve those goals. Planning notwithstanding, the music therapist readily responds to and follows patient initiatives. A snippet of a song—"Just Mollie and me, and baby makes three," from "My Blue Heaven"—that pops up in a patient's mind can create a new train of activity in a music therapy experience.[7] The music therapist responds to bad and good days, sporadic or progressive aphasia, and a host of other daily variables with affirmation and behaviorally appropriate intervention measures.[8] The therapist must be acquainted with an ever-expanding repertoire of songs and be able to "find the best key" for each patient's singing voice.

Just as importantly, singing interventions may be led by people other than music therapists: family members, music specialists, or personnel in group living homes. Though we are not all expert singers, the vast majority of us can recognizably sing a simple song like "Row, Row, Row Your Boat" or "Frère Jacques." Singing with dementia patients is possible in a variety of settings and can involve a variety of people. Many of today's octogenarians grew up with participatory singing and, in many cases, singing can be a substitute communication or expressive system for a patient with dementia.[9] As Cuddy and Duffin write:

> Much musical understanding, unlike the specific knowledge required for expertise at bridge or chess, is held in common by members of a culture. Thus music sparing may be the most available and common form of the sparing of a complex skill in dementia.
>
> *Cuddy and Duffin (2005, 234)*

Though music therapists have specialized knowledge and experience that helps craft a personalized therapeutic experience, no therapist's expertise can supersede a family member's wealth of knowledge about patient tastes, preferences, and personal history. From this perspective, a family member's efforts have an advantage over the therapeutic approach of a licensed music therapist who begins knowledge of the patient from a blank slate.

Thus, singing interventions can be led by people with various connections to the patient and can comprise "singing with" and "singing to" experiences, wherein the patient is respectively active or passive. These may involve singing "Happy Birthday" at a family celebration, singing in a group at a community center or resident facility, singing as an introduction ("Hello, Hazel, how are you today?" to a familiar tune), and many other forms.[10] In a group, the "Hello" song also creates the opportunity for guided improvisation, as participants insert new names for each verse. One favorite song among the English-speaking "greatest generation" is "Don't Sit under the Apple Tree with Anyone Else but Me."[11] With some guidance, those with early and some mid-stage dementias can offer alternate verses ("Don't sit under the maple tree," "Don't eat all of the black-eyed peas," etc.) Finally, dementia sufferers can also enjoy and feel uplifted by informal recital or concert experiences to which they simply listen.

Usually, the choice of songs should be guided by a sense of the patient's background and stated favorites, provided they can express preference. Again, memories are extremely individual, so the hymn tune "Amazing Grace" might convey a maudlin or sad affect for one patient and, for another, the happy days of youth. Philosopher Jerrold Levinson suggested eight potential rewards of listening to music that might be applied to singing with dementia patients:[12] emotional catharsis, apprehending expression, emotional communion, savoring feeling, understanding feeling, expressive potency, emotional assurance, and emotional resolution. With dementia patients, these benefits may take slightly different forms: helping the patient release pent-up emotions ("Too Darn Hot"), suggesting a positive emotion to replace the patient's negative one ("What a Wonderful World"), providing an opportunity to share a laugh over a silly image ("or would you rather be a pig?" from "Swinging on a Star"), enjoying strong feelings expressed in a song ("Oh, What a Beautiful Mornin'"), or helping the patient recognize feelings of happiness or gratitude ("Get Happy," "Put on a Happy Face").[13]

Songs and vocal music can also have unfortunate associations, so even in casual sing-along-type settings participant histories should be screened so that upsetting music is avoided. Today's aged population lived through, and may have participated in, the Second World War. Classical music such as the fourth movement of Beethoven's Ninth Symphony was sometimes used as propaganda by the Third Reich. Noted German conductor Wilhelm Furtwängler conducted a famous performance of the symphony to celebrate Adolph Hitler's birthday in the 1930s.[14] Consequently, "Ode to Joy," a hymn derived from that symphony, might recall negative memories for a Jewish person. Checking patient backgrounds can help determine which songs might spark negative reactions.

Collecting a list of favorite songs from patients while they are capable of supplying them is a good first step when planning to sing with dementia sufferers. People with mild cognitive impairment may not be able to generate a song list independently, but they can usually recognize a song if they hear a well-known phrase or two. In later stages of impairment, a close family member may be able to describe the patient's singing background. Some sufferers, alas, neither have family members who can supply favorite songs, nor can they suggest particular songs themselves. In such cases, music therapists usually begin with a repertoire of songs that were popular when the individual was between eighteen and twenty-five years old (Rio 2009). Of course, even within a single state or nation, geography and culture can greatly influence popular music tastes.

Singing songs from a dementia patient's youth makes sense; if any memory is preserved for this population, it is likely to be long-term memory. Singing songs from youth is also important because it provides the opportunity to reminisce (Brooker and Duce 2000). In a study about group activity with dementia sufferers, Brooker and Duce found that reminiscence therapy sustained a higher level of wellbeing among participants than did "talking group" activities or time spent alone. Without planned activity, they noted, levels of wellbeing quickly deteriorated. Though increased wellbeing after singing is usually short-lived, momentary enjoyment is precious. In my monthly sing-alongs with a mixed group of seniors whose cognitive levels range from no impairment to late-stage dementia, almost everyone can remember good feelings associated with the event, even if they cannot name any of the songs we sing.

My observations are not unique. Difficult as it is to extrapolate generalizable knowledge from singing studies involving dementia patients, "study-specific measures and the qualitative analyses [indicate] that many participants [have] positive gains including lucidity and improved social interaction within session, as well as enjoyment, singing engagement, and carry-over memory and recall from one week to the next" (Davidson and Fedele 2011, 402). Irrefutable proof of direct physical benefits should not be expected in this realm of inquiry. Further, improvements are usually short-lived. Nevertheless, countless experts in the field have witnessed and measured observable, positive effects of singing interventions with dementia patients. The strength of that evidence is sufficient to offer hope to anyone who wishes to give singing a try.

Case histories are invaluable in the assessment of singing interventions. Cuddy and Duffin reported on a patient identified as EN who had always been a deeply devoted amateur musician. EN's mini mental state examination (MMSE) declined slowly over two years. In March 2000, her score was 23; in October 2002, it was 18; and it declined to 14 by April 2003. From January 2004 to August 2004 it remained at 8. These numbers describe a progression from early, through middle, and into late-stage dementia. Family members pointed out tunes that EN was likely to recognize in a Familiarity Decision Test. Along with a Distorted Tunes test, the Familiarity Decision Test was administered in a one-on-one setting with the patient in the fall of 2003 and again in June 2004.[15] An independent observer was present for the Distorted Tunes test. The researchers noted that EN "enjoyed test melodies (that she knew) and hummed or sang along with the tunes long after the test music had stopped" (Cuddy and Duffin 2005, 232).

EN also participated in the Famous Melodies Test developed by W.R. Steinke, which separately assesses recognition of sung and instrumental melodies (Steinke et al. 2001). The complete battery comprises sixty-eight familiar song melodies, thirty-nine familiar instrumental melodies, and eight melodies newly composed for the test. The song and instrumental melodies were intended to be highly familiar for a Canadian sample of normal controls. According to behavioral observations, EN's score for song melody recognition was 86 percent correct and for instrumental melody 64 percent correct. She falsely recognized only one of the eight newly composed melodies; in other words, she knew what she remembered, and mistakenly believed she was familiar with only one of the completely new melodies. Comparable results from normal controls involving amateur musicians aged fifty-nine to seventy-one were 98 percent correct for song recognition (range 91–100 percent) and 89 percent correct for instrumental. Even with an MMSE score of 8, the words of a song such as "Silent Night," "Happy Birthday," or "Frère Jacques" could be a recall cue for the tune itself. In EN's case, singing had the capacity to spark memory.[16] In addition to improving self-esteem and sense of autonomy, recognizing and singing songs can change the way others see and treat the patient. These are substantial gains for those living in a world of diminishment.

In contrast to the individual singing experience reported by Cuddy and Duffin, Davidson and Fedele explored group-singing experiences for persons with dementia (Davidson and Fedele 2011). A sizable literature review prefaces this research report and includes sections on documented benefits of group singing for dementia patients, as well as benefits for neuro-typicals. A QOL measure was utilized in this study to assess the overall impact of the singing program on participants with dementia, and to explore whether attending a group-singing program with a caregiver affects the QOL of the patient. They recruited forty-eight participants, comprising twenty-nine people with dementia and nineteen caregivers.[17] Patient QOL was assessed by the caregivers (Logsdon et al. 2002). To supplement these data, further qualitative comments were also recorded from a checklist of verbal comments made by the caregivers and the singing group facilitator. In addition, the researchers kept detailed observational diaries throughout the sessions (Davidson and Fedele 2011, 206–9).

One important benefit of the group-singing modality is that it is easy and cheap to administer. Further, when singing involves the caregiver, as the Davidson and Fedele study did, communication, pull-away, and resistance behaviors are improved (Hammar et al. 2011). Singing generates better posture, stronger movements, and increased patient awareness of the self and environment (Götell et al. 2003, iii). In a study by Louhivuori and colleagues (2005), patients reported feelings such as inner peace and positive mood after singing.

The Davidson/Fedele singing program ran for six weeks in late 2009; sessions were led by an experienced group-singing facilitator. Each of the two groups met weekly for two hours with an afternoon tea break mid-session. This experiment featured a detailed protocol for the singing sessions. Repertoire was similar for each group, but since the choristers were allowed to suggest songs, repertoires differed slightly. The group from the Maurice Zefert Home (MZH) for Jewish people suggested some Hebrew and Yiddish songs.

Statistics from the AAWA singing group's pre-/post-session questionnaires, across weeks two, four, and six, offered compelling information.[18] Participants in that group were able to recall the activity 93 percent of the time, were able to recall specifics of the session 79 percent of the time, engaged in spontaneous singing after the session 67 percent of the time, and engaged in reminiscent storytelling after the session 60 percent of the time.[19] On the other hand, short-term memory after the session was unchanged 71 percent of the time, and long-term memory after the session was unchanged 100 percent of the time. "No change" at first seems to represent a negative finding; still, no change in long-term memory indicates that no decline was observed for participants.

Data for the MZH singing group's target behavior/outcome observational checklist includes a great many qualitative observations made by the caregivers. Though too numerous to reproduce entirely, these selections will give a general sense of the responses made by the caregivers, who observed patient behavior during and after the singing group.

"He seldom sings; occasionally he mouths the words, but tends mostly to lie back, swaying slightly, with his eyes closed and a smile on his face. He appears totally immersed in the songs. I think the work has a different, but valuable, meaning to him."

"She waves to me during the songs, and smiles a lot."

"Today, I made personal contact with her when she saw others coming for a hug and lined up for one too, arms outstretched."

"She has moved to the front row and is wonderfully present throughout rehearsal."

"His whole face comes alive when he is singing."

"Her spirits were high throughout the whole session."

"She stayed alert and responsive [and] attempted every song."

"In the first week she left the session, saying it was 'awful,' but she has attended every week since then and appears to enjoy it."

"She has begun to pre-empt songs, and she sings in her seat while she is waiting for rehearsal to start."

"She was really enjoying it, and said, 'Music is really good for you.'"

"Singing makes you feel good."

"I should tell everyone if they are ever miserable, to just come in and sing."

"She informed me afterwards that she gets a lot out of the session because singing lifts your spirits and makes you feel happy."

Not all observations were so positive.

"She needs constant energetic input to stay connected to the process."

"She sings along with everything but is rather isolated from the rest for some reason."

"She appeared upset about being given the songbook and muttered loudly to her daughter. Her daughter later told me that she thought she was back at school and was being asked to do schoolwork."

Still, the singing experience was a favorite activity for many members of both groups. For some, it was the highlight of the week.

The findings of Davidson and Fedele, and especially the difficulty they found in quantifying statistically significant health and wellbeing benefits from group singing, are consistent with those of several other studies. Singing may accomplish benefits such as relieving short-term stress; further, as one of their participants mentioned, singing is simply good fun and takes the mind off everyday problems. The most significant benefits occurred during and immediately after the sessions, but singing sessions can also offer the possibility of improved lucidity and wellbeing. Importantly, singing can stimulate feelings of wellbeing even when the participation is slight; a patient does not always need to sing in order to benefit from a group-singing experience. Seeing others enjoy themselves can be infectious.

Clair made this statement about singing with dementia patients.

Singing is integral to the life quality of those who are in progressive dementia and their caregivers. It functions to provide islands of arousal, awareness, familiarity, comfort, community, and success like nothing else can. It is particularly valuable as an intervention because it is accessible to a wide array of individuals, since it has no prerequisites for prior musical skills or training, and it can include persons across cultures and socio-economic strata. It is also effective in a late stage dementia when responses to other stimuli are nonexistent. Singing successfully engages individuals in meaningful purposeful participation through the disease trajectory.

Clair (2000, 93)

In an earlier study, Clair and Bernstein stated that singing participation decreases as dementia progresses, and will eventually cease for patients with late-stage Alzheimer's disease. When enjoyment of singing ends, "activities requiring simple responses that provide vibrotactile stimulation, e.g., a drum, are the most likely to facilitate active music responses" (Clair and Bernstein 1990, 124). Still, singing interventions can draw smiles and nods, even from dementia patients in hospice care.

A Summary of the Ways Singing Can Help People with Dementia

Several benefits associated with singing for this population have been mentioned so far. This section outlines several other important benefits from a selection of additional research studies; as always, the reader is urged to read the reports for more specific information about variables such as participant demographics, singing leaders, types of singing, song repertoire, and frequency of the interventions.

In a 2011 study, Camic and colleagues recruited dementia patient/caregiver pairs to participate in a singing group (Camic et al. 2011). Living at home was one inclusion criterion. Participants were screened for song preferences, and the repertoire included culturally relevant "songs sung down the mine" and songs from life in New Zealand. New experiences are difficult for dementia patients; some participating at-home caregivers worried prior to the study about involving their loved ones in situations that required interaction with others. Post-experiment interviews revealed six themes, the first of which was that the group challenged beliefs and attitudes about whether one or the other member of the pair could sing. Several were surprised to find how easy it was to sing along with a group (Camic et al. 2011, 167). Other benefits mentioned by the caregivers included enjoying the experience and the new opportunity, feeling a sense of security established by a very competent singing facilitator, welcoming of new learning, and experiencing personal changes. The latter category included listening to more music at home, singing the group's songs at home, and going out to concerts for the first time. Previous concerns about protecting loved ones with dementia from misunderstandings and potential ridicule were thus alleviated through this study with singing at its core.

In 2009, Göttell and colleagues studied vocally expressed emotions and moods in communications between caregivers and persons with severe dementia (Göttell et al. 2009). The protocol took place during early morning care sessions, which included toileting, washing, and getting dressed. Participants included nine individuals with severe dementia living in a nursing home in Sweden and five professional caregivers in that setting. The researchers compared three situations to assess the influence of singing in caregiver-directed morning care: the "usual" routine with no music, with background music playing, and with the caregiver singing to and/or with the patient. After the experiment, the "usual" way was characterized as displaying "disjoint vitality," wherein the caregiver expressed positive energy and the person with dementia (PWD) responded weakly and/or in a monotone voice that expressed listlessness, confusion, and annoyance (Göttell et al. 2009, 426).

None of the PWDs in this study could express musical preferences, so the research team pre-sampled test music for the "background music" condition, then evaluated verbal and facial responses. During the actual intervention, "music typically consisted of popular songs from the 1920's through the 1960's, as sung by a male vocalist and accompanied by an orchestra" (Götell et al. 2003, 424).[20] Interestingly, the music seemed to relieve the caregiver of all the responsibility for setting and maintaining a positive emotional tone during the interaction. Compared to the "usual" condition, the PWDs were much more vocally expressive during the background music condition. "Positive emotions were predominant, and no PWD expressed aggression toward a caregiver. Both caregivers and PWDs spoke with warmer and more sonorous voices." Responses during the background music condition were described as "mutual vitality infused with playfulness" (Götell et al. 2003, 427).

The choice of songs utilized in the third condition was left to the will and musical knowledge of the caregivers. Most caregivers sang with words, but some hummed songs as they engaged in the morning routine. None of the caregivers had specific training in singing to persons with dementia; all were licensed practical nurses or mental health nurses who had been caring for these specific patients for a year or more. Most had sung either in a choir, to children at home, or in occasional celebrations. In general, these caregivers chose folk or popular songs from the early twentieth century and, especially, children's and drinking songs.

In this study, singing created an atmosphere that was less light-hearted than in the background music condition. In the singing condition: "There was a sense of mutual vitality, but compared to the light-heartedness of the interaction with background music playing, the dynamic with singing was characterized by a sense of sincerity, openness, intimacy, and even vulnerability" (Götell et al. 2003, 427). One reported interaction underscores the capacity of singing together to reaffirm the personhood of the patient with dementia. Too often, these lovely, fragile individuals are treated as burdens to the caregiver, rather than sources of occasional delight.

When one of the caregivers sang the waltz "Kostervalsen" (the Koster Waltz), whose last line is a proposal of marriage, the PWD responded in a playful manner: "Maja, sweetheart, hey, do you want to marry me?" C[aregiver] sings the words to the song, sounding open, playful, and rhythmic. P[atient] laughs in a delighted manner, and then happily replies "OK. I'll do that."

Götell et al. (2003, 428)

Observers also noted that the singing condition sometimes prompted increased attention and joy, which took the form of making cogent remarks, smiling warmly, rocking in time to the music, joking and making puns, reporting distant and pleasant memories, and singing songs in the native language. The researchers labeled the results of this intervention "mutual vitality infused with sincerity." In early morning care routines with my mother, an altercation could sometimes be avoided by singing a few words of a diversionary song. The Swedish study by Götell and colleagues reminds us to keep singing, if only because we may be caregivers for our aging loved ones one day.

The reader may look to a study by Svansdottir and Snaedal for evidence that singing interventions with dementia patients can result in a reduction of short-term agitation (Svansdottir and Snaedal 2006). Lesta and Petocz studied four female residents with sundowner's syndrome (Lesta and Petocz 2006). As a result of singing patient-preferred songs with a music therapist, observers saw decreases in anxiety and increases in eye contact and in more frequent gesturing toward and touching others. Regarding the common symptom of restless wandering, Lesta and Petocz found that "sitting with the group" behavior improved from 39 percent of the time during pre-intervention to 75 percent during the singing. That increase was sustained into the fifteen-minute period after the intervention. Singing can serve regulative functions, a benefit that can carry over to other activities. Music therapists suggest that improved "sitting with" and lucidity behaviors achieved through a singing intervention can extend into, and thus facilitate, a meeting scheduled after the singing.

Singing is non-invasive and inexpensive. Models of good singing are every-where, vocalizing with a recording is still singing, and singing is cross-culturally effective. Singing can decrease stress, agitation, or nervousness, and can reduce extreme arguing behavior, improve sleep, improve attention and social interaction, and improve language usage. Singing can be used in place of or as an adjunct to other traditional forms of stress reduction such as drug therapy, and may be more advantageous because music interventions usually have no negative side effects. And though not everyone can play an instrument, almost everyone can sing.

In a 2013 review, McDermott and colleagues assessed eighteen studies to learn how music therapy works for dementia sufferers (McDermott et al. 2013). Though only one of the studies that met their inclusion criteria used singing exclusively, most music therapy sessions include singing. Therefore, some general findings are relevant here. A study by Ashida found that small-group intervention using familiar songs to focus on reminiscence—positive memories—was effective in reducing depressive symptoms (Ashida 2000). Physiological changes have also been studied. Two studies found that heart rate variability was improved as a result of music therapy interventions (Raglio et al. 2010, and Okada et al. 2009). Another piece of research recorded decreased heart rate among recipients of music therapy (Ridder and Aldridge 2005). Kumar and colleagues reported increased serum melatonin concentration associated with "a calmer mood" after music therapy, and Suzuki and colleagues observed a reduction of the stress hormone salivary chromogranin A (Kumar et al. 1999, and Suzuki et al. 2004).

Singing out of tune does not completely cancel these benefits. Though singing proficiency is widespread in the general population, 10–15 percent of us exhibit poor singing abilities (Dalla Bella et al. 2007). When reading words presents difficulty, singing on a repeated syllable rather than words (i.e., la-la-la-la-la-la rather than "happy birthday to you") can make the activity accessible for dementia patients. Importantly, singing on "la" can represent the most fluent vocalizations a person with dementia experiences. Finally, Koniari and colleagues published an informative review of literature about dementia patients who can sing but cannot speak. A comparison of speaking and singing shows a common neural activation pattern in the left hemisphere for both, while singing activates additional right hemispheric involvement (Koniari et al. 2012).

In summary, McDermott and colleagues wrote that "singing was a medium for change in seven qualitative and quantitative studies. However it was not possible to consolidate enough evidence to develop a new theory" (McDermott et al. 2013, 792). And since the goal of the McDermott study was the development of a theory, all this data must be contextualized; embedded in these results, however, is the fact that singing featured as an important medium for change.

"Jackie's Voice: Keeping 'Songs of the Self' Alive while Living with Early-Onset Alzheimer's Disease (AD)": A Case Study by Robin Rio, MA, MT-BC

Jackie comes to the clinic with her husband, Fred.[21] He does most of the talking during our greeting in the hallway, because Jackie has a hard time communicating with words. She nods and looks at him with adoration, smiling when she sees Susan and me, her music therapists. When looking at Jackie as she enters the session room and begins to move to the music, you see the picture of health. She is smiling, moving vigorously, and singing along. Jackie is in the middle stage of early onset Alzheimer's disease (AD), with her first symptoms of memory loss at fifty-two years of age. Only 5 percent of people with AD are considered early onset, so the diagnosis is rare, but the course of the disease is the same: a terminal, degenerative illness that typically lasts eight to ten years.

Jackie has played the keyboard as a church musician. She was one of those amazing worship leaders who could play the piano flawlessly while reading a score that may have involved multiple independent vocal lines, while singing a written alto part, and leading a choir. People liked her so much that when she began having problems remembering things, they covered for her at work. She was not officially diagnosed for another five years. Since stopping work, she has been a dedicated volunteer at the zoo, and has taken on the role of piano accompanist for the monthly jam session and sing-along in a group initiative for community members with AD and their care partners. This therapeutic music group is hosted by the university music therapy program leaders and the AD institute's community engagement partners. I came to know Jackie through the group. Her husband provided the details of her social history and illness.

During her first years with AD, Jackie continued to participate and perform with her church, with assistance in tasks like page turning and redirecting when she became distracted or lost her place in the service order. Due to her overall cognitive decline, she could no longer lead from the piano, so she sings in the choir where she is able to follow along with the help of the other singers. Since she can no longer accompany a group on piano for the community monthly jam sessions for people with AD, she attends the events but only participates in singing and drumming. This larger group format does not work as well for her now that she needs more individual support. To best meet her changing needs, I, as her professional therapist from the faculty, and a student therapist offer Jackie weekly individual music therapy at the university clinic.

Jackie's need areas are a result of her cognitive decline. Her husband says that at home she has begun what he calls "aggressive wandering" and becomes extremely anxious, thinking she has missed a choir rehearsal and insisting he drive her to church. On other occasions she has left the house rapidly, before anyone noticed, and hurried down the street as if escaping her home. She is at a risk of failing to find her way back. Fred is becoming a bit overloaded, since he also cares for his elderly parents. One of their adult sons has a serious mental illness, and their other son has significant medical concerns. Throughout the many phases of Jackie's degenerative and terminal illness, there are various needs that require thoughtful attention to her unique abilities and perspectives. She needs value and purpose in her life. In addition to Jackie's needs, her family needs respite and support. Since Jackie is unable to communicate effectively, others must anticipate her needs and interpret what she is trying to say when her words are not making sense. As her condition worsens, music therapists become key resources who help Jackie maintain her own "voice" as she loses her ability to communicate clearly through everyday language.

Effectiveness of Singing for Connecting Jackie's Inner and Outer Worlds

Singing, chanting, and voice work are especially effective for people with AD (Cuddy et al. 2012). Musically using the voice can be tailored to every ability level and preference (Clair 1996 and Gerdner 2005). Favorite music can be sung with and for the person with AD as an aid in reminiscing, reducing anxiety, supporting spirituality, enhancing communication, and nurturing relationships. Singing and music experiences within a social context help Jackie express her inner world and connect with others. The primary focus of this case study is Jackie's vocal work, both her physical, musical sound-making "instrument" and her metaphoric voice, which helps to express her core beliefs and communicate her thoughts and feelings to others.

Developing Rapport and Familiarity

Rapport is a key ingredient in therapy, regardless of the specific ideology and theoretical framework of the therapist or the client's need for treatment (Austin 2008). Voice work can be intimidating, especially if someone is becoming unsure of herself and anxious due to memory loss and brain changes. Feeling a sense of trust and openness with the therapist helps Jackie achieve success. Jackie was already familiar with the therapist from her previous involvement with the monthly AD jam sessions, and she quickly felt comfortable with the structure of individual sessions. Knowing Jackie's profound love of music, especially church music, made it easy to prepare songs for the session. The selection of songs included some she would find familiar and comforting, as well as some that were challenging and would help to maintain some of her advanced musicianship, while supporting Jackie's sense of self through sharing of meaningful music. The individual music therapy process is outlined below (Mercadal-Brotons 2011).

Outline of Individual MT Sessions

Warm-Ups

In order to activate the mind and body for therapy work, movement to music and breath work are incorporated at the beginning of each session (Thaut 2005). Simple dancing, marching, upper body "crossing the midline" motions, stretches, self-massaging, and rhythmic movement were employed for five to ten minutes each session. Warm-ups also provided the therapists with an in-the-moment assessment time that allowed for any small talk and measurement of Jackie's physical and cognitive functioning and mood state on that particular day. Jackie's voice was then warmed up through deep breathing, singing simple scales on vowel sounds, and humming. The actual music varied during the warm-ups depending on this brief and holistic assessment. If Jackie made an observation, such as noticing leaves on the trees outside the window, her comment would be turned into a vocal warm-up using her words and rhythms. If Jackie seemed agitated or anxious, deep breathing with holding tones or a simple, familiar tune was used to calm her. When she was highly energized, music that matched her mood was used to connect with her and support her (Davis et al. 1992).[22]

Playing Instruments

For rhythm and harmony, Jackie played a variety of instruments, such as a hand drum, tambourine, piano, autoharp, or maraca. There were times when she was able to use her voice while playing an instrument, and other times when she had to choose between singing and playing, because it was too complicated to do both. Since Jackie had been a pianist all her life, she was always given an option to play the piano during the session. Even if the piano was becoming more and more challenging, being a pianist remained a familiar and enjoyable role.

Singing Familiar Songs, Chants, and Vocal Improvisations

Jackie possessed a vast, memorized repertoire of sacred and secular songs, and she could often remember these and enjoy them; she was given choices of what she wanted to sing. As her illness required Jackie's music-making to be simplified, she was encouraged to sing a song without accompaniment, often holding hands with the therapists for added physical contact and emotional connection. When she was able, playing piano while the therapists used their voices to sing songs or improvise was also an important part of the session. This activity clearly felt familiar and comfortable to her. Improvised sounds and songs were used to meet Jackie in the moment, by emphasizing a thought or a feeling. Vocal sounds, such as the sound of horses when talking about visiting the country, were also used to make melodies and sound effects or the voice was employed as a melody instrument to sing a tune without words.

Closing

The end of the session was important; Jackie needed time to transition from the music therapy session to her day-to-day life. Sometimes she would become anxious to leave before the end of the session because she was confused about where she was and had the sense she was supposed to be somewhere else. Ending with a closing song helped provide her with a sense of completion and accomplishment. A recap of what was done during the session occurred through simple discussion and in the singing of the closing song, such as the traditional spiritual "He's Got the Whole World in His Hands" when the session focused on faith. Many times, a simple song that was familiar offered the greatest degree of musical success, helping Jackie feel confident and satisfied with her work. Songs with the word "home," such as "Show Me the Way to

Go Home" or "The Banana Boat Song," helped in guiding Jackie through the end of the session.[23]

The Sessions

Over the course of one semester of Jackie's individual music therapy, seven of the music therapy sessions were videotaped and transcribed, with written notes being taken during four other sessions. Session notes and video transcriptions, spanning from August through December 2012, were analyzed for musical content, emotional content, and any words, gestures, or facial expressions that seemed to hold significance for Jackie. Some techniques, such as singing a song and then asking questions about it, re-reading the lyrics after singing a song, or drumming and then stopping to immediately to ask a question, stimulated Jackie's memory and heightened her capacity to express herself. Jackie also was able to spontaneously share many "one-liners" that expressed her personality and wit, and the stimulation provided by movement, melody, harmony, and rhythm seemed to maximize her ability to share her sense of humor. Two main themes that consistently were expressed in her music choices, gestures, and words were relationships and spirituality. The therapists encouraged as much musical and session direction from Jackie as was possible, keeping in mind her need for self-expression, musical-physical-sensory stimulation, and anxiety reduction, while providing the security inherent in a predictable structure.

Within the first month of MT sessions, in order to help bolster Jackie's sense of self, we taught her specific parts of the chant "Not Easily Broken" (Jackert 2012). Voice part 1: "Keep on moving sister, you got to stay strong; Keep on moving brother, you got to stay strong;" voice part 2: "Standing tall, standing tall, standing tall, all the day long." After singing this chant in harmony with her two MTs, I asked Jackie:

R: What makes you feel strong?
J: My husband makes me feel strong.
R: Anything else?
J: I like to sing songs about God and his son. That makes me feel strong.

In the following session, Jackie chooses "Doxology-Old 100th," which begins "Praise God, from whom all blessings flow."[24] While discussing the meaning of this song and life's blessings, Jackie is unable to remember if she is married or not. She remembers a nice man that she is in love with, but forgets the details. I help her remember her husband, and she smiles in recognition. We develop a chant in the moment to capture this important piece of her reality, I'm thankful for my husband, I'm thankful for my kids. Because it is sung with feeling and musicality, it is not like a memory exercise, but a musical statement of core beliefs that she wants to hold on to.

Jackie's family of origin aligns with her consistent theme of relationship in her weekly sessions. At the end of September, when asked what she would like to focus on for the session, she said, "My Mom." She shared how her mom was always there for her when she was a child, and how much she loves her. She brings up her sister Peggy, and how she's a nurse, which "is good, because Peggy and Mom live together and she can take care of her." Her song choices that day were from a songbook collection, and she chose "It's a Small World," "Turn, Turn, Turn," and "I'd Like to Teach the World to Sing," singing harmony while playing piano.[25] The songs represent a specific era in her life and make a connection to her past. During the chanting/song creation at this session, she was able to articulate:

J: I'm thankful for my family. I'm thankful for love. And I'm thankful for Fred, who I'm planning to marry.

Later in the session she remembers she is already married to Fred. She also professes:

J: I'm thankful for Jesus.

As the sessions continue, she remembers other members of her family, usually after singing a song or playing a rhythm. During the first session in October, Jackie sings soulfully while playing piano, then says:

J: "Home on the Range"[26] reminds me of my Dad, who's not around anymore, but he's in heaven . . . He was a hard worker . . . He would go off for a ways . . . he was a . . . like a mechanic . . . for anybody (waving her hands in an effort to communicate) . . . for big trucks.
R: So this song reminds you of him?
J: Yes.
R : It's an old song, isn't it?
F: It's a good song, and nobody dies in it. (She laughs, and we join in laughing.) It's not a sad song.

She sounds young when she's talking and reminiscing, and I can appreciate the value of these memories coming to the surface and being shared.

F: Sometimes I'd go with him . . . he had a giant tire in the back of his truck (more gestures demonstrating the magnitude of this task of her dad's). I loved to watch him.

During this session, Jackie is in great humor, full of one-liners and smiles. She is not usually this talkative, but this day she is enjoying some of her country roots. Her father was a fiddler, and her mother yodeled, and she remembers there were four fiddles and a piano in her home growing up. We show her a vibraslap, which is a fun instrument that creates the sound effect "boing" when struck. She dubs it "out of control." When we demonstrate it again, she says, "They'll come a-runnin'." To help her choose a song when she can't decide, we sit around our drums and rub them, then wiggle our fingers, tapping the drum gently.

R: Let's think of a word that makes you feel good.
J: Friends.
R: Friends!

As we play our drums, we chant the simple phrase, improvising a tune made up of three to four notes.

All Singing: Friends (held for four counts) Friends (held for four counts) Friends . . . Make me feel good!

We continue to repeat this phrase while drumming, singing with long tones, taking deep breaths, and adding harmony. The simple singing/chanting is especially helpful, because we can repeat it as a sung meditation, like the spiritual tradition of Taizé.[27] These shared simple words and phrases become graced with nuance and emotion as the harmonies and rhythms evolve and the confidence of the voice is sustained. The melody, harmony, and rhythm give the words feeling and expression. After several times more, we become quieter, and accentuate each tone. As the drums fade out, we take each other's hands. We meditate on the idea of friends, and Jackie is looking down contemplatively and smiling.

R: When you think of friends, is there any picture that comes to mind?
J: Peggy.

She talks about her sister Peggy being her friend, and I show her the American Sign Language (ASL) sign for friends, which is linking index fingers together, first right finger over left, then left finger over right. She comments that she and her sister are linked together, like the ASL sign. Spontaneously she quietly offers, "I was surprised at how Peggy could take charge and I couldn't." This comment helps the therapists understand some of Jackie's insecurities, and gives voice to what appears to be an unresolved issue. The statement reminded the music therapists to support Jackie further in making decisions and speaking out, even with her limited access to use of language.

In closing, we sing "Kumbaya," a favorite of Jackie's.[28] The style of the song and physical layout of sitting in a circle around drums and guitars remind us of friends around a campfire, coming back to the theme of relationship once again. Jackie sings out with rich tones and clear words, a beautiful tremolo in her voice that is reminiscent of some of the popular torch singers from the 1950s and 1960s. It is easy and comfortable for her, to have each other to sing with, in parts, enjoying the harmony. At the end of the verse, without prompting, Jackie says, "We sound too good." We sing the next verse, "Someone's praying my lord, Kumbaya." Our voices are even stronger, expressing more feeling, and the harmonies even more full and rich. Jackie is using her breath and face fully and expressively, as we repeat the song again, "Kumbaya my lord, Kumbaya . . ." She looks calm, peaceful, not showing any anxiety, only a wholehearted expression of friendship and connection to her self and to her past, while clearly present in the moment.

Discussion

Singing is not a replacement for conversation, but it is a second language to access when direct conversational communication is impaired. Since most of Jackie's conversation was limited to one-word responses or short phrases, spontaneous singing helped her express her thoughts and feelings more fully. When the added texture of rich harmonies, melodies, and rhythms was added to single words or phrases, the few words sung were enlivened, expanding her capacity for expressivity.

Singing familiar songs helped Jackie stay secure in her own personal history, and she remained able to sing lyrics of songs easily since her reading ability was still functional. Although singing song lyrics is not the same as being able to maintain a conversation, Jackie was able to benefit from the language and poetry in the songs, and the sense of satisfaction brought on by using more mature and complex language. Jackie was so connected to her relationships and her spiritual life that there were many songs that supported these prominent themes and helped her to maintain a strong connection with these important aspects of herself.

Finally, singing with other musicians—the MT and the MT student—often fulfilled the familiar and enjoyable role of singing and playing music in a small ensemble. For someone who enjoyed music throughout her life, this "trio" provided a sense of closeness and camaraderie that was enjoyable and musically rich, while working toward her goals in therapy. For all the sessions, Jackie was more relaxed after singing and moving to music, as evidenced by her facial expressions, comments, and behaviors. She was able to access memories and communicate during sessions, and nurtured relationships through the sharing of her life stories. Although her overall condition was deteriorating, her musical ability remained strong, particularly for simple, meaningful songs of faith from her religious and family traditions.

Postlude: Music Care in the Later Stages of AD

When caregiving became especially difficult for Jackie's husband, he began taking Jackie to an adult day care center. At this point, Fred was caring for both of his parents, who were now in hospice care, and helping one of his adult sons with serious medical issues that required extended hospitalization. It was too difficult to schedule Jackie's music therapy sessions at the university clinic any longer, so through the university's clinical outreach program a graduate student provided Jackie with individual music therapy sessions at the adult day care center. During this time, the student therapist used many of the sensory stimulation and supportive music therapy techniques needed to help Jackie respond. When Jackie finally required twenty-four-hour skilled nursing care, she was taken to live at a small group home. Music therapy care will continue for Jackie there as well, with the social and musical information gained in prior years becoming especially useful in providing meaningful music experiences based on Jackie's known preferences and rich musical history.

"Desperately Rediscovering Susan": A Case Study by Annamaria Oliverio, PhD, Music Therapist

Singing is administered as a music therapy intervention during a twelve-month period for a middle-aged woman named Susan recovering from a brain tumor and stroke, the latter of which resulted in some loss of brain function. Background, initial functioning, and areas of need are detailed along with targeted singing interventions. The patient's desired outcome is to be able to sing effectively enough to once again participate in her church choir and ensemble activities. The results of singing interventions indicate significant progress not only in voice quality and control, but also in memory functioning, gross motor movement, gait control, emotional expression, and self-esteem.

Background

Most of the background information regarding Susan's illness was self-reported and based on her physician's assessments. During the time of this case study, Susan, a woman in her middle forties, was recovering from two emergency brain tumor surgeries complicated by a stroke she experienced during the second surgery. She was also undergoing regular chemotherapy sessions. Susan is married and a mother of three young boys, aged nine to thirteen. Her family was also under financial strain due to her surgeries, hospital stays, and treatment. Thus, with the exception of music therapy, no other auxiliary healthcare was being administered at the time her story was documented.

Before her illness, Susan enjoyed a very busy and vital lifestyle. She owned and managed her own vintage women's clothing and jewelry shop and was very active in her church community. Coming from a musical family, she also enjoyed singing in a choir and regularly participated in ensembles as well as singing karaoke with her female friends. As a result of her tumor and stroke, Susan was forced to close her shop and end her previous activities with the church and friends in order to focus her energies on healing. While her spouse helped with the children, he basically remained uninvolved in Susan's recovery because his time was consumed with work and taking care of the household. Her parents live in a different state and visited periodically to help their daughter.

Survival rates for brain tumors vary widely depending on the type of tumor and other factors, including age. Survival rates tend to be highest for younger patients and decrease with age. Also, patients with some types of tumors have relatively good survival rates (Mitchell and Samson 2009). Five-year survival rates for patients with ependymoma (a primary type of brain or spinal cord tumor) and oligodendroglioma (a rare tumor originating in the glial cells of the brain) are, respectively, 85 percent and 81 percent for people aged twenty to forty-four, and 69 percent and 45 percent for patients aged fifty-five to sixty-four. Glioblastoma multiforme (the most common tumor of the central nervous system) has the worst prognosis with five-year survival rates of only 13 percent for people aged twenty to forty-four, and 1 percent for patients aged fifty-five to sixty-four (Krex et al. 2007). Doctors estimated that Susan's oligodendroglioma had been growing for about five to eight years. While Susan's post-cancer prognosis was promising following her two emergency surgeries and chemotherapy protocol, she suffered a stroke during the second surgery. Her neurophysiological functioning was compromised, especially on the right side of her body. Given the fact that Susan was right-handed, she struggled to train her left side to complete fine motor tasks such as writing or using a computer mouse to compensate for her right-side paralysis.

Throughout the year, Susan experienced varying degrees of difficulty moving her right arm, shoulder, leg, foot, fingers, and toes. At the start of music therapy sessions, Susan also indicated that she had difficulty with short-term memory and with expressive and receptive language. She had no family history of stroke and, prior to her tumor, she was otherwise very healthy.

At the time of this case study, Susan was undergoing chemotherapy five days in a row each month and she was on anti-seizure and anti-blood clotting medication. Though she had received some occupational, physical, water, and speech therapies, she identified her major problem areas as speech fluidity, lack of focus, difficulty moving her right side, memory loss, receptive and expressive language, as well as emotional repression. At the beginning of treatment, Susan used a number of diverse walking implements. Walking was arduous. As the year progressed and she regained more gross motor movement in her leg and foot, Susan was able to walk around her house without using her removable leg cast and cane.

Susan's hearing and vision appeared within normal parameters. She also demonstrated good hand–eye coordination, though she had difficulty with finger/hand dexterity on her right side and she was struggling to train her left side. Her affect suggested a combination of alertness and anxiety. Physically, she displayed low stamina and she tired easily, consistent with the side effects indicated on her medications. However, Susan was determined to heal as she exhibited eagerness to interact with the therapist.

Susan loves music and is working very hard to regain gross and fine motor movement in the right side of her body, as well as regaining her voice. She appears very shy and humble, but does not hesitate to attempt new interventions that may be challenging. After she receives chemo, she experiences extreme fatigue and stress, though during visits with her parents she appears significantly happier and more relaxed. Throughout the course of treatment, Susan improves significantly in her self-identified problem areas.

Based on her presenting skills and areas of need as expressed by the client, the overall goals for Susan's treatment plan were to improve gross motor movement, followed by fine motor movement on her right and left sides, to promote expression of feelings, to increase short-term memory, to promote communication, relaxation and distraction from stress, and to improve self-esteem by finding her voice.

The Use of Singing Interventions

Music therapy sessions were conducted at Susan's residence, once a week for an hour. A musical preferences assessment was given during the initial meeting; it determined that Susan appreciated all genres of music listed on the assessment. She indicated being especially fond of Adele's music; prior to her illness, she could sing a number of Adele's songs from memory.[29] At the beginning of treatment, sessions were quite structured and included diverse vocal warm-ups and breathing exercises. Since Susan's breath was very shallow, we focused on relaxation, elongating her breath and learning to take chest-to-belly breaths. By the end of our treatment sessions, Susan was comfortable singing up and down a one-octave scale using one breath, singing half notes. Voice quality and volume were also focuses of the warm-ups. Initially, she sang so softly she could barely hear her own voice. Thus, for a while she used a microphone to better hear her voice, which she claimed sounded different than before the stroke. After several months of voice exercises and singing interventions, both with and without the use of a microphone, Susan became used to hearing her "different" voice and grew confident enough to participate in a lyric composition intervention, which allowed her to express her feelings as well as tell the story of her illness and ongoing recovery. Original music was also composed.

Relaxation and Distraction from Stress

Just as breathing and vocal exercises at the beginning of each session were designed to treat Susan's voice quality and volume, they also relaxed and distracted her from stress and/or pain. In fact, specific vocal warm-ups would often make her laugh out loud, which further improved her mood and ability to relax. For example, "blowing raspberries" made her feel silly and she would giggle through the exercise; but when she sang immediately following, her volume and quality improved noticeably. On days when she was feeling especially tired or stressed, such as the days during and immediately following chemotherapy, Susan preferred singing to more sedative music, usually at the end of the session. Occasionally, she would fall asleep during this intervention.

Gross and Fine Motor Movement

Interventions to improve gross motor movement and gait on the right side included marching rhythmically to the beat of the song while seated. This activity progressed to walking rhythmically while singing either to recorded music, karaoke, or live guitar music. When she was walking to recorded music, Susan preferred reggae songs. Walking rhythmically progressed from holding on to the therapist while listening and following recorded music to match her pace until finally Susan was able to walk on her own rhythmically, singing a song of her choice and following the therapist who was playing the guitar.

Creating her own movements to songs and incorporating American Sign Language helped Susan improve her fine motor movement while singing. For example, she would sign the phrase "ring of fire" to the corresponding Johnny Cash song.[30] She started by making signs and movements to music using her left hand and arm only; however, over the course of the year, Susan began integrating her right hand. To further improve her solo singing and musical independence, she learned to play two- to three-chord songs on the QChord while singing.[31] She used her left hand to play the chords and her right to strum. Singing these songs while playing the QChord improved her self-esteem and willingness to sing solos again.

Improving Short-Term Memory

With Susan, improving short-term memory also led to improvement of overall communication. To that end, Susan began by singing her favorite songs. She quickly realized that if she tried to simply recite the lyrics without the music, she could not remember them. However, as soon as she heard the music, she was able to remember over 75 percent of the lyrics to songs she previously had memorized. For the other 25 percent of the lyrics, we used song games such as fill in the words and name that tune (e.g., singing a familiar song with "la, la, la" instead of lyrics until the client remembers phrases and eventually the entire song and title of the song). Seeing that her long-term memory was allowing her to remember her favorite songs, the therapist encouraged her to take on the challenge of learning new lyrics and new songs. Using the same process of singing games for memorization, Susan learned sixteen new songs from memory, including a song in an American Indian language called "Mahk Jchi" (Heartbeat Drum Song).[32] This song became her favorite to sing while walking to improve her gait.

Singing in a round as well as integrating harmony were also used to help Susan improve her memory and focus. Initially, Susan had difficulty singing her part of the simple song "Row, Row, Row Your Boat" as a round. Furthermore, she had difficulty maintaining her melody line when the therapist sang harmony. However, via multiple repetitions, Susan eventually was able to sing her parts while a totally different part was sung simultaneously (e.g., when singing two-part pentatonic songs). She was also able to recognize her voice quality improvements and identify areas that needed further work.

Promoting Communication and Expression of Feelings

Susan initially struggled to express herself. She would often get stuck in the middle of a phrase, forgetting the words she wanted to use to convey her thoughts. Singing helped her restore speech as she was able to access language through the songs she sang. By singing alone, Susan was able to impact the three main components of language at once, cognition, linguistics and pragmatics, by supporting memory and retrieval of information. Thus, Susan was able to sing words she could not yet remember to speak. However, in Susan's case, once she accessed the words several times through the songs, she was able to retrieve them quite easily in speech.

Once Susan's speech and overall ability to communicate had improved, the next step was to promote her expression of feelings. Together, we created diverse song improvisations, for example attaching new phrases to old songs that allowed her to express how she was feeling in the moment. Pictures were also used to provoke a mood, such as joy, serenity, or loneliness, and inspire the creation of an appropriate chant, jingle, or song parody. During the last two months of treatment, Susan composed lyrics for a song about her relationships, aspirations, worries, struggles, and triumphs during her illness and recovery, for which the therapist composed original music.

Improving Self-Esteem

Singing favorite songs with live music and karaoke accompaniment, along with learning new songs, greatly improved Susan's self-esteem, sense of independence, and self-worth. As she gradually rediscovered her voice, she became more and more willing to challenge herself and test boundaries. Recordings of her voice allowed her to hear her consistent improvement. She was usually very critical of herself, but she also noted her consistently improving voice quality and memory, making her even more determined to progress further. By the end of one year, Susan had recorded a CD of herself singing new songs she had learned and her own original song.

Discussion and Conclusions

Through specific singing interventions and experiences such as vocal warm-ups, movement while singing, improvisation, composition, improvising, composing, listening, and re-creating, Susan was successful at meeting the individualized session objectives and goals she and the therapist created for her treatment plan. Also, because Susan enjoyed all types of musical genres, she was open to singing songs that initially were beyond her comfort zone (e.g., "Mahk Jchi"), in order to meet a new challenge or objective. Even at her most exhausted, Susan always participated in singing interventions to the fullest. As the year progressed and her self-esteem improved, Susan began to groom herself regularly and her social interactions increased. She also felt confident enough to get clearance to drive, so she began to go to church meetings and to visit friends again. Though she had not yet fully returned to ensemble singing, Susan diligently practiced singing songs from her old and new repertoires on her own, between sessions. She is still not satisfied with her singing because she compares it to the way she used to sing, though after listening to recordings of her voice near the beginning of treatment and at the end of the year, Susan acknowledged her significant improvements. At the time her case was documented, Susan was not receiving any other supplemental therapies except music therapy and, of all the interventions employed, singing appears to have played the most significant role in her accomplishments and in improving her quality of life. By the end of therapy, she smiled and laughed regularly, even when she felt pain or fatigue.

"At the End of Life": A Hospice Case Study by Jan Dougherty, MS, RN

MA is an eighty-two-year-old white female who has a ten-year history of progressive Alzheimer's disease, hypertension, and diabetes. MA is now in the advanced stages of her dementing illness, which is characterized by the following: severe short and long-term memory loss, limited verbal abilities, oriented only to self, dependent for all activities of daily life (e.g., bathing, feeding, dressing, toileting), and incontinent of both bowel and bladder. MA meets hospice criteria for advanced dementia using the Functional Assessment Staging Tool (FAST), which outlines the seven stages of cognitive and functional decline associated with Alzheimer's disease (Reisberg 1988). In stages 6 and 7, the scale is further broken down into specific expected functional decline. Patients with dementia qualifying for hospice care must meet the following criteria: FAST stage 7C (cognitive loss and functional decline as outlined above, speech limited to less than a half dozen words per day, unable to walk without assistance), plus one of the following qualifiers: hospitalization in the past six months, recurrent infection or fever, pressure ulcers and/or unexpected weight loss (National Hospice and Palliative Care Organization 2008). MA was admitted to hospice care by her primary care physician following hospitalization for aspiration pneumonia.

MA lives at home with her daughter and granddaughter, who both work but share in caregiving responsibilities to provide the 24/7 care required. MA's family has been very committed to her care, and they desire to keep her at home with the additional aid of hospice caregivers. This Medicare benefit provides MA with physicians, nurses, social workers, hospice aids, chaplains, and volunteers to meet the comfort needs of both the patient and the family caregivers. MA's nurse learned that she loved music throughout her life, as was evidenced by music being played in the background at almost every visit. MA's granddaughter, Laura, provides the bulk of care during the daytime hours. She reports that her grandmother is now sleeping most of the day and, during her waking hours, she tries to meet her comfort needs, including feeding, bathing, continence care, and repositioning her in her bed or lounge chair. Laura expresses her own grief about this once "feisty Irish woman" who loved to tell stories, read books, volunteer, and cook for her family. She feels sad that her grandmother can no longer speak but sees her eyes brighten when Laura is with her. She wants to make sure that her grandmother's final days are good ones, but, beyond the great personal care she provides, Laura does not know what else she can do.

The hospice nurse, Beth, notices that music is almost always playing in the background when she visits MA and her granddaughter. Beth has learned that the memory for music is one of the last areas affected in the brains of people with neurodegenerative diseases such as Alzheimer's disease. Furthermore, she has learned that engaging dementia patients with songs that are familiar, beloved, and well rehearsed throughout life is likely to create positive connections. On one of the visits with MA, Beth begins to ask Laura about her grandmother's music history and learns that MA used to love to sing to her kids and grandkids—especially Irish tunes. Furthermore, Laura knows that her grandmother, a devout Catholic, also liked religious tunes, such as "Amazing Grace."[33] Beth educates Laura about the unique role that music can play in engaging people with advanced dementia and suggests that they discuss how Laura might incorporate music in her grandmother's care. Beth inquires about a favorite Irish tune that Laura recalls her grandmother singing to her and Laura promptly replies, "Grandma loved to sing 'When Irish Eyes

Are Smiling!'"[34] Beth suggests that Laura sing to her grandmother, but Laura quickly says, "My voice is terrible – I can't hold a key." Beth reassures Laura that success is not about the quality of her voice, but rather her intent to have fun and engage with her grandmother.

Beth encourages Laura to sing "When Irish Eyes Are Smiling" during the visit to her grandmother, but she first discusses the importance of meeting MA's basic needs so that she is more likely to focus on the pleasant event of singing rather than being distracted by unmet needs. Beth helps Laura change MA's brief, gives MA a small glass of juice, and seats her comfortably in her lounge chair in the living room. MA is awake but shows no expression; she tracks Laura's voice with her eyes. Laura holds her grandmother's hand and says, "Okay, Gran, I am going to sing a song to you that you used to sing to me! I hope you will join along."

Laura shyly begins to sing the chorus of this favorite song, "When Irish eyes are smiling, sure 'tis like a morn in spring." Laura and Beth see MA lock her eyes on Laura. As Laura continues with the chorus, "In the lilt of Irish laughter, you can hear the angels sing," both Laura and Beth see a twinkle appear in MA's eyes, and a smile begins to form. Laura begins to relax and sing louder, and with confidence she continues, "When Irish hearts are happy, all the world seems bright and gay." MA is clearly connecting with the song. Beth delights as she sees Laura laugh and continue on with the chorus, "And when Irish eyes are smiling, sure, they steal your heart away." At this point, Beth sees MA trying to move her lips. Beth suggests that Laura slowly repeat the chorus again and prompt her grandmother to sing along if she is able. Laura kisses her grandmother, saying, "That was so much fun, let's try it again!" Laura initiates the chorus once again and now, like magic, she sees her grandmother move her lips and slowly hears her voice the lyrics of the chorus. Between laughter and tears, Laura repeats the chorus with MA another three times. As each chorus is repeated, MA begins to sing aloud more of the words, and her smile becomes more prominent. When Laura finishes the tune, she is filled with joy and satisfaction to hear her grandmother's soft voice and see her smile.

Beth encourages Laura to continue on by singing "Amazing Grace." Laura is now filled with much more confidence as she begins, "Amazing grace, how sweet the sound." Beth observes that MA continues to smile at Laura and then, as the song continues, she tries to join in. As Laura repeats the chorus, Beth also notes that MA begins to tap her hand to the rhythm. After finishing a couple of repetitions of this song, Laura remembers that her grandmother used to sing "He's Got the Whole World in His Hands" and spontaneously moves into that song. MA holds a smile and moves her lips with some of the lyrics. She also begins to try to clap along as Laura repeats the chorus several more times. After about ten minutes, Laura stops and says, "I just got my Gran back!"

Beth reviews with Laura the powerful intervention music can continue to offer to MA and suggests that she and her mom begin to try to sing along with

MA for about ten to fifteen minutes during her waking hours. Beth stresses the importance of always making sure that MA's basic needs have been met. She discusses important principles of singing the chorus of familiar songs (instead of the verses) and slowing the tempo. She helps Laura become familiar with behavioral features that support her grandmother's enjoyment of the music experience. Such features include: bright eyes and/or prolonged eye contact; peaceful, alert, or animated facial features; raised eyebrows; laughing/ smiling (or attempts to do so) during the activity; movement of hands, feet, or simply one finger or toe in response to the music (lapping/patting/ tapping); and verbal cues. Verbal cues include attempts to hum, sing/ talk/pray, intelligible/unintelligible expressions with meaning, single words/ phrases ("Yes," "Good"), repetitive phrases or sentences, and silent formation of words, which demonstrates positive meaning related to the activity (Edelman et al. 2007).

Beth reports back to the hospice team about how MA responded to music. She suggests that the hospice aide should sing to MA when providing her bed bath. The aide said that she would try "You Are My Sunshine" and "He's Got the Whole World in His Hands," as these have been pleasurable for many of her patients with advanced dementia. The chaplain quickly notes that he will ask Laura and her mom about other favorite religious songs that were pleasurable for MA. He will also sing them to her during his visits. The team appreciated the ways music played a unique role for MA and her family during her hospice care, and they incorporated it into MA's routine care.

FIGURE 5.1 Informal sing-along. Collection of author.

Plato is credited with saying: "Music gives a soul to the universe, wings to the mind, flight to the imagination, and life to everything." This statement is certainly true for those with advanced dementia, as witnessed by MA's family and hospice team. Despite her debilitated condition, MA's favorite tunes opened her world and her mind beyond the limits of her disease and, for a few moments, allowed MA to be "Gran" once again. Music can be one of the most powerful and positive interventions in people with advanced dementia. Hospice care members should be taught how to utilize music in end-of-life care for people with dementia (see Figure 5.1).

Conclusion

At the present, nothing reverses dementia. Especially for this vexing set of pathologies, intervention goals must address quality of life and wellness, which are difficult to quantify. The brain of a dementia patient who perceives his quality of life positively may not show markers of this wellness level. Still, therapists, researchers, patients, and caregivers regularly affirm the benefits gained from various interventions. No matter how severe the associated cognitive decline, patient wellbeing can be nourished in a supportive environment, just as it can be diminished in a neutral or malignant one.

In multiple research studies, singing individually and in groups has been shown to improve quality of life for many people with dementia. Ideally, music therapists, certified professionals trained to utilize musical experiences with the patient to address the many deficiencies associated with dementia, should be available to anyone who might feel the benefits. Unfortunately, dementia is prevalent enough that demand exceeds availability of professional music therapists. Many people caring for patients in various stages of cognitive deterioration have no access to music therapists and have little guidance about how best to use singing with dementia patients. Why is the use of the singing voice not a more natural option for caregivers?

Caring for a person with dementia can be physically and emotionally exhausting, so much so that various tools have been created to help study this phenomenon. In 1980, Stephen H. Zarit and colleagues published a popular self-report measure to help assess caregiver burden (Zarit et al. 1980). Family caregivers regularly report depression, stress, and isolation. Some have tried various approaches to improve vexing problems such as resistance, agitation, and aggression, with success that seems short-lived. Many caregivers share a "walking on eggs" sense of helplessness that can be intensified if the person with dementia is a family member. In 2013, the Alzheimer's Association (United States) began funding a project featuring an interactive web-based caregiver support tool (iSupport) that is accessible via computer, tablet, and mobile phone.[35]

Importantly, dementia patients are not the only benefactors of singing. Even if the ill person seems unaware that singing is taking place, the caregiver can experience many benefits of singing that have been articulated throughout this book. Singing can improve quality of breathing by encouraging deeper breaths. Singing can voice feelings that are often left unexpressed. Singing in groups can give the caregiver the chance to share experiences, stresses, and helpful information with others facing the same challenges. Singing may increase oxytocin uptake. And for the dementia sufferer, as Bannan wrote:

> The holistic, tangible nature of group singing depends on the survival of channels of musical and social intelligence on which participation depends. These seem to outlive the verbal and logical domains that so easily represent the means by which we label people as active, social beings.
>
> *Bannan and Montgomery-Smith (2008)*

One's sense of selfhood can be nurtured through singing relationships. The average family member might "reach" their loved one with dementia by singing the songs from her youth. In my music and health class, quite a few graduate-age university students have related the ways that singing 1940s and 1950s songs created a sense of connection with a grandparent who suffered from dementia, even if the grandparent could no longer recognize the singer. Music therapist and professor of music therapy Robin Rio provides a user-friendly guide, complete with recommended songs and other activities, in her book (Rio 2009). Especially helpful in this guide are suggested plans for a singing session, chordal accompaniments, and full texts for seventeen songs, including "After the Ball," "All through the Night," "Arirang," "Cielito Lindo," "Hava Nagila," "Waltzing Matilda," and "When Irish Eyes Are Smiling."[36] Her longer list, with titles only, comprises more than 175 songs. Rio also suggests thirty-two artists whose recordings are likely to be recognized by seniors with dementia, including the Andrews Sisters, Gene Autry, Tony Bennett, Xavier Cugat, Doris Day, Nelson Eddy, Ella Fitzgerald, Mario Lanza, Elvis Presley, Tito Puente, and Hank Williams, Sr.

As Ruth Finnegan documents, many music-making opportunities are hidden from research projects; they simply involve volunteer musicians committed to improving quality of life or sharing individual talents with all sorts of groups (Finnegan 2007). Finding group-singing opportunities that can include dementia patients may be as simple as checking the offerings of municipal or county adult recreation centers, churches, apartment complexes, or senior resident facilities. Several organizations have invested in large-scale research initiatives aimed at making group singing available to dementia patients and their caregivers. The Alzheimer's Society of the United Kingdom (2014) offers a service called "Singing for the Brain" (SFTB) for people with dementia or Alzheimer's and their caregivers who come together to sing in a group. Music sociologist Mariko Hara reported on fifty SFTB groups in the UK (Hara 2011). Importantly, this is not a project during which music therapy is delivered; these are informal group-singing events. SFTB fits in with several areas important in dementia care and the aims of the

Alzheimer's Society: peer support, activity, stimulation, and raising awareness.[37] Hara reported as an insider; she participated in an SFTB group for eight months and spent another six months observing and generating her research report. One of her vignettes will be shared here; it underscores the potentially transformative power of singing in these groups.

Laura is a care-receiver who knows many songs and who regularly sings and dances in the group sessions. Her demeanor is always joyful and cheerful during these times. Hara met Laura and her caregiver (Laura's husband) at a supermarket after one session. In that context, writes Hara:

> When I went to say hello to them she didn't recognize me, nor my name (in the session, everyone has a name tag) and she looked a bit puzzled. Her energy level was much lower than I was used to and her attention was not very focused. In short, she seemed to be a totally different person from the Laura I knew from the session.
>
> It seems that the SFTB sessions enable Laura to be a very different person from the Laura I met outside the sessions. In the sessions she is always very confident and cheerful when interacting with others, she is alert and accurate about the words she sings and easily follows the facilitator's instructions when it comes to challenging activities such as singing in parts. It seems that SFTB sessions allow her to reconnect to the enjoyment of being with others and the joy of taking the initiative. Out of this context, she is not as cheerful or confident as in the sessions.

The changes wrought by group singing thus may be short-lived. Still, as Hara (2011) noted, the SFTB sessions also have what she called positive "spin-off" effects:

> Kelly told me that it takes all morning to get her husband ready for the SFTB session. This preparation then becomes an event in itself within their daily life. Another couple always arrives at the venue half an hour early to feed the swans on the river before the session. Lisa told me that on the way home from the SFTB sessions she and her mother continue singing the songs from the session. Peggy (a carer) told me that her mother, Nichola, sleeps very well in the car after the one hour of constant singing . . . For the participants with dementia, their memories of "a good time" in SFTB sessions obviously do not last long; therefore, extending the effect with spin-offs becomes very important for their everyday life both for themselves and their carers.

Finally, the SFTB group can help rekindle relationships that have been disrupted by dementia. One participant, Lisa, related that her mother had always had a great sense of humor. "When mum makes me laugh, it is quite touching. This is when I meet 'old mum' . . . Those moments are very important for me."

Chances are, everyone will eventually know and love someone who suffers from a form of dementia. Many of us will suffer its effects ourselves. My sincere hope is that this chapter contributes to increased singing opportunities for everyone, and for dementia patients in particular.

Film Illustrations

The Music Never Stopped (2011), *Away from Her* (2007), *On Golden Pond* (1981), *A Song for Martin* (2001), *The Savages* (2007), *Aurora Borealis* (2006), *The Notebook* (2004), *Iris: A Memoir of Iris Murdoch* (2001), *Firefly Dreams* (2001), *Age Old Friends* (1989).

Video Illustrations

"Please Don't Stop the Music," Dr. Amy Clements-Cortes "Don't Stop the Music" at Toronto Reference Library March 11, 2013. Presented by the Baycrest Centre for Education on Aging, www.youtube.com/watch?v=SogJE-XSAlo, accessed 30 December 2014.

Scott Tonkinson, MM, MT-BC, "Music Therapy for the Elderly," www.youtube.com/watch?v=59bMEot4RfY&list=UU4jYX8KOQtvKCxrAe3wx-gA, accessed 29 December 2014.

Discussion Points

NOTE: Until the patient becomes familiar with you, it is best to have a family member or other caregiver present when visiting a person with dementia. Always ask permission before visiting or singing, and be ready to stop the song at the first sign of sadness or distress.

1. Speak with someone who has a loved one suffering from loss of cognitive function. Offer to help create a list of songs that were meaningful to the patient when she was between eighteen and twenty-four years old. If the patient's history is not known, select a few upbeat songs from the top forty of that chronological period. Offer to visit the patient and, if allowed to visit, offer to sing a song from the list for or with her. If the patient or her representative agrees, sing the song softly. Note the patient's response to the song.
2. Create a possible song list for a patient who grew up in Mexico, Poland, or Korea. If the opportunity arises to visit a patient from one of these countries, learn one or two songs, even if you must sing them on a neutral syllable such as "la." How did the patient respond to your attempt to sing songs from his home country?
3. Brainstorm ways that your advocacy might help a person who has early-stage Alzheimer's disease find ways to sing with a group.

Notes

1 Generally speaking, behavioral qualitative research is the type gathered via open-ended questions or self-reporting. Assessing a person's feelings about receiving chemotherapy would be considered qualitative research. Quantitative research, on the other hand, addresses more objective methods of measurement such as blood pressure, glucose levels, and heart rate.

2 Psychologists Tom Kitwood and Kathleen Bredin developed Dementia Care Mapping (DCM) in the early 1990s. DCM is an observational tool that considers the care of people with dementia from the viewpoint of the person with dementia. These results can assist with the development of person-centered care. DCM involves observation continually over several hours during a waking day. Every five minutes, several measures are recorded, the main measure being the Wellbeing/Illbeing value, expressed numerically from most negative to most positive ($-5, -3, -1, +1, +3, +5$, respectively).

3 As with all research referenced here, the original study must be consulted for complete information.

4 It bears repeating that experimental groups are recruited to be as homogeneous as possible in order to reduce the number of variables that could invalidate results. People who met these inclusion criteria may not exhibit the same behaviors as other people with the same illnesses. This is a given in the quest for generalizable knowledge.

5 MMSE's insensitivity to mild cognitive impairment inspired the creation of the Montreal Cognitive Assessment (MoCA, available at mocatest.org), which has replaced the MMSE in some situations.

6 The experiment itself measures QOL.

7 Walter Donaldson wrote the music to "My Blue Heaven" in 1924 and George A. Whiting supplied lyrics soon afterward.

8 To get the best sense of music therapists at work, read the case studies below and see the video list at the end of the chapter.

9 I witnessed one exemplary hospital technician using her own singing to soothe a dementia patient undergoing a fifteen-minute EEG, a procedure which stretches patients' ability to remain still and avoid fidgeting with more than twenty contacts attached to the scalp with a sticky gel. Banner Desert Hospital Adult Progressive Care 4A, Phoenix, AZ, 24 June 2014.

10 Cuddy and Duffin (2005: 230) point out the difficulty in determining whether group-singing activities reveal that musical abilities are spared in dementia, or whether patients respond to simple stimulation in group settings. Most music therapists would suggest that a combination of the two scenarios is most likely.

11 An updated version of the English folk tune "Long, Long Ago," "Don't Sit under the Apple Tree" features lyrics by Lew Brown and Charles Tobias and premiered in 1939.

12 Levinson's article targets rewards associated with listening to music that evokes negative emotions, but this list comprises general benefits that might be present in a singing intervention. Jerrold Levinson, "Music and Negative Emotion," in *Music and Meaning*, ed. J. Robinson (Ithaca, NY: Cornell University Press, 1997), 226, n23. For applications in healthcare, see Norton (2008).

13 Composer/lyricists, respectively, are Cole Porter, Bob Thiele/George David Weiss, Jimmy Van Heusen/Johnny Burke, Richard Rodgers/Oscar Hammerstein II, Harold Arlen/Ted Koehler, and Charles Strouse/Lee Adams.

14 A congratulatory handshake from Joseph Goebbels, Reich Minister of Propaganda, to Furtwängler is a complex testament to the tensions of those times. See Zucher (2005).

15 The Familiarity Decision Test, comprising ten familiar (vocal and instrumental) works, is the first examination in the 1998 version of the University of Montreal Musical Test Battery. Ten unfamiliar vocal and instrumental examples were utilized in the Distorted Tunes Test.

16 Cuddy and Duffin (2005) stress the idiosyncratic nature of the case study method. It will detect patterns of loss and sparing if they exist—patterns that may be quite specific to the individual (234).

17 Eleven PWDs, their eleven caregivers, and one additional caregiver who attended alone were recruited from Alzheimer's Australia-Western Australia. Eighteen residents with dementia and seven volunteer support workers were drawn from Maurice Zeffert Home, a residential facility for elderly Jewish people.

18 The acronym is derived from the organizing society, Alzheimer's Australia-Western Australia.

19 See full article for consideration of multiple variables required to fully contextualize these findings.

20 The caregivers stated that prior to participation in this study they had never listened to music while performing the morning care routines.

21 The names have been changed.

22 The iso principle is a technique wherein music is matched to the client's mood.

23 "Show Me the Way to Go Home" was written in 1925 by the English songwriting team of James Campbell and Reginald Connelly (pseudonym, Irving King). "Day-O" (the Banana Boat Song) is a traditional Jamaican folk song that was first popularized in the US by Harry Belafonte.

24 The Doxology text was written in 1674 by Bishop Thomas Ken; the tune Old 100th first appeared in a Genevan psalter in 1551, during the Protestant Reformation. It is usually attributed to Loys Bourgeois (ca. 1510–60). This tune is among the best known in Protestantism.

25 Composer/lyricist and dates are, respectively: Robert B. Sherman/Richard M. Sherman 1964, Pete Seeger late 1950s, Rose Malka Freidman/Roger Cook/Roger Greenaway 1971.

26 Daniel Kelley/Brewster M. Higley, 1870s.

27 Taizé refers to a location in France and to the ecumenical repertoire of music composed for worship at a pilgrimage site there.

28 "Kumbaya" is a religious folk song featuring Gullah dialect spoken by certain residents of the South Carolina/Georgia Sea Islands. It was first recorded in 1926.

29 Adele Laurie Blue Adkins (b. 1988) is an English singer-songwriter who won Grammy awards for Best New Artist and Best Female Pop Vocal Performance in 2009.

30 "Ring of Fire" is a country music song written by June Carter Cash and Merle Kilgore and popularized by Johnny Cash on the album *Ring of Fire: The Best of Johnny Cash* (1963).

31 The Suzuki QChord® Digital SongCard Guitar.

32 "Mahk Jchi," a song by Ulali, a Native American women's a cappella group, was featured on the group's 1994 recording of the same name.

33 John Newton's hymn text "Amazing Grace" was first published in 1779. The tune most commonly associated with the text is New Britain. The text/tune pairing dates to 1835.

34 First published in 1912, the song was written by lyricists Chauncey Olcott and George Graff, Jr., and composer Ernest Ball.

35 Dolores E. Gallagher-Thompson and colleagues will work with the World Health Organization to conduct a trial with 430 users in Bangalore, India, where Internet penetration is high and collaboration is secured with the National Institute of Mental Health and Neuro Science (NIMHANS) Alzheimer's research center. Their hope is to reduce caregiver stress. www.alz.org/research/alzheimers_grants/for_researchers/overview-2013.asp?grants=2013gallagher, accessed 14 July 2014.

36 Composers and composition dates, respectively, are Charles K. Harris 1892, traditional Welsh 1784, Korean folk song, Qirono Mendoza y Cortez 1882, traditional Israeli 1918, traditional tune arranged by Christina Macpherson and A.B. Paterson 1893; and Ernest Ball, Chauncey Olcott, and George Graff, Jr., 1912.

37 Hara here describes the words of southwest region manager, ALZ Society.

References

Alzheimer's Association. 2014. "Alzheimer's Myths." www.alz.org, accessed 2 June 2014.

———. "Diagnosis of Alzheimer's Disease and Dementia." www.alz.org, accessed 4 June 2014.

———. "Seven Stages of Alzheimer's." www.alz.org, accessed 19 June 2014.

———. "Tests for Alzheimer's Disease and Dementia." www.alz.org, accessed 6 December 2014.

———. "Types of Dementia." www.alz.org, accessed 2 June 2014.

———. "What Is Dementia?" www.alz.org, accessed 2 June 2014.

Alzheimer's Society of the United Kingdom. 2014. "Dementia Brain Tour." http://alzheimers.org.uk, accessed 9 July 2014.

Ashida, S. 2000. "The Effect of Reminiscence Music Therapy Sessions on Changes in Depressive Symptoms in Elderly Persons with Dementia." *Journal of Music Therapy* 37: 170–82.

Austin, D. 2008. *The Theory and Practice of Vocal Psychotherapy: Songs of the Self.* London/Philadelphia, PA: Jessica Kinglsey Press.

Awofeso, N. 2005. Bulletin Board: "Re-defining Health." *Bulletin of the World Health Organization* 83.802: 802, www.who.int/bulletin/bulletin_board/83/ustun11051/en/, accessed 22 September 2014.

Bannan, N., and C. Montgomery-Smith. 2008. "'Singing for the Brain': Reflections on the Human Capacity for Music Arising from a Pilot Study of Group Singing with Alzheimer's Patients." *Journal of the Royal Society for the Promotion of Health* 128.73: 73–8.

Banner Alzheimer's Institute. 2014. "Alzheimer's Prevention Initiative." http://banneralz.org, accessed 22 June 2014.

Brooker, D., and L. Duce. 2000. "Wellbeing and Activity in Dementia: A Comparison of Group Reminiscence Therapy, Structured Goal-Directed Group Activity and Unstructured Time." *Aging & Mental Health* 4.4: 354–8.

Camic, P.M., C.M. Williams, and F. Meeten. 2011. "Does a 'Singing Together Group' Improve Quality of Life of People with a Dementia and Their Carers?" *Dementia* 23.12: 157–76. http://dem.sagepub.com/content/12/2/157, accessed 22 September 2014.

Centers for Disease Control and Prevention (US). 2014. "Health-Related Quality of Life: Well-being Concepts." www.cdc.gov/hrqol/wellbeing.htm#eight, accessed 22 September 2014.

Clair, A.A. 1996. *Therapeutic Uses of Music with Older Adults.* Michigan: Health Professions Press.

———. 2000 "The Importance of Singing with Elderly Patients." In *Music Therapy in Dementia Care,* ed. D. Aldridge. London: Jessica Kingsley, 81–101.

Clair, A.A., and B. Bernstein. 1990. "A Comparison of Singing, Vibrotactile and Nonvibrotactile Instrumental Playing Responses in Severely Regressed Persons with Dementia of the Alzheimer's Type." *Journal of Music Therapy* 27.3: 124.

Crowe, B.J. 2009. "Review of *Music: Promoting Health and Creating Community in Healthcare Contexts,* edited by J. Edwards. Newcastle, UK: Cambridge Scholars Publishing, 2007." *Music Therapy Perspectives* 27.1: 69–71.

Cuddy, L.L., and J. Duffin. 2005. "Music, Memory, and Alzheimer's Disease: Is Music Recognition Spared in Dementia, and How Can It Be Assessed?" *Medical Hypotheses* 64: 229–35.

Cuddy, L., J. Duffin, S. Gill, C. Brown, R. Sikka, and A. Vanstone. 2012. "Memory for Melodies and Lyrics in Alzheimer's Disease." *Music Perception* 29.5: 479–91.

Dalla Bella, S., J.-F. Giguère, and I. Peretz. 2007. "Singing Proficiency in the General Population." *Journal of the Acoustic Society of America* 121.2: 1182–9.

Davidson, J.W., and J. Fedele. 2011. "Investigating Group Singing Activity with People with Dementia and Their Caregivers: Problems and Positive Prospects." *Musica Scientiae* 15: 402–22. DOI: 10.1177/1029864911410954.

Davis, W.B., K.E. Gfeller, and M. Thaut. 1992. *An Introduction to Music Therapy: Theory and Practice.* Dubuque, IA: Wm. C. Brown.

Edelman, P., B.R. Fulton, D. Kuhn, M. Gallagher, J. Dougherty, and C.O. Long. 2007. "Assessing Quality of Life Across the Continuum of Dementia: Two New Observational Tools for Researchers and Practitioners." *Alzheimer's Care Today* 8.4: 332–43.

Finnegan, R.H. 2007. *The Hidden Musicians: Music-Making in an English Town.* Cambridge, MA: Wesleyan University Press.

Gerdner, L.A. 2005. "Use of Individualized Music by Trained Staff and Family: Translating Research into Practice." *Journal of Gerontological Nursing* 31.6: 22–30.

Götell, E., S. Brown, and S.L. Ekman. 2003. "The Influence of Caregiver Singing and Background Music on Posture, Movement and Sensory Awareness in Dementia Care." *International Psychogeriatrics* 15.4: 411–30.

———. 2009. "The Influence of Caregiver Singing and Background Music on Vocally Expressed Emotions and Moods in Dementia Care: A Qualitative Analysis." *International Journal of Nursing Studies* 46.4: 422–30.

Hammar, L.M., A. Emami, E. Götell, and G. Engström. 2011. "The Impact of Caregivers' Singing on Expressions of Emotions and Resistance during Morning Care Situations in Persons with Dementia: An Intervention in Dementia Care." *Journal of Clinical Nursing* 20.7–8: 969–78.

Hara, M. 2011. "Expanding a Care Network for People with Dementia and Their Carers through Musicking: Participant Observation with 'Singing for the Brain.'" *Voices: A World Forum for Music Therapy* 11.2. https://voices.no/index.php/voices/article/view/570/459, accessed 14 July 2014.

Jackert, L. 2012. "Not Easily Broken." *Daughters of Harriet: From the Heart.* CD, www.earthtonesmusictherapy.com, accessed 30 December 2014.

Kitwood, T., and K. Bredin. 1994. "Charting the Course of Quality Care." *Journal of Dementia Care* 2.3: 22–3.

Koniari, D., H. Proios, K. Tsapkini, and L.C. Triarhou. 2012. "Singing but Not Speaking: A Retrospect on Music–Language Interrelationships in the Human Brain since Otto Marburg's Zur Frage der Amusie (1919)." *Advances in Psychology Research* 87: 239–48.

Krex, D., B. Klink, C. Hartmann, A. von Deimling, T. Pietsch, M. Simon, M. Sabel, J.P. Stinbach, O. Heese, G. Reifenberger, M. Weller, and G. Schackert. 2007. "Long-Term Survival with Glioblastoma Multiforme." *Brain* 130.10: 596–606.

Kumar, A., F. Tims, D. Cruess, M.J. Mintzer, G. Ironson, D. Lowenstein, R. Cattan, J.B. Fernandez, C. Einsdorfer, and M. Kumar. 1999. "Music Therapy Increases Serum Melatonin Levels in Patients with Alzheimer's Disease." *Alternative Therapies in Health and Medicine* 5.6: 49–57.

Kumar, S.P. 2012. "Reporting of 'Quality of Life': A Systematic Review and Quantitative Analysis of Research Publications in Palliative Care Journals." *Indian Journal of Palliative Care* 18.1: 59–67.

Lesta, B., and P. Petocz. 2006. "Familiar Group Singing: Addressing Mood and Social Behaviour of Residents with Dementia Displaying Sundowning." *Australian Journal of Music Therapy* 17: 2–17.

Levinson, J. 1997. "Music and Negative Emotion." In *Music and Meaning*, ed. J. Robinson. Ithaca, NY: Cornell University Press.

Logsdon, R.G., L.E. Gibbons, S.M. McCurry, and L. Teri. 2002. "Assessing Quality of Life in Older Adults with Cognitive Impairment." *Psychosomatic Medicine* 64.3: 510–19.

Louhivuori, J., V.M. Salminen, and E. Lebaka. 2005. "'Singing Together': A Cross-Cultural Approach to the Meaning of Choirs as a Community." In *Cultural Diversity in Music Education: Directions and Challenges for the 21st Century*, eds. P.S. Campbell, J. Drummond, P. Dunbar-Hall, K. Howard, H. Schippers, and T. Wiggins, 81–94. Bowen Hills, Queensland: Australian Academic Press.

McDermott, O., N. Crellin, H.M. Ridder, and M. Orrell. 2013. "Music Therapy in Dementia: A Narrative Synthesis Systematic Review." *International Journal of Geriatric Psychiatry* 28: 781–894.

Mercadal-Brotons, M. 2011. "Music Therapy and Dementia: A Cognitive-Behavioral Approach." In *Developments in Music Therapy Practice: Case Study Perspectives*, ed. A. Meadows. New Hampshire: Barcelona Publishers.

Mitchell, D.A., and J.H. Sampson. 2009. "Toward Effective Immunotherapy for the Treatment of Malignant Brain Tumors." *Neurotherapeutics* 16.3: 527–38.

National Hospice and Palliative Care Organization. 2008. "Caring for People with Alzheimer's Disease and Other Dementias: Guidelines for Hospice Providers." Revised May 2008. www.nhpco.org/sites/default/files/public/Dementia-Caring-Guide-final.pdf, accessed 30 December 2014.

National Institute of Neurological Disorders and Stroke. 2014. "Dementia: Hope through Research. Treatments." www.ninds.nih.gov, accessed 22 June 2014.

Norton, K. 2008. "How Music-Inspired Weeping Can Help Terminally Ill Patients." *Journal of Medical Humanities* 32.3: 231–43.

Okada, K., A. Kurita, B. Takase, T. Otsuka, E. Kodani, Y. Kusama, H. Atarashi, and K. Mizuno. 2009. "Effects of Music Therapy on Autonomic Nervous System Activity, Incidence of Heart Failure Events, and Plasma Cytokine and Catecholamine Levels in Elderly Patients with Cerebrovascular Disease and Dementia." *International Heart Journal* 50.1: 95–110.

Raglio, A., O. Oasi, M. Gianotti, V. Manzoni, S. Bolis, M.C. Ubezio, S. Gentile, D. Villani, and M. Stramba-Badiale. 2010. "Effects of Music Therapy on Psychological Symptoms and Heart Rate Variability in Patients with Dementia: A Pilot Study." *Current Aging Science* 3.3: 242–6.

Reisberg, B. 1988. "Functional Assessment Staging (FAST)." *Psychopharmacology Bulletin* 24: 653–9.

Ridder, H.M., and D. Aldridge. 2005. "Individual Music Therapy with Persons with Frontotemporal Dementia: Singing Dialogue." *Nordic Journal of Music Therapy* 14.2: 91–106.

Rio, R. 2009. *Connecting through Music with People with Dementia: A Guide for Caregivers.* London: Jessica Kingsley.

———. 2013. "Music Therapy in Dementia Care." At the 24th Annual Arizona Geriatrics Society Fall Symposium: The New Era of Alzheimer's Disease. *Arizona Geriatrics Society Journal* 18.1: 4–6.

Steinke, W.R., L.L. Cuddy, and L.S. Jakobson. 2001. "Dissociations among Functional Subsystems Governing Melody Recognition after Right-Hemisphere Damage." *Cognitive Neuropsychology* 18.5: 411–37.

Stix, G. 2010. *Scientific American* 302: 50–7.

Suzuki, M., M. Kanamori, M. Watanabe, S. Nagasawa, E. Kojima, H. Ooshiro, and D. Nakahara. 2004. "Behavioral and Endocrinological Evaluation of Music Therapy for Elderly Patients with Dementia." *Nursing and Health Sciences* 6.1: 11–18.

Svansdottir, H., and J. Snaedal. 2006. "Music Therapy in Moderate and Severe Dementia of Alzheimer's Type: A Case–Control Study." *International Psychogeriatrics* 18.4: 613–21.

Thaut, M. 2005. *Rhythm, Music, and the Brain: Scientific Foundations and Clinical Applications* (Studies on New Music Research). New York: Routledge.

Zarit, S.H., K.E. Reever, and J. Back-Peterson. 1980. "Relatives of the Impaired Elderly: Correlates of Feelings of Burden." *Gerontologist* 20: 649–55.

Zorn, J. 1990. Jacket Notes. *The Carl Stalling Project: Music from Warner Bros. Cartoons, 1936–1958*, Vol. 1. Stalling and the Warner Bros. Orchestra.

Zucher, S. (producer). 2005. *Great Conductors of the Third Reich: Art in the Service of Evil*. New York: Bel Canto Society.

6

SINGING AND RELIGION[1]

> The most powerful feeling with a liturgy is the prayer that seeks for nothing special, but is a yearning to escape from the limitations of our own weakness and an invocation of all Good to enter and abide with us.
>
> *George Eliot,* Daniel Deronda, *1876*

The first several chapters of this book provided clinical information to support the claim that singing is good for you. Like the others in Part 2, this chapter focuses on a widespread condition or activity made better by singing or some other form of sustained vocalization. We need look no further than religious practice to find evidence that humans intuitively make singing a part of life. The chapter begins by examining the ways melodious vocal sound has been documented in esoteric religious practices. In that section, indigenous non-Western healing and shamanic work will also be mentioned. The next part illustrates historical and current singing practices in five major faiths—Hinduism, Buddhism (with brief visits to Confucianism and Daoism), Judaism, Christianity, and Islam—with one vocal form for each.[2] Authoritative estimates suggest that, in the year 2000, practitioners of these five faiths accounted for 77 percent of the nearly 6 billion people in the world, and nearly 90 percent of those who practice any religion whatsoever (Hitchcock 2004, 61, 8–9).

A chapter such as this must address several complex ideas. What is faith, and how is it related to religion? A universal definition of faith evades anyone's best efforts; still, describing oneself as Buddhist, a member of a Presbyterian church, or atheist is understandable to most people. Religious faith is distinct from the faith we have in airplanes to convey us safely from place to place. With that sort of faith, we believe an expected result will occur with enough frequency to offset the occasional surprise or disappointment. Further, despite having our faith shattered on occasion, humans have the capacity to believe again. Those whose faith in human or physical nature has been damaged beyond restoration are sometimes even described with pathological terms such as paranoid or depressed.

Religious faith is different from that more common type. Trusting that humans can have encounters with a deity or group of gods, a cosmic intelligence, or a master plan for the universe is the primary tenet of religious faith. The religious believer expects not to be limited to everyday awareness of the physical and emotional world, but to have access to special knowledge associated with her faith. Religious faith comprises symbolic behaviors such as prayer/meditation and singing/chanting to underscore and heighten religious experiences. This kind of faith has many variations. Some believe that religious faith provides assurance of a joyous life after physical death, while others believe that achieving an enlightened state is the most important goal of earthly life. And finally, some people lead faithful lives—devoted to serving the Christian God, for example—but do not embrace an institutional religion. They have faith in divine wisdom or a harmonic universe, but this belief is personal and is enacted alone. In this chapter, being religious implies belonging to a community of believers with similar convictions. Religion refers to a set of beliefs, ceremonies, and rules used to worship and commune with a divinity: a god such as Shiva or group of gods like the Greek pantheon, God, G-d, or other forms of the divine.

What makes a song or recitation religious or spiritual? Stephen Marini answers this question succinctly: "The harnessing of musical expression to mythic content [i.e., religious belief] defines sacred song" (Marini 2003, 4). And while it is perhaps easiest to recognize a religious song by its text, Marini's "mythic content" can also be expressed by non-texted vocal or instrumental music presented in a special context—a church or other holy place, an event such as a funeral, or a healing ceremony. Context, then, is crucial to a conversation about faith and religion. Songs or song-like presentations from the five exoteric religions discussed here can appear in confusing places. In 1830, French composer Hector Berlioz ironically quoted the Dies irae (see Figure 6.1), a part of the Catholic requiem mass, in a symphonic movement entitled "Dream of a Witches' Sabbath."[3] The composer's ironic use of this tune in a pagan context was powerful because its original meaning was well known to most people in the audience. Mass media, on the other hand, have made it possible for religious melodies to be used out of context often enough that original meanings are unknown or disregarded. Today, collegiate bands play the opening of the Dies irae melody to discourage football opponents before a fourth down.[4]

Composer Aaron Copland's version of the American Shaker tune "Simple Gifts" has underscored television advertisements that conflict with the non-materialistic life originally celebrated in the song.[5] Elsewhere, a recording of "indigenous" religious singing is, in fact, a commercial product imagined by a record producer in order to sell CDs or Internet downloads. Understanding spiritual

Di-es i-rae, di-es il-la sol-vet   sae -   clum in fa-vil-la te-ste   Da-vid   cum sy-bil-la.

FIGURE 6.1 Beginning of "Dies irae" chant sequence, *Liber Usualis*, ca. thirteenth century CE.

song therefore often involves negating the ways it has been used out of context in popular culture. In fact, as Philip Bohlman argues, religious music has no meaning at all if local context is removed; only "in situ" (in its original place) can one experience the sounds and the feelings associated with songs of faith (Bohlman 1997).[6]

A final complexity in this chapter has to do with vocabulary, since the terms "singing" and "music" are not embraced by all faith groups. Adhān, the recited Islamic call to prayer, is a form of Qur'anic recitation. Non-Muslims might identify that iconic recitation as a song, but Muslims do not perceive it in that way. For music associated with every belief system discussed here, a potential dichotomy therefore exists between "meaning" and "seeming." Bohlman's crucial perspective, that the meaning is contingent upon contexts and constituents, will guide this chapter. Care has been taken here to retain appropriate terminology, even though readers are asked to adopt the broadest possible perspective on the use of the human voice to produce sustained vocalizations in religious settings. I ask you to think of bhajan, adhān, spirituals, niggunim, and the like as vocal genres related to each other through religion and the inflected voice.

With those caveats in mind, we can turn to this chapter's main purpose, to consider the ways faith, health, and singing intersect in faith communities. I begin with a discussion of esoteric religions—"mystical, symbolic, hidden, or initiatory ways of connecting with God or the cosmos." Jeff Levin's survey provides the framework from which several traditions of esoteric spiritual healing will be examined (Levin 2008). Next, historical and current vocalizing practices in five major exoteric faiths, representing the "public face" of religion, will be represented. From a perspective that seeks to honor all people and beliefs, this chapter examines selected ways people use sustained, melodious speech in religious activity, and some of the roles these vocalizations play.

Singing in Esoteric Traditions

"Esoteric spiritual paths . . . typically have associated with them particular beliefs and practices related to health, healing, and medicine," writes Jeff Levin (2008, 102). Understanding the difference between esoteric and exoteric religions is aided by Levin's list of beliefs that are present in some form among esoteric believers. Regarding *anatomy and physiology*, esoterics believe in subtle forces within the body not normally acknowledged in clinical medicine—such as qi or yogic chakras—through which healing life force flows.[7] Regarding *classification of illness and causality*, esoteric believers acknowledge that thought forms (e.g., past life, karma, or chakra imbalances) cause illness. Esoteric religions also share *attribution of illness* to three key concepts: congestion (e.g., of the colon or respiratory system), imbalance (e.g., of bodily fluids or humors), and harmful relationship to cosmic forces (e.g., being born when the planets are disadvantageously aligned) (Levin 2008, 108). Finally, esoteric *therapeutic modalities* share reliance on subtle, energy-based forms: the highly focused attention of a shaman, treatment with unusual gadgets or substances, and shifts in consciousness, spiritual states, or ways of life.

Esoteric healing practices are evident in most accounts of ancient civilizations, they have remained important throughout human history, and they are still viable among members of non-industrialized cultures today. Some are masked in secrecy; others are open to outside observers. Many emphasize singing, chanting, and reciting. First in the present discussion are the mystery schools, which comprised secret cults that flourished in Ancient Greece in the final centuries before the Common Era. Devoted to mythical Olympian healers such as Chiron, Achilles, and Asclepius, these cults offered transcendent experiences that probably evolved from tribal ceremonies. Asclepius, the Greek god of medicine and healing, is mentioned in Homer's *Iliad* around the eighth century BCE. This documentation suggests that Asclepius was a renowned healer and a historical figure before he was considered a god. After his elevation to god status, temples bearing his name were built throughout the Mediterranean region. Pilgrims journeyed to these shrines for healing through late antiquity. Even Hippocrates (460–ca. 370 BCE), a historical figure central to the change from mystical to rational medicine (ca. fifth century BCE), was initiated at the Asclepian Temple whose ruins are pictured in Figure 6.2.

Alex Hardie writes that the various mystery cults involved appeals to the senses of smell, hearing, and vision. "A large body of evidence in literary and epigraphical sources, vase paintings and mosaics testifies to the presence of the full range of instruments (stringed, wind, and percussive) in mystery music." Hymns ascribed to Orpheus, Pamphos the mythical poet, and Musaeus, the legendary polymath, are also known to have figured prominently in mystery rituals (Hardie 2004, 16–17).

The mystery school most closely associated with singing honored the consummate Greek musician-healer Orpheus, son of the muse Calliope and the Thracian king Oeagrus. Tradition holds that Orpheus lived prior to the Trojan War, in the twelfth or eleventh century BCE. Orpheus famously defied death by descending to Hades to rescue Eurydice, his wife, who died on their wedding day. The very

FIGURE 6.2 Panorama, historical ruins of the Asclepieion, Kos Island, Greece. MNStudio/ Shutterstock.

FIGURE 6.3 Orpheus (left) with his lyre. Bell-krater (bowl for mixing wine and water),
ca. 440 BCE. Classical Greek, Attic. Image copyright © The Metropolitan
Museum of Art. Image source: Art Resource, NY.

embodiment of music's affective power, Orpheus wielded the beauty of his voice
to accomplish this task. When he sang, it is written, ghosts wept and Sisyphus took
a hiatus from his perpetual labors; consequently, the rulers of the underworld found
his prayers impossible to resist.[8] Ted Gioia argues that Orpheus reformed musical
healing by trading the shaman's primary healing instrument, the drum, for the less
"primitive" lyre (Gioia 2006, 75).[9] With Orpheus, argues Gioia, a new era in music
healing was initiated (see Figure 6.3).

Orphism, a mystery school, was practiced by about the fifth century BCE.
Cornerstones of this cult included "clear perception and knowledge ... along
with the instrument of Apollo, the lyre." Edward Lippman continues: "Orphism
remained mystical; its aim was to purify the soul; its prophet [Orpheus], although
often considered to be the son of Apollo, was a Thracian musical magician"
(Lippman 1964, 47). Orphism's goal of purifying the soul was accomplished by

abandoning its Dionysian heritage of orgiastic dance, associated with the evocative aulos (an ancient wind instrument). The lyre was preferred by Orphics; "words can be combined with the lyre but not with the aulos" (Lippman 1964, 49). In other words, the aulos appealed to the body, while the lyre engaged the mind.

In ancient Greece, "mousikē" referred to the business of the Muses, rather than a sounding entity. The physical world, they believed, was ordered by inaudible "music" sometimes described as harmony. The mysterious cosmic ratios preventing the planets from colliding were mirrored in musical proportions—2:1 produces the octave and 3:2 renders the fifth. Orpheus thus inspired this mystery school in its efforts to make sense of the arresting power of accompanied song.

Through their teachings, these mystery school philosophies influenced later Greek writers, as well as exoteric religions. Greek philosophy,

> represented primarily by Plato's and Aristotle's writings on ethics, informed the attitudes toward music of a number of important Muslim and Jewish philosophers, such as al-Kindī [ca. 801–873 CE], the Ikhwān al-Ṣafā, Salomon Ibn Gabirol (1021–1069), Judah ha-Levi (c. 1066–1145), and Maimonides (1135–1204); interestingly, Gabirol and ha-Levi were also singers. These writers probed the uses of music in a balanced and ethical life.[10]

Orpheus, who sang of great mysteries and accompanied himself on a lyre whose strings corresponded to the harmony of the moving stars, inspired a religion that relied equally on voice and lyre.

Another category of esoteric religion comprises the multi-branched Gnostics, a group influenced by the monotheistic Zoroastrian religion and philosophy of ancient Persia (see Figure 6.4). Gnosticism is a vague term that refers to early Christian groups, as well as larger groups that were unrelated to Christianity. Hitchcock writes:

> The Sassanian Empire [224–651 CE] encompassed Persia from the Euphrates River east and stretched to the Caucasus in the north, the Hindu Kush in the east, and north almost as far as Tashkent in today's Uzbekistan. The Sassanians practiced Zoroastrianism, since the 3rd century the official religion of Persia.
>
> *Hitchcock (2004, 335)*

Hymn singing at marriage and other ceremonies is bound with Gnostic traditions that flourished in the first centuries of the Common Era (Moda 2013). The Essenes were a Jewish community living in the desert near the Dead Sea. This Gnostic group appears to have recorded what are now called the Dead Sea Scrolls around the fourth century BCE. Eric Werner examined the Scrolls soon after their discovery between 1947 and 1956 and noted four musical references. Werner described a set of marginal notations that likely helped govern the recitation of scriptural lessons: two references to musical instruments, and what appears to be a note about alternate singing between male and female choirs (Werner 1957). This latter singing reference was also documented by Philo of Alexandria (20 BCE–40 CE) when he described the Gnostic Therapeutae, a healing and singing order of Jewish monastics: "Then, when each chorus of the men and each chorus of the women has feasted separately by itself, like persons in the bacchanalian revels, drinking the pure wine of the love of God, they join together, and the two become one chorus" (Philo 2013). These Gnostic groups clearly sang in worship and addressed performance practice in writing.

Another esoteric religion comprises the Brotherhoods tradition, which originated early in the Common Era, though it did not flourish until medieval times. Bernard of Clairvaux (1090–1153), a French reformist theologian and monk, founded one such brotherhood, the Knights Templar. These monks were the warriors of the Crusades, bent on protecting Christian pilgrims and their sacred places in the Holy Land from an increasing Muslim influence (Grevatt 2013). Bernard was keenly interested not only in sung worship, but also in its style.

> The chant . . . should be quite solemn, nothing sensuous or rustic. Its sweetness should not be frivolous. It should please the ear only that it might move the heart, taking away sorrow and mitigating wrath. It should not detract from the sense of the words but rather make it more fruitful.[11]

Brotherhoods also emphasized perfection and balance, to which end their interest in alchemy is attached. Rather than changing base metals into gold as commonly thought, however, these adherents of secret wisdom hoped to achieve enlightenment and immortality by purifying their bodies with herbal elixirs. The philosophies of the itinerant Swiss healer and Brotherhoods adherent known as Paracelsus (Theophrastus Phillippus Aureolus Bombastus von Hohenheim, 1493–1541) combined practical and folk medicine, alchemy, and the teachings of several bishops.

Modern Freemasonry, revived in 1717, owes its origins to the Knights Templar and other Brotherhoods. Musical specifics of the Masonic ritual are shrouded in the secrecy that characterizes this guild. About the group that famously attracted Mozart (1756–91), Stanley Sadie wrote that hymns and songs for unison singing typified early meetings, and that operatic melodies were often re-texted for those purposes.[12] Religion and singing clearly retained their centrality in Freemasonry and healing may also have been important in this outgrowth of the Brotherhoods tradition.[13]

In India, esoteric Eastern mystical traditions combined writings from sacred sources and ancient Greece and engaged in speculative and practical healing applications in the first centuries of the Common Era. Documentation of these principles may be seen in writings of the Indian sages collectively known as Patanjali, who codified known yoga practices sometime between the second century BCE and the third century CE in a book of aphorisms known as *The Yoga-Sûtra* (Carman 2004). Supernormal powers linked with advanced meditative practice are described in that work. Yoga and music are intimately connected through the essential Eastern mystical concepts of the Divine. A later work of Sanskrit verse, *Saṅgīta-ratnākara*, by early-thirteenth-century scholar Śārṅgadeva, describes this link:

> The *Saṅgīta-ratnākara* is one classic source among many speaking of God as the embodiment of music and of music as an integration of science, art, and yoga that offers both Hindu musicians and listeners a way to spiritual liberation. The treatise describes the *rasika* as the enjoyer of aesthetic bliss; with devotion (*bhakti*) and spiritual wisdom (*jñāna*), this knower of music resonates deeply with the divine vibrations that are the basis of the universe. For centuries, Hindu musicians have envisioned Shiva and other forms of God as the musical shimmering of cosmic consciousness, a mysterious harmony, deep and pervasive.[14]

Other Eastern mystical traditions, including Āyurvedic medicine and various healing forms associated with Buddhism, have also survived and flourished in some modern communities.

A final category of esoteric religion is both ancient and contemporary. The healing activities of specialized individuals in indigenous religions are sometimes called by the generic term shamanism, although literal shamanism originated in Siberia, Manchuria, and Central Asia. Regardless of the nomenclature, efforts at healing probably accompanied humans' earliest group-living experiences; healing ceremonies can include musical components such as singing, chanting, and drumming. Mystical healing occurs in these systems in response to the trance states achieved by the shaman. David Roche wrote that in South Asia:

> Trance remains an enduring sign of successful connection to a macrocosmic reality . . . Music accompanies ceremonies or performances in which bodily expressions, such as convulsions and anesthesia, signal dramatic shifts of consciousness. Such musical contexts represent culturally condoned enactments of spiritual metamorphosis.[15]

Lippman connects Roche's report of convulsions with medical and ritual rites in ancient Greece.

> Thus music is both a cure and a cause of the agitation . . . These rites are evidently quite like the epileptic fits of the shaman, the dancing epidemics of the Middle Ages, the seventeenth-century outbreaks of tarantism, or the uncontrollable jerking of American revivalist meetings; probably in every case, religion is an essential factor.
>
> *Lippman (1964, 46–7)*[16]

In indigenous religious or shamanistic practice, ritual acts can include prayer and chanting, herbalism, drumming, laying on of hands, psychological counseling, and facilitation of inner work such as periods of silence.[17]

A 1992 documentary film directed by Maurice Dorés entitled *Seven Nights and Seven Days* provides a narrated account of a ndepp (healing) ceremony in Rufisque, Senegal. In the film, a ndeppkat (traditional healer) cures a new mother who is disinterested in caring for her child. The healing power of the ndepp is attributed both to the shaman's activities and to community participation in the healing rituals. The week-long process centers upon the female shaman and includes spitting of sour milk, animal sacrifice, singing, and chanting. After the ritual concludes, the new mother accepts her role and begins to nurture her baby. Ethnomusicologists and anthropologists, too numerous to name here, have contributed a wealth of published reports about indigenous healers such as these (Turner 2000, Wissler 2007, and Wissler 2009). Importantly, modern writings carefully situate all observations in culture and place as they address contexts of shamanic activity.

Pat Moffitt Cook documents extensive fieldwork experiences with shamans and other healers in *Music Healers of Indigenous Cultures* and its accompanying CD recording (Cook 2004).[18] Her report of a Huichol peyote shaman offers specifics about a culture of around 16,000 persons who have preserved their faith practices for centuries, despite Aztec and Spanish conquests and efforts to Christianize them (Cook 2004, 53). Huichols live in the Mexican states of Jalisco and Nayarit, in the Sierra Madres. Religion pervades every aspect of Huichol life and shamans—called mara'akame—are seen as "living gods." Ritually ingesting buttons from the peyote cactus attunes the healer with "the heart of God." Among the Huichols, whose name derives from a word meaning doctors or healers, men and women alike are shamans. The entire culture is devoted to achieving communion with the divine. Exposure to hallucinogenic peyote begins in infancy, since nursing mothers are expected to ingest peyote if they or their husbands are active in the community. Songs are frequently acquired while the healer is in a trance state; the symbiotic relationship with peyote or other substances that release or enhance the power of the song, and vice versa, is a crucial element of healing. Cook summarizes that "Chants and songs pray to the deity and request healing," and a mara'akame elaborates, "The creator gave me the gift to treat the chest and stomach" (Cook 2004, 55).[19] One marker of the healer's special relationship with their creator is their receipt of song.

To summarize this discussion of esoteric religions, the healing power of singing is embodied as the all-powerful gift of the Greek god Orpheus, whose legendary healing status was perpetuated in various mystery school traditions. Ancient Greek writers such as Plato and Aristotle, informed by Orphic and Pythagorean mystery schools, in turn influenced Judaism and Islam. Gnosticism, another esoteric religion sometimes entwined with Judaism and Christianity, originated in ancient Persia (present-day Iran). Gnostic singing concerns were documented in the Dead Sea Scrolls in the fourth century BCE and in writings of Philo of

Alexandria around the turn of the millennium. The inherently musical nature of modern Freemasonry may be traced back to medieval Brotherhoods traditions such as those of Bernard of Clairvaux and Paracelsus. Eastern mysticism, familiar to modern yoga practitioners, considers one deity to be the embodiment of music, and chanting to be one path to spiritual liberation and good health. And in shamanism, representing perhaps the most ancient of musical healing traditions, chanting is an avenue by which practitioners achieve trance states. Receiving songs and performing them in rituals grant shamans access to healing powers. It is now time to turn attention to the more institutionalized practices of faith.

Vocal Melody in the Most Populous Religions

In contrast with esoteric religions, this section addresses standardized systems of expressing belief in an innate connection between humans and a supreme God or a pantheon. As opposed to those mysterious and/or secret societies discussed previously, exoteric religions are understandable by most people and do not require leaders or adherents to have special powers. Healing in exoteric religions is often discussed metaphorically, rather than practically as in esoteric faiths. Singing or the melodious use of the voice is no less central in exoteric religions. As in the previous paragraphs, this section is full of potential missteps of interpretation and representation. Fully aware that these topics deserve deeper attention than these brief summaries provide, I offer evidence that the world's most populous religions rely heavily on the power of singing or reciting in their practices.

Hinduism, Buddhism, Confucianism and Daoism (the latter two representing Chinese indigenous religions), Judaism, Christianity, and Islam will be addressed, with remarks on origins, descriptions, and primary texts; comments about proliferation and syncretization; and discussion of a few of the roles attributed to singing, chanting, or tonal recitation. Each section closes with a vocal form characteristic of that religion. Because capturing the essence of any faith system in a few words is a forlorn hope, indeed, incompleteness may be expected. Again, the author's perspective is one of respect for all belief systems. Finally, these faiths will be examined in an order whose chronology is open to question.

Hinduism

The word Hindu ("Sindhu") originally referred to the Indus River, the land around it, and its people: Harappans, a well-documented urban culture flourishing between 2800 and 1500 BCE (see Figure 6.4). And though the Indus River is the ancient birthplace of the religion, the Ganges is the greatest of all rivers to Hindu people. Water is revered in Hinduism for its literal and metaphorical powers to create, sustain, cleanse, and heal. Hinduism embraces great diversity and reveres many gods, but maintains an uncomplicated view about the supreme God, Brahma. Synonymous with divinity, Brahma is everywhere and permeates all existence and all things. For Hindu faithful: "The soul itself cycles through several lives, and the spark of divinity shows itself in many different beings, from the lowliest insect to a great spiritual leader" (Hitchcock 2004, 74).

Aryans, light-skinned migrants speaking an Indo-European language, arrived in the Indian subcontinent from the northwest around 1800 BCE and either mingled with the Harappan culture or replaced it.[20] Aryans brought with them the four Vedas—Rigveda (Rgveda), Yajurveda, Sāmaveda, and Atharvaveda—Hinduism's canonical religious and cultural texts.[21] Hindus believe that the Vedas have existed forever. The oldest is the Rigveda, comprising 1,028 metrical hymns encompassing 10,462 verses in praise of the early Hindu gods. Compilation of the Rigveda dates from ca. 1500 BCE in present-day Pakistan, around the same time that the Vedic system of religion took hold in India. Ancient traditions and the divine pantheon of Hinduism are spelled out in these texts.

Today's world comprises approximately 850 million adherents of the Hindu faith, the majority of whom account for 65 percent of the South Asian population. India and Bali are currently the only nations with dominant Hindu populations, but Nepal, Bangladesh, Indonesia, Sri Lanka, Pakistan, Malaysia, the United States, South Africa, and Myanmar are also homes to sizable numbers of Hindu faithful.[22] Dispersion of Hinduism owes much to beggar poet-singers (mendicants) who traveled around South India between the sixth and ninth centuries CE, and the northern areas between the thirteenth and seventeenth centuries. Along trade routes, the empires of Srivijaya (600s–800s) and Majapahit (1200s–1500s) brought Hinduism and Buddhism to island Southeast Asia.

Devotion to or union with God (bhakti) is a central tenet of Hinduism, though these faithful are not bound together by strict doctrine. In fact, the belief system has been characterized as versatile, flexible, and absorbent (Hitchcock 2004, 74). Characteristically, Hindus accept and celebrate the tremendous diversity of the world's belief systems; "let noble thoughts come to us from all sides," invokes the Rigveda 1-89-I (Griffith 1896). The Indian caste system, which stratifies society and specifies each caste's distinctive obligations to society as a whole, draws on Hindu Vedic thought. Faithful performance of rituals and obligations ensures higher status in the next life; reincarnation is thus the only deliverance from an onerous caste to a higher one.

Manifold divine entities each personalize one aspect of Divinity, Brahma, or God, and "the performance of music (sangīt) has nearly always been associated with divine experience in India, beginning with chants uttered by the seers and sages of Vedic times."[23] Alison Arnold characterizes the role of Hinduism in South India as follows:

> Religious feelings have run deep and steady in South India from time immemorial to the present day . . . Hindu religious traditions, including rituals, customs, sacred images, and stories, pervade everyday life and all the arts. On every street and lane, Hindus sing in worship of the goddess in her

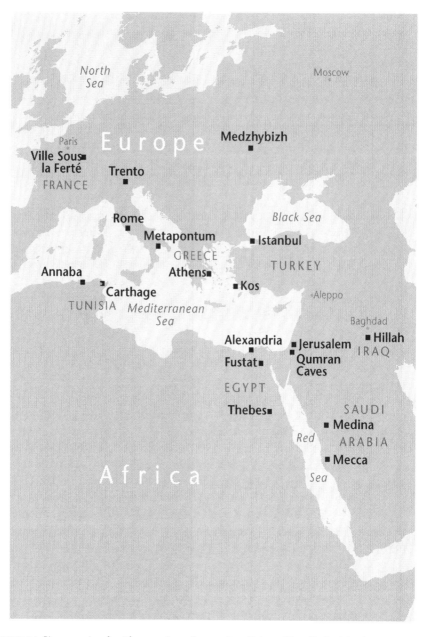

FIGURE 6.4 Sites associated with esoteric and exoteric religions: **Kos** (Asclepieion), **Metapontum** (Pythagoras' adulthood), **Athens** (Plato), **Persia** (Zoroastrianism), **Qumran Caves** (Dead Sea Scrolls), **Alexandria** (Philo), **Ville Sous la Ferté** (monastery, Bernard of Clairvaux), **Harappa** and **Mohenjo-daro** (ancient Hindu settlements, Indus River Valley), **Bodh Gaya** (site of the Buddha's enlightenment), **Tibet** (Buddhism), **Jerusalem**

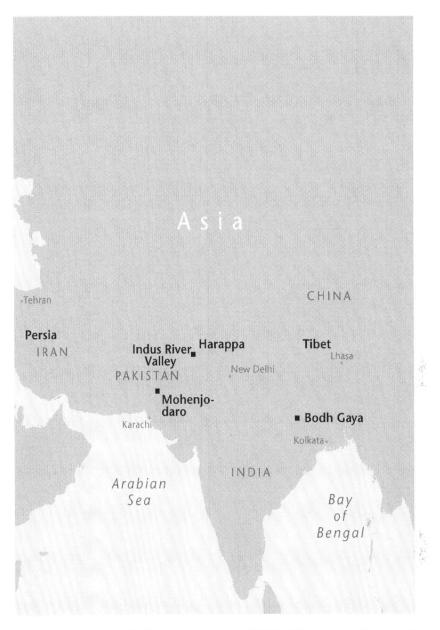

(sacred to Jewish, Christian, and Muslim faithful), **Hillah** (ancient Babylon), **Rome** (Roman Catholicism), **Thebes** (possible site of Hebrew captivity in Egypt), **Fustat** (Maimonides' adulthood), **Medzhybizh** (site of Hasidism), **Istanbul** (Constantinople, Eastern Catholicism), **Annaba** (Hippo) and **Carthage** (St. Augustine's adulthood), **Trento** (Council of Trent), **Mecca** and **Medina** (sacred Muslim sites). Dreamline Cartography, 2014.

many forms and in praise of the deities Shiva and Murugan, and offer flowers to incarnations of Vishnu such as Rama and Krishna. About three-quarters of India's people are Hindu, though *Hindu* is an umbrella term that covers a rich variety of identities.[24]

Bhakti doctrine underscores both hearing praises to God and the singing of God's holy names. Bhajan is a generic term for popular Hindu religious songs, of which there are thousands, in many languages.[25] Ritual environments, per se, are not required for this vocal activity; bhajans may be performed inside or outside, in the temple or the home. Neither is performance of bhajans limited to high castes. The only requirement is to perform Nama Sangeerthana, a musical recitation of a god's names; naturally, the words outweigh the music in importance. The prosody of bhajan texts either conforms to or is influenced by traditional Sanskrit forms.[26]

Guy Beck writes that Hinduism may have been practiced by seers and sages—shamans—as early as 4000 BCE.[27] Sacred texts such as the Vedas "are said to have been heard by sages in trance and to embody the eternal primeval sound that brought about the creation of the cosmos."[28] If the singer or musician is dedicated to bhakti, union with God, then the musical product creates that connection for listeners and the musician alike. So singing a bhajan with proper intention, or focus, insures a blessing for the devotee's musical activity.

No musical or melodic formula dictates the bhajan; musicians and religious leaders are free to create new additions to the repertoire. Still, Brahmins (priests—members of the highest caste), take great care to preserve the Vedic texts perfectly, since errors in recitation are said to bring catastrophe. Brahmin singing, when executed properly, praises, instructs, and preserves. These accomplishments underscore Hindu identity and cohesiveness. Beck also stresses the sense of communal harmony derived from sacred singing. "Most religious music is a group endeavor," he writes, "with a choir seated close to a lead singer." Proximity while singing has been shown to enhance group cohesion.[29]

Hinduism, to summarize this brief exploration, is not founded by any particular prophet, embraces totality of life and divinity, recognizes and honors the wisdom of other faiths, requires holy intention when adherents seek bhakti or union with God, and encourages all believers to sing, preserve, and perform bhajans.[30]

Buddhism

The historical figure known as the Buddha ("enlightened one," Siddhartha Gautama) was born to a Hindu family in present-day Nepal sometime between the mid-sixth and mid-fourth centuries BCE, during a period of religious experimentation and questioning of Vedic Hinduism. K.N. Upadhaya offers one narrative of the relationship between Hinduism and early Buddhism:

[Buddha] heralded a powerful movement repudiating the Brahmanical religion of rituals, ceremonies, and caste distinctions. As against the traditional
faith in God, soul, and active indulgence in worldly life, he preached the
philosophy of atheism, anattaa (soullessness), and world-renunciation. It
seems that these ideas, when forcefully championed by a powerful personality like the Buddha, posed such a serious challenge to traditional Indian
[Hindu] thought that the need was at once felt to put [the latter's] house
in order and meet the challenge by readjusting and remodeling its views in
the light of the new developments. Such an attempt seems to be made in
the *Bhaqauadqiitaa* [ca. 5th–2nd centuries BCE, a 700-verse scripture that is
part of the Hindu epic *Mahabharata*] which tries to shake off some crude
elements of the traditional orthodoxy like animal sacrifice and external
ceremonialism, reduces the rigor of caste, opens the gate of holy life to all
without distinction, recognizes the equality of all professions, and com-
promises with the changing order of things while sharply reacting at the
same time against renunciation or abandonment of worldly duties, atheism,
and anattaa.

Upadhaya (1968)[31]

In these ways, Hinduism and Buddhism are historically and theologically linked.

The Buddha himself allowed women to follow his teachings, but males more
often have adopted the monastic life in Buddhism. Buddhists have lived in monasteries since ca. 550 BCE, and by 232 BCE such institutions were established
throughout the Indian subcontinent. Adherents heard the Buddha's teachings
orally until the last decades before the Common Era, when they were preserved
in the Pāli Canon. A vernacular language in contrast to the elite Sanskrit of the
Vedas, Pāli is the liturgical language of Theravada, the oldest surviving branch of
Buddhism. Buddhism was the largest religion in South Asia until ca. 500 CE, after
which time a revived Hinduism regained its majority. Tenth-century invasions
from the north, which brought Islam to the region, further diluted Buddhism's
presence in northern India.

Buddhist missionaries reached China, mainly from the northwest, sometime
during the first century of the Common Era. There, Buddhism flourished into the
thirteenth century, when a new resurgence of Confucianism predominated. In the
late fourth century, contacts with China brought Buddhist teachings to the Korean
peninsula and, from there, to Japan. In the latter country, Buddhism adapted to
popular beliefs such as Shintoism. "Around the 7th century, Buddhist-influenced
cultures extended from Java to Nepal and from Afghanistan to Japan."[32] Francesca
Tarocco offers a brief explanation of this diaspora:

For centuries, India was at the centre of the development and diffusion
of Buddhist doctrine and religious practice. However, by the 13th century, Buddhist institutions had almost disappeared in India and Central

Asia, only to be partially revived during the 20th century. After the decline of Buddhism in India, Southeast Asian societies looked to Sri Lanka for doctrinal inspiration and guidance. As its notions of rulership appealed to the monarchs of Cambodia, Thailand, Burma (now Myanmar) and Laos, Buddhism was adopted as the official ideology. Until very recent times, in China as well as in Japan, Buddhism was alternatively embraced or rejected, and underwent periods of fortune as well as fierce persecution.[33]

The Buddha's original preference for vernacular languages both personalized and facilitated the spread of his teachings. In 2000, approximately 1.1 billion Buddhists lived in Asia alone. The ten countries with the largest Buddhist populations, again based on data from the year 2000, were China, Japan, Thailand, Vietnam, Myanmar, Sri Lanka, Cambodia, India, South Korea, and Taiwan (Hitchcock 2004, 8–9).

Buddhists believe that the five senses bring wisdom, but also desire and delusion. Early monks heard the dhamma (dharma in Sanskrit; "unvarnished truth") from the Buddha himself. They committed them to memory, taking care to retain prosody and poetic qualities such as alliteration and assonance (Allon 1997). A text of the Pāli Canon, the *Cullavagga*, reports that, after the death of the Buddha, a senior monk invited others to "sing together the *Dhamma* and the *Vinaya* (monastic discipline)."[34] Early Buddhists considered art and music to be inappropriately sensual, but the community gradually allowed instrumental or other sonorous punctuations of the monastic routine.[35] Chanting—in the form of prayer, hymn, or mantra—is central in the liturgy; it conveys both praise and prayer and brings out individual awareness of the Buddha.[36]

Chanting can have a double edge, however. The seventh of the Buddha's ten precepts, which warns against the potential distractions of music, dictates that even metrical regularity should be interrupted so that chant does not sound too much like "music." As Wei Li points out, however, the practice of chanting links Buddhists to the spiritual world, contributes solemnity to rituals, and inspires faith. The benefits of Buddhist chanting can extend beyond comprehension of the sutras (aphorisms that tie concepts together). Chanting can promote clear utterance and a mighty thoracic cavity.[37]

Throughout their intensive, graded study, novices receive focused training in chanting, which imparts health and spiritual benefits. Even if initiates cannot comprehend the teachings, sonic repetition inspires mindfulness and supports memorization and understanding over time. About Theravada Buddhism, Paul Greene writes: "Musical features of *paritta* chant give an aural shape to recited passages that affects the way the words are heard, experienced, and contemplated." Further, these particular chants codify the Buddha's teachings in sonic praxis. Still, most Buddhists do not consider paritta to be music (Greene 2004, n7). Qualities that outsiders might describe as musical—a shapely tune, regular meter, vocal style, modal or harmonic orientation, and instrumental punctuations—have nonetheless become important in today's Buddhism (Greene 2004, 47). Its spread outside the

Indian subcontinent provides the opportunity to shift focus to another ancient locus of the religion, China.

Indigenous Chinese Religions and Buddhism

Tsao Penyeh writes that Daoism drew its sources from Chinese soil and established itself as an indigenous tradition. Of the two traditions discussed here, Daoism is the more challenging to summarize.[38] It coalesced during roughly the same time as Confucianism, between the sixth and second centuries BCE. The Daoist holy book, *Daodejing*, was written between 300 and 240 BCE by the legendary— perhaps mythological—Lao Zi (Lao-tzu, ca. 604–521 BCE), who was thought to be an older contemporary of Confucius. *Zhuangzi* is another important set of writings by Master Zhuang (369–286 BCE). Daoism was inspired by the ancient nature religions of China. It contributed folk animism, the theory of yin and yang, the wuxing (five elements or phases), and the philosophical concept of wuwei (non-interference), developed by Laozi and Zhuang. "Dao" refers to both the elusive, united force of the universe and also a way or path to be followed.

Confucius (K'ng Fu-tzu), born in 551 BCE, was more a philosopher than a religious leader. His principal teachings established a worldview and an idealized social order that developed into a state religion during several periods of China's subsequent history. Faithfulness, sincerity, honesty, and thoughtfulness characterize this philosophical system. Confucian teachings are contained in his *Book of Analects (Lun Yun)* and elsewhere. While Daoism inspired adherents to become passive vessels of the universal Dao, Confucianism provided rules governing external behavior. Both systems were well established when Buddhism entered the land in the first century CE.

Wei Li explains that Chinese Buddhist fanbei (liturgical chanting) can be divided into two major types. Song (reciting) is like the recitative portions of Western opera; it employs one syllable for each musical tone. Zan (singing), on the other hand, is more hymn- or songlike. Depending upon the available singers, fanbei can be a single tune or can involve improvisation on that tune. Fanbei occurs both within and outside monastic settings.

Rural far eastern Buddhist communities also expect chant, often influenced by regional folk music traditions, to be performed at daochang (memorial ceremonies). In these settings, writes Wei, Buddhism blends with folk religion. Because they were also sung at secular festivals, Buddhist tunes absorbed elements of theatrical and instrumental music over time. These rural religious people believe in the healing power of chant. A Burmese monk living in the US reported that "rural folk [in Myanmar] are superstitious. If they have an epidemic they think evil spirits are terrorizing them. They ask monks to chant all these suttas" (Quoted in Greene 2004, 51).

Though Buddhism faded in India during the Middle Ages, it thrived in Tibet. Practice of Buddhism flourished in the "hundreds, eventually thousands, of monasteries [that] came to be built in the remote reaches" after Samye monastery, the first in Tibet, was completed in 779 CE (Hitchcock 2004, 184–5). As religions do the world over, Tibetan Buddhism has evolved to reflect the contexts of its people. A result of rigorous training, chanting among Tibetan monks is much lower in pitch than the average Westerner is accustomed to hearing. Recordings of Tibetan Buddhist chanting are abundantly available today and groups of monks have toured Western countries, so the perpetuation of chanting the dharma of the Buddha has persisted and also absorbed a twenty-first-century flavor. Intoning or chanting lends power to the spoken word and that mystical force has been adapted to its diverse locations, while the parameters of original Buddhist teaching have remained influential.

To summarize, Buddhism teaches people a path to end suffering by the elimination of its causes: greed, hatred, and delusion. Some people consider Siddhartha Gautama to be the fourth Buddha. He achieved enlightenment in Bodh Gaya in the fifth century BCE. His teachings were at first preserved by collective musical vocalizations that eventually absorbed the vernacular languages of new locations. This respect for vernacular languages has made Buddhism readily transferable outside its country of origin. Buddhist liturgy is primarily vocal and is sometimes accompanied by percussion and melodic instruments. Liturgical chant is heard both within and outside liturgical settings, and great care has been taken not only in the textual preservation of the Pāli Canon but also in its musical delivery, which affects reception and understanding of the Canon.

Judaism

For Jews (Hebrew: Yĕhūdhī), history begins with God's creation of the world, as related in the first book of the Torah: Bereishit, the biblical Genesis.

1. In the beginning [was] God's creation of the heavens and the earth.
2. Now, the earth was astonishingly empty, and darkness was on the face of the deep, and the spirit of God was hovering over the face of the water.
3. And God said, "Let there be light" and there was light.
4. And God saw the light that it was good, and God separated between the light and between the darkness.
5. And God called the light day and the darkness He called night, and it was evening and it was morning, one day.

Complete Jewish Bible (2014)

Judaism differs from the other religions highlighted in this chapter because it has a national base. Ancient Palestine/Israel, the birthplace of Judaism, is generally defined as "the territory now covered by modern Israel, Jordan, Lebanon and the southern part of coastal Syria."[39] This religion is also intended for a particular set of people; Jews do not seek to convert the world to Judaism. Contrary to that of

Hinduism and Buddhism, the Jewish diaspora was initiated by forced uprooting of a people and their capture into slavery in the eastern Mediterranean region.

Sometime in the second millennium BCE, the patriarch Abram (Abraham) followed God's command to relocate from Ur in the ancient Mesopotamian city-state of Samaria to Hebron in the land of Canaan—present-day Israel/Palestine. Abram worshipped only one God. His grandson, Jacob, renamed "Israel" after wrestling with an angel, had many sons, each of whom fathered one of the twelve tribes of Israel. As related in the book of Shemot (Exodus), Jacob's progeny were so numerous and successful that an unnamed Egyptian pharaoh punished them first with heavy taxation and, later, enslavement. These watershed events foreshadowed much Jewish experience. The Exodus from Egypt, led by Moses, is consequently a central narrative of Judaism. Its recounting provides the theological basis for belief in a G-d who delivers people from bondage into liberation. In their worst periods of oppression and genocide, Jews have found inspiration in this important narrative.

Israelite history of Jerusalem begins around 1000 BCE, although archaeological findings suggest that the earliest settlement there dates between 4500 and 3500 BCE. Around 587 BCE, armies of Nebuchadnezzar, the Babylonian king, burned down the First Temple in Jerusalem and all remaining Judeans were exiled in Babylon.[40] The Torah, comprising the first five books of Moses with commentary, was compiled during Babylonian captivity in the sixth century BCE. By 68 CE, Judea was a protectorate of Rome; destruction of the Second Temple by Roman Emperor Titus in 70 CE accompanied the capture of Jerusalem and Judea.

Mizrahi Jewish people remained in Babylon after the destruction of the First Temple. In the Common Era, Ashkenazi Jews arose in Italy and began settling the Rhineland by the ninth century. By the eleventh century, they had established cultural hegemony there and spread to Eastern Europe. Another branch of differentiated Jewish musical practice is represented by the Sephardi culture, which flourished under Muslim and then Christian control in medieval Spain, and, later, North Africa (Idelson 1931–2). Millions of Jews migrated to the Americas in the twentieth century as a result of Nazi persecution. In 2000, the world's Jewish population was estimated at upwards of 13 million. Countries with the greatest numbers of Jewish people included the United States, Israel, Russia, France, Argentina, Canada, Brazil, Britain, Palestine, and Ukraine.

The earliest documentation of religious music among Jewish ancestors is archaeological and iconographic (dating from the 12th through 8th millennia BCE) and scriptural. Discerning between actual musical instruments and symbolic ones in biblical and other writings has received prolonged attention from historians and archaeologists. The term "psalmos," referencing the striking or plucking of the strings of a musical instrument, was first applied to ancient Hebrew verse by translators of the Old Testament into Greek. Nevertheless, the actual sound of Old Testament music is anyone's guess.[41] According to Eliyahu Schleifer, liturgy did not include music at all during the patriarchal period (ca. 1800–ca 1500 BCE), but songs and instrumental music are mentioned in scripture as early as Genesis 31:27 (Schleifer 1997).

Secular music, often associated with upper-class excess, is mentioned "with reproach" in the Bible. Sacred music is first documented in conjunction with the period of the First Temple (2 Samuel 6, 1 Chronicles 6:16–17) (Schleifer 1997, 16). From the rabbinic period (300–600 CE onward), orthodox Jewish liturgical singing has featured males only. This practice was established by several talmudic scriptures which equated woman's voice (kol isha) with sexual enticement. Observant Jewish men are thus prohibited from hearing women sing in public worship. Nevertheless, the presence of female singing is documented early in scriptural accounts, notably in the victory song of Miriam, Moses' sister, at the defeat of the Egyptian army at the Red Sea (Exodus 15:20–21). Women likewise play important roles in Hasidic musical tradition, to be discussed below.

Traditional Jewish music is performed at religious gatherings, whether liturgical or paraliturgical. Liturgical services take place either three or four times daily—depending upon the day—and texts are performed in styles that range from relatively plain to highly melodic.[42] The five basic sections of liturgical worship are the singing of biblical texts such as psalms; the shema' yisrael ("Hear, O Israel") and its benedictions; the 'amidah, comprising blessings and performed silently and individually at first, then by the leader; the order of supplications (seder tahanunim); and the reading of the Torah. The performance of the traditional service is extremely flexible and varies by location and subgroup. It is thus marked by change. Edwin Seroussi writes that "a main trend in this process of change is the continuous 'musicalization,' [that] is, the expansion of the truly 'musical' sections."[43] Jewish people are and have historically been musical.

Seroussi notes two other important distinctions about Jewish music. First, musical instruments are excluded from the synagogue.[44] The second accounts for the rich absorption of host cultures' music: liturgical texts, codified millennia ago, may be sung in liturgy to new melodies.[45] Liturgical music thus readily absorbs musical influences from outside the synagogue and a multitude of cultures. The reverse is also true. Schleifer wrote: "The essence of the Jewish experience with history has been that Jews have moved like peddlers from community to community, carrying their musical merchandise with them" (Schleifer 1997, 49). Even in times of persecution, Jews have simultaneously dispersed their own musical traditions even as they absorbed elements of host cultures. As Kay Kaufman Shelemay expressed it: "If any characteristic of Jewish secular and liturgical music repertoires challenges the myth of continuity in Jewish music, it is the widespread presence of contrafacta, pre-existing melodies borrowed from outside the Jewish cultural orbit" (Shelemay 1997, 302).

One esoteric religion, Kabbalah, has been reserved for this discussion of Judaism. Though Kabbalah may be traced back to the period of the Second Temple (516 BCE –70 CE) in Jerusalem, its extensive development began in the twelfth century (Idel 1997, 160 n2). Kabbalah is the body of literature associated with Jewish mysticism. One kabbalistic principle that has influenced many other religions is the indivisibility of the body/mind unity. It follows naturally that healing and belief are similarly associated.

The writings of Moses ben Maimonides (1135–1204), a Sephardi Jew born in Córdoba, Spain, are important sources of Kabbalah's flowering in the medieval period. This noted rabbinic codifier, philosopher, and physician, eventually settling in exile in Fustat, Egypt, wrote in *Eight Chapters*:

> If the humor of black bile agitates him (i.e., if he suffers from melancholy), he should make it cease by listening to songs and various kinds of melodies, by walking in gardens and fine buildings, by sitting before beautiful forms and by things like this which delight the soul and make the disturbance of black bile disappear.
>
> *Quoted in Kaplan (2002, 15–16)*

Maimonides may have been referring to instrumental or vocal music. Moshe Idel provides translations of several kabbalistic documents that refer more specifically to singing in the temple. "They made their voice pleasant by singing the song in a lovely, pleasant, clear and good voice. They pronounced their speech with a significant melodic movement" (quoted in Idel 1997, 167). In addition, cantillation marks such as the shalshelet, which signals a long and elaborate string of pitches, musically enhance the interpretation of the Torah. And finally, Idel comments on the role of cantillation: "Music, including its ritualistic performance, is a technique to liberate the soul from its prison, namely, Nature, rather than a technique to refine the intellect and prepare it for purer forms of intellections" (Idel 1997, 180). Kabbalah represents an ascetic branch of mystic Judaism, a movement which many feel influenced modern Hasidism.

Hasidism (from the Hebrew "pious," "pietism") traces its origins to the Enlightenment period, when Rabbi Israel ben Eliezor (Baal Shem Tov, 1698–1760) instituted a movement in present-day Medzhybizh, Ukraine. The Hasidic *niggun* (pl. niggunim) may be extracted from Jewish musical genres to serve as an example here. Philip V. Bohlman comments on the importance of the musical elements of niggunim, first sung in Poland and Ukraine in the 1700s.

> Hasidism was a spiritual movement in which disciples expressed ecstatic pietism through devotion to a charismatic rabbi and forms of worship that established a more direct communication with God. Words were regarded as a hindrance to forming such communication because they drew attention to themselves.[46]

Music and dance were primary vehicles for this form of devotion. The Hasidic niggun features a spiritually powerful melody that utilizes easily memorized vocables (lie-lie-lie, for example) instead of lyrics.

Since its beginnings, Hasidism has embraced the creation of new niggunim based on melodies from outside Jewish tradition. Any melody can be used as a vehicle for spiritual connection, though those composed by newcomers to the faith community may be less potent at first. Even mundane niggunim may be redeemed when sung in sanctity, however. Schliefer offered a tri-level hierarchy of niggun creation: the lowest level comprises expressions of pure joy and the next level includes liturgical songs that express inward meanings of prayers. Highest in this system are niggunim created by the Hasidic leaders and saints. These express ideas related to kabbalistic ideals, a clear link with earlier Jewish mysticism (Schleifer 1997).[47]

Within Hasidism, women play the important role of preserving niggunim through oral tradition. Ellen Koskoff has studied this process in a New York community (Koskoff 1989). "Lubavitchers," she writes of this group, "believe that one of the most effective vehicles for achieving devekuth (adhesion of the soul to God) is through the vocal performance of specific [niggunim] in correct social/religious contexts" (Koskoff 1989, 214).[48] Niggunim may be heard at weddings, Sabbath meals, and in individual moments of prayer and contemplation.

Orthodox Jews have separate laws for men and women; men are required to go to synagogue at specific times. Lubavitchers share with other orthodox Jews the belief that a woman's voice is a serious distraction to the real purpose of a man's life, namely, the study of Jewish law and the fulfillment of a deep relationship to God.[49] Consequently, Lubavitcher women believe they are endowed with more natural self-discipline than men; men must have external structures imposed by the keeping of rituals.

To summarize, Judaism, in contrast to the other religions examined here, is for a specific nation and people. Jewish people consider the faith to be as old as human habitation of the world. Liturgical texts can be sung to new melodies. This fact, together with the diasporic patterns of Jewish history, accounts for the wide range of Judaic musical styles. The reverse is also true; Jewish flavor characterizes much popular music whose places of origin were densely inhabited by Jews. Examples of this syncretic relationship may be seen in American Broadway musical theater songs, beginning in the late nineteenth century and extending through the works of Richard Rodgers, Oscar Hammerstein II, Irving Berlin, Leonard Bernstein, and Stephen Sondheim (Most 2004). Jews are historically musical people and though roles in synagogue have been gendered male, Jewish song composers of both sexes have provided foundational contributions to American popular music.

Christianity

Rooted in Judaism and thus sharing many essential scriptural and theological tenets such as monotheism, Christianity was inspired by the life and teachings of Jesus of Nazareth (Judea), whose birth to Jewish parents coincides roughly with the beginning of the Common Era. Believed by Christians to fulfill several prophecies of the Hebrew Bible, Jesus offered an avenue for unity with God that was not based on heredity or nationality.[50] Like other religions, Christian theology is heavily nuanced depending on culture and history. In general, believers acknowledge Christ as savior of all people, proclaim that belief, and try to live according to his teachings. Jesus' self-sacrifice to a local Roman governor, Pontius Pilate, and his subsequent resurrection are foundational Christian beliefs. The Christian deity comprises God, Jesus Christ, and the Holy Spirit.

Paul the Apostle (originally Saul of Tarsus, 2–46 CE), a converted Jew, wrote that Jews, Gentiles, slaves, free people, males, and females are equal in the sight of God.[51] In Matthew 5:3–12 (Sermon on the Mount), Jesus (a Hellenized version of the Hebrew Yeshua or Joshua) welcomed marginalized people among those included in the kingdom of God. This equality has been variously interpreted, extended, and transformed throughout Christian history. Though Christianity eventually shared the Jewish injunction against female singing in public, Catholic women composed and performed important vocal and instrumental music at least as early as the ninth century, if not earlier, in cloistered, monastic settings.

After his crucifixion, the resurrected Jesus appeared to his disciples and left them with these words, recorded in the book of Matthew 28:18–20:

> And Jesus came and said to them, "All authority in heaven and on earth has been given to me. Go therefore and make disciples of all nations, baptizing them in the name of the Father and of the Son and of the Holy Spirit, and teaching them to obey everything that I have commanded you. And remember, I am with you always, to the end of the age."[52]

Christianity's mission of converting the world's population has driven its dispersion, but also has brought it into troubling relationships with capitalism and colonialism.[53] During the colonial period, Western European nations—England, Spain, or Portugal, for example—acquired colonies rich in exotic resources, then followed initial colonization with the dispatch of Christian missionaries. The British Empire's colonial and Christianizing efforts at one time extended to North and South America, Africa, Asia, Australia, and Antarctica.[54] Isaac Watts's Anglican hymn which begins "Jesus shall reign where'er the sun, Doth his successive journeys run; His Kingdom stretch from shore to shore, Till moons shall wax and wane no more" may thus be viewed as a lyrical celebration of Christianity's mission, and a reflection of a British Empire upon which the sun never set.[55] Worldwide missionary efforts, pursued by Baptist denominations, the Church of Jesus Christ of Latter Day Saints, Roman Catholics, and other Christian groups, persist into the twenty-first century.

The teachings of Jesus, together with his recorded miracles related to healing, led twentieth-century music therapist and historian Ruth Boxberger to characterize Christianity as a religion of healing.[56]

> Christianity introduced the most revolutionary and decisive change in the attitude of society towards the sick . . . it taught that disease was not a disgrace or sin, nor was the sick man inferior . . . When Christianity became

the religion of the state, society assumed the obligation to care for its sick members.

Boxberger (1962, 147)

Christianity was inspired by a man who lived simply and publicly denounced the acquisition of earthly power. How did this faith develop into a religion so often associated with politics and capitalism? First, Christianity did not arise in a vacuum; its parent religion, Judaism, was well established by the time of Jesus. For at least a century and probably more after Christ's death around 30 CE, Judiasm and the nascent Christianity often shared worship spaces and experiences.

More consequential to Christianity's rise in Western Europe was the fact that the Kingdom of Judea came under Roman rule in 6 CE. From Christ's death in the fourth decade CE until 313, Christians experienced periods of tolerance, though often Christianity was punishable by death because it flew in the face of the established Roman religion. In 313, Roman Emperor Constantine I and Eastern Roman Emperor Licinius ratified the Edict of Milan, which finally ensured tolerance for Christians throughout the Roman Empire (Cockburn 2006). Constantine constructed a residence for the bishop in Rome, a magnificent church (Basilica Salvatoris), and another basilica on Vatican Hill, where St. Peter was martyred and the Vatican now stands. As the Roman Empire collapsed, Christianity adopted its infrastructure, one that partially retained the arrangement of the ancient Roman state. Constantine also set a future dichotomy in motion when he established Istanbul (Constantinople) as the capital of the Byzantine Empire, which included Turkey, Greece, Central Asia, the Eastern Mediterranean, and Egypt.

Today, Roman and Eastern Orthodox Catholicism are two of three main branches of Christendom. The third, Protestantism, arose early in the sixteenth century as a reaction to medieval Roman Catholic doctrines, practices, and hierarchies. Thirty-three percent of the world's religious people were estimated to be Christians in 2000 (Hitchcock 2004, 8–9). Countries with the highest populations of Christians include the United States, Brazil, Mexico, China, Russia, the Philippines, India, Germany, Nigeria, and Democratic Republic of Congo.

The earliest recorded Christian music resembles pagan and Jewish customs of singing at mealtimes (Fassler and Jeffrey 1992). Early Catholic liturgy featured sung scriptures, responses, and prayers, often performed in leader/response style. Also central to Jewish worship, the 150 biblical Psalms of David have formed the core of much Christian singing. Reappearing in late-seventeenth-century English parish churches, psalmody—the singing of psalms—was dispersed via that country's colonization of the New World. Pilgrims arrived at Plymouth Rock, Massachusetts, in 1620 with psalters compiled and printed by Henry Ainsworth (Amsterdam, 1612). New psalters followed in the seventeenth and eighteenth centuries, including the colonial publication *Whole Booke of Psalmes*, commonly known as the *Bay Psalm Book*.[57] Not until 1698 was music published in this influential collection, which underscores the fact that the melodies for psalm singing were transmitted via oral tradition. Usage of newly composed texts—called hymns rather than psalms—varies widely, especially among the Protestant denominations of Christianity.

Christian monasticism has its origins in first-century Christian practices of the esoteric Essenes and Therapeutae. Shortly after the conversion of Constantine, and "in a search for more 'rigorous and heroic' spirituality than emerging civic Christianity," the first Christian monastic communities arose in the deserts of Egypt (Fassler and Jeffrey 1992, xx). Established by Coptic (Egyptian) Christians, these first monasteries provided the foundation for much Christian monastic living in Europe.[58] Churches and basilicae in Rome required liturgies, and monasteries were established to insure regular celebration of divine offices. Religious orders, both male and female, have played crucial roles in the documentation and preservation of worship materials, including chants and songs.

Writings by Church Fathers document the centrality of singing in early monastic life and also its power over humans. In the fourth century CE, St. Basil of Rome and St. John Chrysostom of Greece inquired into the power of singing, for example as practiced by David, the Old Testament psalmist (related in I Kings and elsewhere). In his sermons, St. Augustine (354–430) left a wealth of detail about psalm singing in Hippo and Carthage. He also recorded his own moral dilemma regarding singing in *Confessions*:

> At one time I seem to myself to give [singing] more honour than is seemly, feeling our minds to be more holily and fervently raised unto a flame of devotion, by the holy words themselves when thus sung, than when not; and that the several affections of our spirit, by a sweet variety, have their own proper measures in the voice and singing, by some hidden correspondence wherewith they are stirred up. But this contentment of the flesh, to which the soul must not be given over to be enervated, doth oft beguile me ... Thus in these things I unawares sin, but afterwards am aware of it ...
>
> At other times, shunning over-anxiously this very deception, I err in too great strictness; and sometimes to that degree, as to wish the whole melody of sweet music which is used to David's Psalter, banished from my ears, and the Church's too; and that mode seems to me safer ... Yet again, when I remember the tears I shed at the Psalmody of Thy Church, in the beginning of my recovered faith; and how at this time I am moved, not with the singing, but with the things sung, when they are sung with a clear voice and modulation most suitable, I acknowledge the great use of this institution. Thus I fluctuate between peril of pleasure and approved wholesomeness ... Thou, O Lord my God, hearken; behold, and see, and have mercy and heal me, Thou, in whose presence I have become a problem to myself; and that is my infirmity.
> *Quoted in Pusey (2013)*

The singing, both inspiring and distracting to Augustine, was performed by males. Much of the subsequent millennium's Catholic approach to female singing may be deduced from this passage by Augustine's contemporary, Cyril of Jerusalem (fourth century), who advised nuns to pray "so that their lips move, but the ears of others do not hear . . . And the married woman should do likewise."[59] Nonetheless, the twelfth-century abbess and mystic Hildegard of Bingen enjoyed widespread notoriety for her vocal and instrumental compositions and her preaching tours. Especially in Italy after the Council of Trent (1545–63), cloistered nuns sang in convents whose perforated walls allowed sound to travel outside. The Council's enclosure of nuns was highly unpopular in cities such as Siena, Rome, and Bologne, and restrictions were eased by the end of the sixteenth century (Monson 1992).

As it does in all spiritual practice, song unites, encourages, and binds like-minded people together. Especially within the institution of North American slavery, spiritual song played all those roles. Efforts to convert slaves from indigenous African beliefs to Christianity were neither widespread nor consistently guided by idealistic Christian principles. Often, enslaved people were taught biblical principles in an attempt to control them. Of the many religious musical forms evolving from this period in United States history, the African American spiritual is distinctive. The spiritual genre is a type of folk song that arose in eighteenth-century Protestant worship meetings called revivals. In early American hymn publications, the term spiritual was applied to folk-inspired sacred music, while "hymn" or "psalm" referred to more "learned" (notated) genres of religious song.

Spirituals are Protestant music; Catholicism was a minority religion in the eighteenth-century US. Spirituals therefore reflect many of the principles that guided Martin Luther (1483–1546) and others toward the reform of Catholicism: justification by faith (rather than by what Luther considered corrupt practices such as the sale of indulgences), the idea that a believer is freed from Church rules by Christ's Gospel, the valuation of vernacular worship instead of the Catholic preference for ecclesiastical Latin, and prominence of music in worship.

In the spiritual, West African musical traditions merge with and absorb not only Christian principles but also Anglo-American hymn style. Enslaved people articulated their own hopes of deliverance from slavery through the exile narratives of prominent Hebrew heroes and martyrs. One such song provides biting commentary on the hypocrisy so evidently displayed by the white master class in antebellum America (see Figure 6.5). Characteristically for its genre, "O Daniel" mixes social commentary in the verse with the chorus's hopeful remembrance of the biblical Daniel's terrifying night in a lion's den. As told in the Hebrew Bible's book of Daniel, chapter 6, the imprisoned man emerged unharmed because he never ceased to pray for God's deliverance. Its two discrete parts also indicate this spiritual's genesis in oral-tradition environments such as revivals, where "wandering choruses" such as "Didn't my Lord deliver Daniel" were spontaneously attached to hymns about other topics. In the second half of the twentieth century, African American spirituals became sources of US national pride and appeared widely in school, university, professional, and choir programming. African American spirituals

FIGURE 6.5 "O, Daniel," African American spiritual, in William Francis Allen, Charles Pickard Ware, and Lucy McKim Garrison, *Slave Songs of the United States* (New York, 1867), 94.

now represent not only black Americans but also English-language Protestantism, due to their publication in a huge array of denominational hymnals.

To summarize, Christians believe that Jesus Christ fulfilled Judaic prophecies and offered religious salvation to all people. The Gospel of Jesus differentiates Christianity from its parent, Judaism. Like the other religions examined here, Christianity is founded on age-old principles that have been reinterpreted, corrupted, dispersed, and reinvented in ways representing diverse environments. Singing, with few exceptions, characterizes Catholic and Protestant worship experiences. The textual content of Christian vocal music is widely diverse. Some forms preserve ancient, chant-based liturgy based on conceptions of a distant, benevolent, and just God. In contrast, some Protestant music emphasizes personal relationships with God, facilitated by Jesus. Perhaps more than any other music discussed here, Protestant music has absorbed popular musical influences and enjoys notable commercial success in the mass media.

Islam

Islam arose in the Arabian peninsula, which was gradually inhabited in the first centuries of the Common Era by Arabic nomads.[60] This Bedouin lifestyle necessarily maximizes the resources available in desert ecosystems; wide expanses of grazing land and water are necessary for feeding livestock such as camel, sheep, and goats. Historically, Bedouins differentiated into familial tribes, within which fierce solidarity reigned. Warfare among tribes over land, livestock, and power was common. Each tribe worshipped distinct gods, and each god was associated with a phenomenon of nature. Nevertheless, all tribes worshipped Allah—a removed, distant deity (Hitchcock 2004, 335). During the month of Dhul-Hijah, the month for the hajj or pilgrimage to Mecca, tribal differences were set aside and many gods were worshipped. Mecca, often called the navel of the Earth, is traditionally considered the place the biblical Adam went after arriving on earth at Mount Budh, in India or Ceylon.

By the sixth century, two factors had arisen which paved the way for Islam. First, trade routes through major Middle Eastern cities—Cairo, Jerusalem, Damascus,

Baghdad—passed through Mecca and Yathrib (Medina). As elsewhere, these cities responded to newfound wealth with enjoyment of material goods. Also significant in this watershed was the fact that, by the sixth century, the Arab peninsula was surrounded by monotheist religions: Zoroastrianism, Judaism, and Christianity. Bedouins increasingly converted or otherwise absorbed monotheism, in addition to two other principles shared by these religions: faith in prophets and reliance on divinely inspired scriptures.

Muhammad ıbn 'Abd Allāh, the prophet who eventually united the Arab world under Islam, was born around the year 570 to the Quraysh, a tribe that dominated Mecca. The Quraysh were the caretakers of the holy destinations of the hajj: the Kaaba (a sacred structure which houses the pre-Islamic Black Stone) and Zamzam (the spring believed to have provided water for the biblical Abraham's son, Ishmael). Muhammad eventually married Khadija and, with her, had six children, of whom only the four girls survived. Khadija and her youngest, Fatima, were the first women to proclaim faith in Allah; thus, these two provide the ideal Islamic female models.

Sensing a crisis brought about by materialism and spiritual confusion in Mecca, Muhammad retreated for silent meditation in the year 610. This was the time of Muhammad's Night of Power, when Jibril (Arabic for Gabriel the angel) commanded him to "recite."

> In the Name of God, the Compassionate, the Merciful
> RECITE thou, in the name of thy Lord who created;
> Created man from CLOTS OF BLOOD:
> Recite thou! For thy Lord is the most Beneficent,
> Who hath taught the use of the pen;
> Hath taught Man that which he knoweth not.
>
> *Rodwell (1876)*

Thus begins the Qur'an, the central religious text of Islam, which was revealed to the Prophet over twenty-two years. Originating with Allah, these scriptures were transmitted by Jibril to Muhammad. Muhammad preached theology of one God, the wrongfulness of paganism (in the destruction of all idols may be seen the Muslim injunction against representative statuary or paintings in mosques), and the necessity to cleanse his society from the corruption of materialism. He defended widows, orphans, and the poor, and preached of heaven and hell, the balance of power between men and women, and ethnic equality. Muhammad taught coexistence with Jews and Christians, and, like the latter, Muslims hope to convert others to Islam.

The word Qur'an stems from the Arabic quaraa (to recite, to read). This holy book of Islam comprises 114 chapters called suras, each of which contains verses (ayat), meaning "signs" or miracles. The Qur'an was at first preserved orally; memorizing the Qur'an is still the greatest act of devotion a Muslim can undertake.

The entire Qur'an was not notated until the mid-seventh century. Jewish and Christian patriarchs—Abraham, Isaac, Jacob, Moses, David, Solomon, and Jesus—and Mary, Jesus' mother, are revered in the Qur'an.

In the early 620s, Muhammad experienced a Night Journey in which he traveled on horseback through the heavens to Jerusalem. Through this journey, he joined the community of prophets of Judaism and Christianity. All three religions would afterward share Jerusalem as a holy city. Also during that Night, Muhammad received direction to pray five times a day: at sunrise, noon, afternoon, dusk, and before sleeping. His home in Medina was the first mosque, and Muhammad was its imam, religious and political leader. He also acted as prophet, statesman, military leader, and judge.

Persecuted in Mecca because of his tribe's wealth, Muhammad was welcomed into Madinat al-Nabi, today's Medina. Islam accords to this arrival the beginning of Islamic history. The year 628 found Muhammad back in Mecca after several military battles. His hajj in 632 was his last, by which time as many as 30,000 had embraced Islam. In Hitchcock's words: "Religious unification now transcended tribal diversity with a commitment to peace" (Hitchcock 2004, 351).

"Islam, literally an act of surrender, is related to words for peace and reconciliation. A Muslim is one who surrenders to Allah, who seeks to follow and implement God's will" (Hitchcock 2004, 314). Islam holds five pillars or tenets: 1) bearing witness (shahada): "There is no god but Allah and Muhammad is the Messenger of Allah," 2) group praying or worshipping (salat), which is more blessed than that performed individually, 3) "purification" (zakat) which has come to mean tithing and almsgiving, 4) sawm—fasting during Ramadan, and 5) hajj, pilgrimage to Mecca, which is a sacred duty. The world's Islamic population comprised 20 percent of all religious people in the year 2000. Countries with the highest number of Muslims include Indonesia, Pakistan, India, Bangladesh, Turkey, Egypt, Iran, Nigeria, China, and Algeria (Hitchcock 2004, 8–9).

Though there is no statement in the Holy Qur'an explicitly condemning music, the legal status of music has been continually discussed. The simple chanting of the Qur'an and the call to prayer have an uncontested lawful status, and certain types of devotional singing have been variously tolerated within the different schools of Islamic law.

Outsiders might perceive the iconic call to prayer, adhān, as something akin to singing. Adhān was instituted by the Prophet to distinguish Islamic practice from that of other religions, and from melodious recitation of the Qur'an (Bohlman 1997, 78). It is recited five times daily, loudly and in public. Muezzins call the faithful to worship by reciting "Come and pray, come and flourish, there is no god but Allah. Allahu akhbar!" All Muslims must pray with intention.

As Eckhard Neubauer and Veronica Doubleday have written: "Strictly speaking, the words 'Islamic religious music' present a contradiction in terms. The practice of orthodox Sunni and Shi'a Islam does not involve any activity recognized within Muslim cultures as 'music.'"[61] Consequently, reciting will be used here to refer to the melodious, sustained speech involved in these central tenets of Islam.

Adhān is highly diverse in practice because it typically absorbs the local flavor surrounding the mosque. Still, unifying factors include the influence of Egyptian style, the use of Arabic as the language of Muhammad's divine inspiration, and the widespread use of dhikr, repetitive vocalizations of the names of God. The call to prayer is always performed by a single male voice without accompaniment. Recorded adhān emerged in the twentieth century and continue to be utilized by some mosques. Scott Marcus elaborates on the diversity of styles employed by reciters. Some locations favor basing adhān on maqāmāt (singular maqām), a set of pitches, like a mode or scale, characteristic of Arabic classical music. Some adhāns are more musically influenced by respective locality, and others employ a minimal number of pitches.

> While the text of the call is fixed (an additional line is added in Shi'ite communities), the melodic component is left to the individual caller. Each caller tends to develop his own unique, often highly complex and artistic, rendition, which he then uses day in and day out. At least three normative models have emerged. One version is based on the melodic mode called *maqām rāst* . . . variations of this model prevail in present-day Cairo . . . While renditions in *maqām rāst* or *maqām hijāz* tend to be highly melismatic and virtuosic, a third model, referred to by some as the *adhān shar'ī*, is syllabic and uses only two notes, a whole step apart. The caller simply alternates between these two notes.[62]

Marcus relates his surprise upon hearing, while in Cairo, "the two-note call, rendered by someone with a surprisingly poor voice," instead of the artistic, beautiful renditions he had come to expect. He recollects:

> The *nāy* maker, perceiving my reaction, offered the explanation that the usual *mu'adhdhin* was not present; he had been called away to his village. The call that day was therefore being given by someone who worked in a neighborhood bakery. "It is a long way from the baker's oven to becoming an artist" (*min al-furn lil-fannān*). Clearly, mosques seek a *mu'adhdhin* with a beautiful, even virtuosic voice; but the *nāy* maker assured me that both fine and poor voices are acceptable before God.[63]

Numerous recordings of adhāns are available online.[64] Where there is a mosque, there is a recited call to prayer, and these reflect the individuality of the reciter, as well as the culture surrounding the mosque. Prayer and vocality are thus inseparable in Islam.

Muhammad ibn 'Abd Allāh, to conclude, united the Arab world under Islam. Muslims are called publicly to pray, five times on most days, by loud, sometimes electronically broadcast adhāns recited by muezzins who are overwhelmingly male, although female imams are accepted in some countries. Though not considered music, this familiar invocation to prayer utilizes many of the melodic capabilities of the human voice. Individual style and virtuosity are recognized. Though adhāns reflect the cultures surrounding individual mosques, unifying factors include the influence of Egyptian style, the use of Arabic as the language of Muhammad's divine inspiration, and the widespread use of dhikr, repetitive vocalizations of the names of God.

Conclusion: The Cultural Work of Belief-Based Singing

This expansive chapter has revealed that spiritual or religious singing, reciting, and chanting play several important metaphysical and practical roles in belief communities. Ancient Greek followers of Pythagoras (sixth century BCE) saw congruity between the numerical proportions that produce musical harmonies and those that govern other aspects of the natural world.[65] In that view, planetary orbits were synchronized according to their proportionate speeds and fixed distances from the Earth. Similar ratios were present among the components of the musical scale—what we call do, re, mi, fa, so, la, ti, do. Scales and the music exemplifying them thus reflected a central truth about the universe—a "music of the spheres." Pythagoreans credited this notion to ancient Semitic people ("Chaldeans") or Babylonians, who in turn may have influenced the Jewish belief in an "orderly cosmos hymning praise of the Creator."[66] In some of our oldest documented histories, then, natural phenomena such as music's overtone series reflect a purposive, intelligent system believed to embody universal wisdom or God.

Variations of this belief abound. The King Bushmen of Botswana consider falling stars to be gifts from the gods, gifts that manifested on Earth as songs. Hindus believe that earthly music resonates sympathetically with divine vibrations. Shiva is one identity of the Hindu God whose presence is not symbolized by any iconic representation. Instead, for centuries, "Hindu musicians have envisioned Shiva and other forms of God as the musical shimmering of cosmic consciousness."[67]

Second, many faiths hold that singing helps believers "tune in" with a deity. Singing intensifies and empowers praise and prayer. It is, therefore, one way that Jews experience denekut, or joining with the soul of G-d. The niggunim of Hasidic Jews often comprise nonsense syllables precisely because more literary texts distract from the desired communion with G-d. Chanting likewise brings out individual awareness of the Buddha for his followers, and memorizing and reciting the Qur'an is the greatest act of devotion a Muslim can undertake. Singing marks places where divine presence is desired in many faiths. Zoroastrians sang at weddings and other ceremonies, as do Freemasons, a likely offspring of Zoroastrianism. Singing contributes solemnity to Buddhist rituals. Jews, Christians, and other religious people request God's blessing and presence at mealtimes, weddings, or in meditative moments through song.

Philip Bohlman articulates a third consideration: "singing substantiates religious experience" (Bohlman 2000, 8). So in song the feeling of belief becomes tangible, and, further, since religious feeling is often profound and multi-layered, song can stand for an entire narrative tracing the journey from enslavement to freedom, for example. June Boyce-Tillman relates a "fine Jewish story" describing the origins of the niggun.

> The rabbi goes to the woods to celebrate his ritual. He finds the place, lights the fire, and sings the service. God says: "It is enough." The rabbi goes to the woods to celebrate the service. He finds the place but has forgotten how to light the fire. God says: "it is enough." The rabbi can no longer find the wood but he sings the service. God says, "It is enough." The rabbi can no longer remember the words of the service. But he sings the tune. God says: "It is enough."
>
> *Boyce-Tillman (2000, 136)*

In this way, ancient ritual is reduced to intention and metaphorical act; spiritual singing, chanting, and reciting likewise become deeply symbolic acts of faith.

Fourth, song or recitation is generated deep within the human body and resonates in many parts of our anatomy—chest cavity, pharynx, throat, nasal passages—as it passes outward to the external world. This physical connection between inner and outer, paired with the inherent expressivity of a melody with or without text, gives the believer tangible ways to identify with her faith. Australian Aboriginal people believe that one role of didjeridu or yiraga (the latter translated as "windpipe") is to accompany the soul of the deceased to the "other side" (Turner 2000, 49). David Turner related the words of one subject, interspersed with his own commentary:

> Singing was like playing the didjeridu, he said. The words may come out from the mouth but the "echo" comes from deep down in your guts. Singing was also like didjeridu playing in another way, I reflected. It took you out of yourself to transcend the pain of grief you felt on the loss of a loved one.

"Lord, I want to be a Christian in my heart," one American folk hymn attests. Singing reinforces that metaphor with physical sensation.

Music's power to change human behavior, the essence of the Greek ethos theory, is a fifth cultural accomplishment of religious singing. In the words of American singer Bernice Johnson Reagon: "Songs are a way to get singing. The singing is what you are aiming for and the singing is running the sound through your body. You cannot sing a song and not change your condition" (quoted in Walton 1991, 255).[68] Every belief system discussed here recognizes the power of the inflected voice. Esoteric and indigenous faiths rely upon the extraordinary power of chanting, sometimes in combination with medicinal agents such as peyote buttons, to heighten and sustain the trance. These powerful shifts in consciousness, similarly observable in Buddhist chanting and other meditative practices, are expected, desired, and culturally condoned. In addition to intensifying trance states, mystical singing promotes spiritual liberation in kabbalistic rituals. The goal in these performances is not to refine the intellect and prepare it for purer thought processes, but to liberate the soul from its prison, that prison being Nature. Music offers Hindu musicians, as well as their listeners, a path that leads to spiritual liberation and proximity to God. The *Saṅgīta-ratnākara* (*The Jewel Mine of Music*), written in 1240 by Śārṅgadeva, teaches that God is the embodiment of music, and that music integrates the disciplines of science, art, and yoga.[69] Jeff Titon describes the effect of singing in an Old Regular Baptist worship service: "The music is literally moving; it activates the Holy Spirit, which sends some people into shouts of ecstasy, swoons, shakes, holy dance, and trance" (Titon 2002, 160). No greater acknowledgment of singing's power over humans need be sought than its capacity to distract from, as well as intensify, worship.

A sixth commonality among religions is that singing is an act of praise, directed toward the divine. The Vedas (1500 BCE and following) contain hymns praising early Hindu gods. The singing of God's names is revered in many faiths. Hindus call this musical recitation—wherein God's attributes are variously named—Nama Sangeerthana, the singing of which benefits both the singer and the listener. Islam features dhikr, repetitive vocalizations of the names of God. Praise may be its own end or may be functional. Hindu faithful perform rituals and obligations such as Nama Sangeerthana to ensure higher caste status in the next life. Ritual singing is important for the rebirth of the soul. In "Nirgun bhajan," hymn of the formless divine, a musician sings and accompanies himself on the bowed fiddle:

> Such hymns convey beliefs in a deity without attributes, yet their texts focus not on the deity, but on the transitory nature of life, the inevitability of death, the temptations of maya—this world of illusion—and the importance of devotion for the rebirth of the soul.[70]

In addition to its metaphysical attributes and powers, singing has a seventh, practical purpose, to preserve and transmit scripture and holy writings, and to instruct apprentices about them. The Vedas and other Hindu sacred texts not only praise but also educate. Prior to preservation of the Buddha's teachings in the Pāli language, Buddhist monastic ritual comprised "singing together the dhamma." Musical features of paritta chant give an aural shape to recited passages. The music component of that chant affects the way the words are heard, experienced, and contemplated. The melodic shapes of the Buddha's teachings were retained as perfectly as possible for this mnemonic purpose. The Dead Sea Scrolls contain marks that indicate cantillation and choral singing. And on the ways Islam and musical sound are related, Regula Qureshi wrote:

> The fact is that musical sound plays a highly significant role in articulating the singularly verbal message of Islam, both in its universal quranic form and also in the form of vernacular devotional poetry. What expresses Muslim identity, or experience or faith, is a dynamic of living communication through words being sounded and heard . . . The words of the quaranic message; words that explain and interpret the message; words that praise God and his messenger; words that convey the believer's submission, the literal meaning of "Islam." Presenting these words musically renders the message more articulate and intense, as well as acoustically and aesthetically compelling. Indeed, musical recitation is integral to Islam's essentially oral approach to religious texts.
>
> *Qureshi (2000, 25)*

Apart from its pedagogical usefulness, the health benefits of singing appear frequently in religious documentation. Shamans sing or chant both in preparing for and during healing ceremonies. Kabbalists believed strongly in mind/body unity, which can be seen in Maimonides' prescription for alleviating melancholy with song and other art forms that delight the soul (Kaplan 2002, 15–16).

Buddhists acknowledge that chanting produces a mighty thoracic cavity; several studies to date have shown that the blood pressure of Buddhist monks was at its lowest while they were chanting (Weil 2008).

> To many Buddhists [in China], reciting scripture, or "reading a text," is itself, in a broad sense, meditation. It is considered a way to purify the mind, eliminate ignorance, and absorb the essence of Buddhist teachings. To achieve this goal, Buddhists must hold themselves erect and concentrate on reciting in a clear voice. In addition, breath control becomes significant, especially when phrases are long and uninterrupted, as in a rendering of zhou—Chinese transliteration of mantras based on Pāli or Sanskrit. Thus, the longer the expiration, the better the reciter. This skill, considered a good indication of meditative skills, requires years of exercises.[71]

And in today's rural Myanmar, people ask monks to chant suttas (aka sutras, discourses attributed to the Buddha or a close disciple) to appease the evil spirits causing an epidemic (Greene 2004).

These advantages play a host of helpful roles when believers express religious faith in communities. In Islam, group prayer or worship is considered more blessed than that performed by an individual. Group singing, like other forms of group music making, produces a sense of belonging. Hindus see musical harmony as instantiation of communal harmony. Shared tastes are on display when singers unite in groups, and shared beliefs only strengthen those bonds. Beverly Patterson writes that

> some, and perhaps many, Primitive Baptists invest the singing in their churches with meaning related to religious identity, identity not only as Primitive Baptists but even more as children of grace, members of the true church that is separate from the world and that transcends the boundaries set by denominations and nations.
>
> *Patterson (1995, 39)*

Margarita Mazo writes about Molokans (i.e., "milk drinkers"), a group of non-Orthodox Russian Christians: "Singing is a keystone of the Molokans' self-identity. It epitomizes Molokan religious experience and social life to such an extent that most adults in the community consider the continuity of their singing a critical factor for their survival as Molokans" (Mazo 2000, 83). Relative to this philosophy, Alex Khalil stated: "The voice projects history and genealogy through its very sound" (Khalil 2009). So shared experience—of the metaphysical or of biological, regional, and ethnic identity—empowers song in corporate religious experiences. Religious singing can articulate boundaries between self and other or, in Stephen Marini's words, differentiate between liminality and communitas (Marini 2003, 321–2). Its cohesive properties notwithstanding, religious song can also bridge cultural boundaries between diverse groups, as it has in diasporic music such as the Hasidic niggunim, which readily absorbs musical influences from other cultures to which the faith has extended.

One final aspect of the important cultural work performed by spiritual singing will be addressed here. Spiritual singing and its attendant benefits help people endure hardship of all types: being misunderstood, homesickness, questioning the meaning of life and identity, and bereavement. Further, since songs are particularly good at concealing multiple meanings once absorbed into local practice (Bohlman 1997), religious singing has become a tool to voice resistance within colonialism, slavery, genocide, and other institutions featuring dominating and dominated classes. Enslaved people in antebellum America communicated the desire for freedom in the spiritual "Go Down, Moses." Holocaust victims expressed solidarity with Jewish song as they were herded to gas chambers, and the structure of Christian hymns was utilized in black Africans' resistance to apartheid, a fact readily apparent in music by black South Africans today (Bohlman 1997, 73). In this way, religious song can be an effective tool to cope with unspeakable trauma. Faith communities, whether numerous or few in adherents, tap the power of singing, chanting, or reciting to intensify individual and group experiences, to worship and teach about religion, and to improve the quality of life or wellness of believers.

Musical Illustrations

Bhajan: Nirgun bhajan, "Hymn of the Formless Divine," *Garland Encyclopedia of World Music*, accessed 31 December 2014.

Buddhist chant: *Lama Chöpa: A Buddhist Tantric Celebration*, Monks of Dreprung Loseling Monastery, 1999.

Niggunim: Yaakov Mazor, ed. 2004. *The Hasidic Niggun as Sung by the Hasidim*, Anthology of Music Traditions in Israel vol. 17, 2 CDs. Jewish Music Research Centre, Jerusalem.

Spiritual: Paul Robeson, "Didn't My Lord Deliver Daniel," arr. Moses Hogan, *On My Journey: Paul Robeson's Independent Recordings*, Smithsonian Folkways 2007.

Adhān from Mecca: www.youtube.com/watch?v=qvUMtvxrgco; **adhān from the Philippines** www.youtube.com/watch?v=AW-RXRS7fV4; both accessed 31 December 2014.

Discussion Points

1. In the 2010 film *Secretariat*, the 1967 Edwin Hawkins Singers' version of a mid-eighteenth-century hymn (Phillip Doddridge's "O Happy Day") under-scores Big Red's capture of the second jewel in horse racing's Triple Crown. What are the tangible effects (cultural work) of this gospel music in the con-text of a horse race? Relate Bohlman's perspectives about religious singing and context to your thoughts about this cinematic moment.
2. In historical or contemporary news reports, search for ways people have used sacred song or chant to foster hope or solidarity in catastrophic situations.
3. Research one form of religious singing that absorbs influences from non-religious music. How do practitioners of that genre justify borrowing from popular music (for example) in the construction of sacred song?

Notes

1 All dates in this chapter reflect the Gregorian calendar.
2 Any attempt to draw firm boundaries between esoteric and exoteric religions is likely to misrepresent some faith systems; I have observed the division only gener-ally. Kabbalah, a Jewish esoteric form, will be addressed in the section on Judaism. Chinese native philosophical systems or religions, representing 23.5 percent of the world's religious adherents in 1900 but only 6.3 percent in 2000, will be represented here by Confucianism and Daoism, both of which will be addressed in the section on Buddhism. When Buddhism entered China, it absorbed many of the practices and philosophies of China's indigenous religions, whose tenets had provided the roots from which Confucianism and Daoism arose.
3 The text associated with this ancient tune begins "Day of wrath, that day shall dissolve the world into embers, as David prophesied with the Sybil."
4 *Grove Music Online*, s.v. "Dies irae," by J. Caldwell and M. Boyd, accessed 28 December 2014.
5 "The United Society of Believers in Christ's Second Appearing, popularly known as Shakers or Shaking Quakers, was a millenarian community under the leadership of Ann

Lee (1736–84) of Manchester, England, who emigrated to America in 1774." *Grove Music Online*, s.v. "Shakers," by V.F. Yellin and H.W. Hitchcock, accessed 28 December 2014.

6 Of course, "being there" physically does not always insure spiritual or religious understanding.

7 In neo-Confucian Chinese philosophy, qi (air, breath) is the life force that makes everyone unique. In traditional Chinese medicine, qi is life force or energy that flows among unseen meridians in the body and balances bodily components: organs, tissues, veins, nerves, cells, and consciousness, for example. Chakra (wheel) refers to energy centers in the body where psychic forces and bodily functions merge and interact with each other. Chakras are prominent in some forms of Hinduism and Buddhism. Emphasis mine. *Encyclopædia Britannica Online*, s.v. "qi" and "chakra," accessed 19 July 2013.

8 Ovid's first-century description of the powers of Orpheus may be found in Chapter 1 of this book.

9 He draws a distinction between more primal musical-magical practice from the East and this more "cultured" (in Western perception) form of healing. I do not intend to perpetuate Western chauvinistic attitudes about shamanism by referencing Gioia's point here.

10 *Garland Encyclopedia of World Music*, s.v. "Assessing Spiritual Value: Is Music Good or Bad?" eds. V. Danielson, S. Marcus, and D. Reynolds, accessed 31 December 2014.

11 Bernard's letter to Abbot Guy, *Grove Music Online*, s.v. "Bernard of Clairvaux," by Mary Berry, accessed 18 June 2013.

12 *The Oxford Companion to Music*, s.v. "Freemasonry and music," by Stanley Sadie, accessed 18 July 2013.

13 National Library of Medicine, US National Institutes of Health, s.v. "Paracelsus," www.nlm.nih.gov/exhibition/paracelsus/paracelsus.html, accessed 18 June 2013.

14 *Garland Encyclopedia of World Music*, s.v. "Religious and Devotional Music, South Area [of India]," by Alison Arnold, accessed 31 December 2014. Hinduism and bhakti doctrine will be explored more fully in the section on exoteric religions.

15 *Garland Encyclopedia of World Music*, s.v. "Music and Trance," by David Roche, accessed 31 December 2014.

16 Tarantism was a form of "dancing sickness," common in sixteenth- and seventeenth-century Italy, thought to be caused by a tarantula (wolf spider) bite.

17 Researchers have become interested in physiological changes experienced by adherents of shamanistic religions. See Gingras et al. (2014).

18 Also see the website for her *Open Ear Center: Dedicated to Sound and Music in Healing*, www.openearcenter.com, accessed 31 December 2014.

19 Track 11 of the accompanying CD is a Mara'akame "Song for Petitioning the Gods for Healing" recorded in the 1940s, which features calls sung by the shaman and refrain/responses sung by a group comprising, according to my hearing, males and females.

20 Some experts question the ethnic origin of Aryan and argue the term simply denotes upper class, from the Sanskrit "arya," meaning noble or distinguished.

21 *Garland Encyclopedia of World Music*, s.v. "Vedic Chant," by Wayne Howard, accessed 19 June 2013.

22 *Garland Encyclopedia of World Music*, s.v. "South Asia, Religious Practice," by Alison Arnold, accessed 18 June 2013.

23 *Garland Encyclopedia of World Music*, s.v. "Religious and Devotional Music, Northern Area [of India]," by Guy Beck, accessed 31 December 2014.

24 *Garland Encyclopedia of World Music*, s.v. "Religious and Devotional Music: South Area [of India]," by Alison Arnold, accessed 31 December 2014.

25 It is also a genre of religious ritual performed throughout India. Philip Bohlman (1997, 77) points out that bhajans have been reconfigured in the twentieth century partly in response to mass media such as the cassette industry in South Asia.

26 *Grove Music Online*, s.v. "India, VI, Religious Music, Hindu," by Robert Simon, accessed 6 June 2013.

27 *Garland Encyclopedia of World Music*, s.v. "Religious and Devotional Music, Northern Area [of India]," by Guy Beck, accessed 31 December 2014.

28 Ibid. Compare Homer's discussion of the harmony of the spheres, eighth century BCE, and the ancient Greek theories of cosmic ratios that govern the universe.

29 See chapters 2 and 4 of this book, and Vickhoff et al. (2013) for discussions of singing in groups.

30 Incorporation of bhajan into Hindu pop music has been problematized by scholars such as van Maas (2009–10).

31 Also see Upadhaya (1998).

32 *Grove Music Online*, s.v. "Buddhist Music," by Francesca Tarocco, accessed 20 June 2013.

33 Ibid.

34 Ibid.

35 *Garland Encyclopedia of World Music*, s.v. "Buddhism in Northern India," by Guy Beck, accessed 31 December 2014.

36 Discussing the manifold benefits of another central practice, meditation, lies outside the scope of this chapter. Recent studies document Buddhist meditation's capacity to enhance attention and the awareness that all things are interconnected—qualities which promote empathy. Summarized in DeSteno (2013).

37 *Garland Encyclopedia of World Music*, s.v. "Religious Music in China, Buddhism," by Wei Li, accessed 31 December 2014. See also Skingley et al. (2014).

38 This section is informed by the following articles in *Grove Music Online*: "Daoism" by Tsao Penyeh; "East Asia, 3. Aesthetics, Cosmology, and Religion" by D.W. Hughes and S. Jones; and "China IV, Living Traditions" by A.R. Thrasher and others. I also relied on two entries by K. De Woskin in the *Garland Encyclopedia of World Music*: "Religious Music in China, Overview" and "Music and Aesthetics in Ancient China."

39 *Grove Music Online*, s.v. "Jewish Music," by E. Seroussi et al., accessed 24 June 2013.

40 The musical history of Mesopotamia is relevant in any examination of early Jewish history. See *Grove Music Online*, s.v. "Mesopotamia," by A. Kilmer, accessed 8 August 8, 2013.

41 Several websites list scriptural locations where vocal and instrumental music are mentioned.

42 *Grove Music Online*, s.v. "Jewish Music," by E. Seroussi et al.

43 Ibid.

44 As they have for cantillation, rules about instrumental music have varied historically. Musical instruments were, for a short time, allowed in some Ashkenazi synagogues in the eighteenth century, for example, and are allowed in some synagogues today.

45 *Garland Encyclopedia of World Music*, s.v. "Music in the Religious Experience of Israeli Jews," by E. Seroussi, accessed 31 December 2014.

46 *Garland Encyclopedia of World Music*, s.v. "Jewish Music in Europe," by P. Bohlman, accessed 31 December 2014.

47 Hasidic niggunim reflect the kabbalistic mysticism of Rabbi Isaac Luria Ashkenazi (1534–72), who lived in Safed in the Galilee region of Ottoman Palestine.

48 Lubavitch in Russian means "city of brotherly love." Chabad-Lubavitch is currently one of the best known Hasidic movements of orthodox Judaism.

49 Koskoff (1989) provides talmudic citations for this law.

50 The virgin birth, for example, is foretold in Isaiah 7:13–14 and its fulfillment is recounted in the New Testament book of Luke 1:26 and following.

51 Galatians 3:28.

52 New Revised Standard Version Bible (1989).

53 Bruno Nettl writes: "Beginning with the establishment of colonial empires by nations of Western Europe from the 16th century to the 18th, colonialism received increased

impetus in the race for colonies during the late 19th and early 20th centuries." *Grove Music Online*, s.v. "Colonialism," by B. Nettl, accessed 9 July 2013.

54 The Dutch East India Company was founded in 1602 and is considered the world's first multinational corporation. It supported Christian missions in Asia, its primary sphere of influence. It was dissolved after bankruptcy in 1800.

55 The hymn was first published in Watts's *The Psalms of David* (1707).

56 For example, John 11:1–45 recounts the restoration of life to Lazarus. The healing of the hemorrhaging woman is recorded in Mark 5:25–34, Matthew 9:18–26, and Luke 8:40–56. The healing of "Legion," the man possessed by demons in the territory of Gadara, is described in Matthew 8:28–34.

57 Cambridge, MA, 1640, 3rd ed. 1651; published thereafter as *The Psalms, Hymns, and Spiritual Songs of the Old and New Testament*.

58 St. Anthony (251–356) was born to a Christian family in Egypt. A monastery commemorating his life of Christian service was founded a century after his birth in Egypt.

59 Quoted in *Grove Music Online*, s.v. "Women in music," by Judith Tick, accessed 31 December 2014.

60 Today, the Kingdom of Saudi Arabia covers about 80 percent of the Arabian peninsula.

61 *Grove Music Online*, s.v. "Islamic music," by V. Doubleday and E. Neuebauer, accessed 31 December 2014.

62 *Garland Encyclopedia of World Music*, s.v. "The Muslim Call to Prayer," by S. Marcus, accessed 31 December 2014.

63 Ibid.

64 Adhān from Mecca, www.youtube.com/watch?v=qvUMtvxrgco; adhān from the Philippines www.youtube.com/watch?v=AW-RXRS7fV4; both accessed 31 December 2014.

65 *Grove Music Online*, s.v. "Music of the Spheres," by J. Haar, accessed 6 August 2013.

66 Ibid.

67 *Garland Encyclopedia of World Music*, s.v. "Conservative Sanskrit Musical Treatises and Innovations," by Alison Arnold, accessed 31 December 2014.

68 Reagon is founder of the acclaimed female vocal ensemble Sweet Honey in the Rock.

69 *Garland Encyclopedia of World Music*, s.v. "South Asia, Religious Practice," by Alison Arnold, accessed 18 June 2013.

70 *Garland Encyclopedia of World Music*, s.v. "Uttar Pradesh" [the most populous state in India] and "Mendicant Musicians' Music," by Edward O. Henry, accessed 31 December 2014. Mendicant is a polite word for beggar.

71 *Garland Encyclopedia of World Music*, s.v. "Religious Music in China, Buddhist," by Wei Li, accessed 31 December 2014.

References

"Adhān from Mecca." Uploaded 6 Nov. 2006. Posted by Muslim Makkah, www.youtube.com/watch?v=qvUMtvxrgco, accessed 22 October 2013.

"Adhān from the Philippines." www.youtube.com/watch?v=AW-RXRS7fV4, accessed 22 October 2013.

Allon, M. 1997. *Style and Function: Study of the Dominant Stylistic Features of the Prose Portions of Pāli Canonical Sutta Texts and Their Mnemonic Function*. Tokyo: International Institute for Buddhist Studies.

The Bay Psalm Book (The Psalms, Hymns, and Spiritual Songs of the Old and New Testament). 1640. Cambridge, MA.

Berlioz, H. 1960. *Symphonie fantastique*, movement 5. New York: Breitkopf and Härtel.

Bohlman, P.V. 1997. "World Music and World Religions: Whose World?" In *Enchanting Powers: Music in the World's Religions*, ed. L.E. Sullivan. Cambridge, MA: Harvard University Press.

————. 2000. "Introduction." In *Music in American Religious Experience*, eds. P.V. Bohlman, E.L. Blumhofer, and M.M. Chow. New York: Oxford.

Boxberger, R. 1962. "Historical Bases for the Use of Music in Therapy." In *Music Therapy 1961: Eleventh Book of Proceedings of the National Association for Music Therapy*, 147. Lawrence, KS: National Association for Music Therapy.

Boyce-Tillman, J. 2000. "Sounding the Sacred: Music as Sacred Site. The Search for a Universal Sacred Music." In *Indigenous Religious Musics*, eds. K. Ralls-Macleod and G. Harvey. Aldershot: Ashgate.

Carman, J.E. 2004. "Yoga and Singing: Natural Partners." *Journal of Singing* 60.5: 433–41.

Cockburn, A. 2006. "The Gospel of Judas." *National Geographic Magazine*, http://ngm. nationalgeographic.com/2006/05/judas-gospel/cockburn-text.html, accessed 31 December 2014.

The Complete Jewish Bible, translated from Hebrew. Bereishit–Genesis–Chapter 1, www. chabad.org/library/bible_cdo/aid/8165, accessed 31 December 2014.

Cook, P.M. 2004. *Music Healers of Indigenous Cultures: Shaman, Jhankri, and Néle*. Bainbridge Island, WA: Open Ear Press.

————. *Open Ear Center: Dedicated to Sound and Music in Healing*, www.openearcenter.com, accessed 31 December 2014.

DeSteno, D. 2013. "Gray Matter: The Morality of Meditation." *New York Times*, www.nytimes. com/2013/07/07/opinion/sunday/the-morality-of-meditation.html?smid=fb-share&_r=1&, accessed 31 December 2014.

Eliot, G. 1876. *Daniel Deronda*. London: Blackwood.

Fassler, M., and P. Jeffrey. 1992. "Christian Liturgical Music from the Bible to the Renaissance." In *Sacred Sound and Social Change: Liturgical Music in Jewish and Christian Experience*, eds. L.A. Hoffman and J.R. Walton, 84–123. Notre Dame, IN: University of Notre Dame Press.

Gingras, B., G. Pohler, and W.T. Fitch. 2014. "Exploring Shamanic Journeying: Repetitive Drumming with Shamanic Instructions Induces Specific Subjective Experiences but No Larger Cortisol Decrease Than Instrumental Meditation Music." *Public Library of Science (PLoS) One* 9.7. DOI: 10.1371/journal.pone.0102103.

Gioia, T. 2006. *Healing Songs*. Durham, NC: Duke University Press.

Greene, P.D. 2004. "The Dhamma as Sonic Praxis: Paritta Chant in Burmese Theravada Buddhism." *Asian Music* 35.2: 43–78.

Grevatt W.K. 2013. "Mystics, Warriors, and the Grail: Exploring the Sacred Medieval Psyche." *Psychological Perspectives: A Quarterly Journal of Jungian Thought* 56.1: 61–73.

Griffith, R.T.H., translator. 1896. *Sacred Texts, Rig Veda*, www.sacred-texts.com/hin/rigveda/rv01089.htm, accessed 19 June 2013.

Hardie, A. 2004. "Muses and Mysteries." In *Music and the Muses: The Culture of 'Mousikē' in the Classical Athenian City*, eds. P. Murray and P. Wilson, 11–38. London: Oxford University Press.

Hitchcock, S.T., with J.L. Esposito. 2004. *Geography of Religion: Where God Lives, Where Pilgrims Walk*. Washington, DC: National Geographic Society.

Idel, M. 1997. "Conceptualizations of Music in Jewish Mysticism." In *Enchanting Powers: Music in the World's Religions*, ed. L.E. Sullivan, 160. Cambridge, MA: Harvard University Press.

Idelson, A.Z. 1931–2. "The Kol Nidre Tune." *Hebrew Union College Annual* 8.9: 493–509.

Jewish Virtual Library. "Ancient Jewish History: The Twelve Tribes of Israel." www.jewish-virtuallibrary.org/jsource/Judaism/tribes.html, accessed 24 July 2013.

Kaplan, L. 2002. "An Introduction to Maimonides' 'Eight Chapters.'" *Edah Journal: Inquiries in Jewish Ethics* 2.2, online.

Khalil, A. 2009. "Music of the Desert Fathers (of Arizona): Negotiating Religious, Ethnic, and National Identities." Paper presented at the 35th Annual Conference of the Society for American Music, Denver, CO, March 2009.

Koskoff, E. 1989. "The Sound of a Woman's Voice: Gender and Music in a New York Hasidic Community." *Women and Music in Cross-Cultural Perspective*, ed. Ellen Koskoff, 213–23. Urbana: University of Illinois Press.

Levin, J. 2008. "Esoteric Healing Traditions: A Conceptual Overview." *Explore* 4.2: 101–12.

Lippman, E. 1964. *Musical Thought in Ancient Greece*. New York: Columbia University Press.

Maimonides. 2002. *Eight Chapters*, 5, trans. R. Weiss. Quoted in L. Kaplan, "An Introduction to Maimonides' 'Eight Chapters.'" *Edah Journal: Inquiries in Jewish Ethics* 2.2.

Marini, S. 2003. *Sacred Song in America: Religion, Music, and Public Culture*. Urbana: University of Illinois Press.

Mazo, M. 2000. "Singing as Experience among Russian American Molokans." In *Music in American Religious Experience*, eds. P.V. Pohlman, E.L. Blumhofer, and M.M. Chow. New York: Oxford.

Moda, J.J. 2013. "The Marriage Ceremony of the Parsis." *Zoroastrian Rituals: Wedding*, http://avesta.org/ritual/zwedding.htm, accessed 17 June 2013.

Monson, C.A. 1992. *The Crannied Wall: Women, Religion, and the Arts in Early Modern Europe*. Ann Arbor: University of Michigan Press.

Most, A. 2004. *Making Americans: Jews and the Broadway Musical*. Cambridge, MA, and London: Harvard University Press.

New Revised Standard Version Bible. 1989. New York: The Division of Christian Education of the National Council of the Churches of Christ in the United States of America.

Patterson, B.B. 1995. *The Sound of the Dove: Singing in Appalachian Primitive Baptist Churches*. Urbana: University of Illinois Press.

Philo. *De Vita Contemplativa*, xi, http://humweb.ucsc.edu/gweltaz/courses/history/hist_5B/Lectures/therapeutae.pdf, accessed 17 June 2013.

Pusey, E.B., translator. 2013. *Confessions* Book X. *Project Gutenberg's Confessions of St. Augustine*, www.gutenberg.org/files/3296/3296-h/3296-h.htm, accessed 26 June 2013.

Qureshi, R.B. 2000. "When Women Recite: 'Music' and Islamic Immigrant Experience." In *Music in American Religious Experience*, eds. P.V. Bohlman, E.L. Blumhofer, and M.M. Chow. New York: Oxford.

Reagon, B.J., with B. Moyers. 2000. *The Songs Are Free*, VHS. New York: Mystic Fire Video. Quoted in J. Walton. 1991. "Women's Ritual Music." *Music in American Religious Experience*, eds. P.V. Bohlman, E.L. Blumhofer, and M.M. Chow, 256. New York: Oxford.

Rodwell, J.M. 1876. *The Qur'ân: Sacred Texts*, www.sacred-texts.com/isl/qr/096.htm, accessed 31 December 2014.

Sadie, S. 2013. "Freemasonry and Music." In *The Oxford Companion to Music*. *Oxford Music Online*. Oxford University Press, www.oxfordmusiconline.com/subscriber/article/opr/t114/e2681, accessed 18 July 2013.

Schleifer, E. 1997. "Jewish Liturgical Music from the Bible to Hasidism." In *Sacred Sound and Social Change: Liturgical Music in Jewish and Christian Experience*, eds. L.A. Hoffmann and J.W. Walton, 13–58. Notre Dame, IN: University of Notre Dame Press.

Shelemay, K.K. 1997. "Mythologies and Realities in the Study of Jewish Music." In *Enchanting Powers: Music in the World's Religions*, ed. L.E. Sullivan, 299–318. Cambridge, MA: Harvard University Press.

Skingley, A., S. Page, S. Clift, I. Morrison, and S. Coulton. 2014. "'Singing for Breathing': Participants' Perceptions of a Group Singing Programme for People with COPD." *Arts and Health* 6.1: 59–74.

Titon, J.T., ed. 2002. "North America/Black America." In *Worlds of Music: An Introduction to the Music of the World's People.* Belmont, CA: Schirmer/Thomson Learning.

Turner, D.H. 2000. "From Here into Eternity: Power and Transcendence in Australian Aboriginal Music." In *Indigenous Religious Musics*, eds. K. Ralls-Macleod and G. Harvey, 35–55. Aldershot: Ashgate.

Upadhaya, K.N. 1968. "The Impact of Early Buddhism on Hindu Thought: With Special Reference to the Bhagavadgiitaa." *Philosophy East and West* 18: 163–73.

———. 1998. *Early Buddhism and the Bhagavadgita.* Delhi.

van Maas, S. 2009–10. "Pop and Polytheism." *Journal of the Indian Musicological Society* 40: 84–92.

Vickhoff, B., H. Malmgren, R. Åström, G. Nyberg, S.-R. Ekström, M. Engwall, J. Snygg, M. Nilsson, and R. Jörnsten. 2013. "Music Structure Determines Heart Rate Variability of Singers." *Frontiers in Psychology* 4.334. DOI: 10.3389/fpsyg.2013.00334.

Walton, J. 1991. "Women's Ritual Music." In *Music in American Religious Experience*, eds. P.V. Bohlman, E.L. Blumhofer, and M.M. Chow, 256. New York: Oxford.

Weil, A. 2008. "Music for Health?" www.drweil.com/drw/u/QAA400483/Music-For-Health.html; referencing "Gregorian Chanting Can Reduce Blood Pressure and Stress," [London's Daily] *Mail Online* (May), www.dailymail.co.uk/sciencetech/article-563533/Gregorian-chanting-reduce-blood-pressure-stress.html, accessed 1 August 2013.

Werner, E. 1957. "Musical Aspects of the Dead Sea Scrolls: For Curt Sachs on His 75th Birthday." *Musical Quarterly* 43.1: 21–37.

Wissler, H., director. 2007. *Kusisqa Waqashayku (From Grief and Joy We Sing).* www.queros-music.com.

———. 2009. "Grief-Singing and the Camera: The Challenges and Ethics of Documentary Production in an Indigenous Andean Community." *Ethnomusicology Forum* 18.1: 37–53.

SELECTED TIMELINE OF VOCAL HEALING MILESTONES FROM MYTHOLOGY AND HISTORY

Every reasonable effort has been made to ensure accuracy, though many dates are speculative. Mentions of "music" which plausibly included singing are included. See also Figures 1.1 and 3.3.

NOTE: Non- and pre-linguistic usages of singing to promote health are noted only occasionally in modern reports of what are considered to be relatively continuous traditions (e.g., Native American).

BCE

Antiquity	From the earliest times, Chinese people sang, danced and played such instruments as bone flutes and clay vessel flutes to request rain and other survival needs from supernatural forces.
ca. 4000	Hinduism may have been practiced by seers and sages (shamans).
ca. 3100–539	In ancient Babylon society, the gods and music were closely connected. Music was used in liturgy, chants, and education.
3100	Worship of Osiris began in Egypt.
ca. 3000	Ancient Egyptians used music to summon the gods; musicians held the same status as priests and healers.
ca. 3000	According to Chinese mythology, Ling Lun, the imperial music master, was sent to study music practices west of the Ounloun mountains.
ca. 3000–2000	The pyramids were built in Egypt; Stonehenge was built in England.
ca. 2700	Ancient Egyptian instruments including clappers were preserved.

ca. 2323–2150	Princess Seshseshet is pictured playing harp and singing to her husband in the tomb of Mereruka at Saqqara.
ca. 2300–1700	Hindu priests performed dances, recited incantations, and used amulets to cure patients.
ca. 2300	Egyptian songs about the shepherd's lot preserved.
ca. 2000	The first known music theory texts were recorded in Mesopotamia (the region between the Tigris and Euphrates rivers). Cuneiform tablets preserved details about musicians and musical instruments.
ca. 2000–1800	In Greece, the philosophy of disease changed from magical to religious origins. Ancient scholars believed diseases came from the gods.
ca. 1766	Elite and common people sang and danced as a means of self-expression, influencing one another, in the Shang and Zhou dynasties of China.
ca. 1650	The ancient Egyptian Papyrus Westcar contains five stories about miracles performed by priests and magicians. Isis and four other goddesses are sent to help Reddedet with childbirth. The goddesses transformed themselves into musicians and assisted with the birth.
ca. 1600–1200	Nomadic Hebrew tribes utilized chants, laments, dirges, welcome songs for heroes, war songs, and work songs. Vocal music calmed and excited the passions.
ca. 1600–1200	In Anatolia during Hittite rule, cuneiform tablets preserved festival songs, performed as solos or in choruses, e.g., "Song of the God of the Favorable Day," which symbolizes a battle with the Storm God. In funerary rituals musicians sang to an accompaniment on the lyre.
ca. 1500–1200	The Rigveda was compiled in Pakistan around the same time that the Vedic system of religion took hold in India.
ca. 1400	Artists who painted tombs in the Valley of the Kings (Egypt) studied the classical authors and wrote psalms of their own.
ca. 1400	Hurrian cult songs were preserved on tablets at the ancient site of Ugarit (Ras Shamra, Syria).
ca. 1400	Traditional date for the construction of the Oracle at Delphi. Pindar (522–433 BCE, in *Paean* 8), related that the Third

	Temple's architectural features included sirens whose songs provoked the gods to bury the temple in the earth.
ca. 1300	Egyptian songs about workers in the field preserved in the tomb of Paheri at El-Kab.
ca. 1200–800	The earliest documentation of religious music among ancestors of Jewish people was preserved in archaeological and iconographic forms.
12th or 11th century	According to tradition, Orpheus lived prior to the Trojan War.
ca. 1100	Clay flutes, stone chimes, and bronze bells were preserved in the royal tombs of China's northern Henan province.
ca. 1040–970	The harp playing of the Hebrew David, singer of psalms, cured King Saul's melancholy.
ca. 1000	Wenamun's tribulations were alleviated only by the presence of a female Egyptian singer at Byblos.
ca. 1000	King David employed professional musicians to provide vocal and instrumental music for the First Temple.
ca. 1000–600	The *Shih Ching*, edited by Confucius, was the first Chinese classic containing poetry to be sung.
ca. 800	A Sumerian hymn detailing a story of human creation was preserved on a tablet.
8th century	In his epic poem *Iliad*, Homer mentions Asclepius, the Greek god of medicine and healing, and references singers as mourners. In *Odyssey*, Homer relates an image of Achilles singing by his tent. His is the first mention of sirens singing in order to lure sailors to their doom. He also calls on the nine Muses in *Odyssey*.
Late 8th century	Hesiod (Homer's successor and composer of didactic epics) wrote about music in *Works and Days*; he bids the Muses to sing the praises of Zeus. In *Theogony*, the Muses appear as singers and dancers.
ca. 700	A Greek vase in the "Geometrical Style" depicted the mourning of the dead within Greek society.
ca. 650	Terpander, lyrist and lyric poet of the Lesbos, calmed crowds in Sparta with his music.

650–400	The Homeric hymn to Hermes portrayed Hermes' invention of the lyre. In fifth-century Greece, singing to the lyre was associated with schoolboys and their teachers, and was thought to promote a sense of justice, moderation, and courage.
ca. 612	Sappho, Greek lyric poet, trained well-born girls on Lesbos in works dedicated to Aphrodite, the Graces, and the Muses. In *Dialogue on Love*, Plutarch wrote that Sappho "speaks words mingled truly with fire, and through her songs, she draws up the heat of her heart." Among surviving works are wedding songs sung antiphonally by males and females.
ca. 600	Arion of Methymna founded the first dithyrambic choir of fifty boys and men. Dithyramb is an ancient Greek hymn sung and danced in honor of Dionysus.
ca. 597	Oriental Jewish populations retained their liturgies, even while exiled in pagan surroundings.
582	With the inclusion of nomoi (an ancient Greek genre that sometimes featured singing), music became a part of the Pythian games in Greece.
ca. 570–495	The life of Greek philosopher Pythagoras. Though Homer and Hesiod referenced it earlier, Pythagoras is credited with the concept of music of the spheres. He and his followers developed theories about musical consonances and planetary movements.
ca. 550	Damon of Athens reportedly viewed music as a means of moral indoctrination and group identifier.
mid-6th century	An image of Orpheus first appeared in a sculptured panel.
ca. 500–350	Pythagorean philosophers believed music had a social and ethical role similar to its role in the governance of the individual body. Good health was considered a result of the body's numerical equilibrium.
5th century	Greek tragedy arose out of choral performance in Athens; the most acclaimed composers were Aeschylus, Sophocles, and Euripides.
ca. 496–406	Greek tragic poet Sophocles led the choral paean celebrating the defeat of the Persians at Salamis. He wrote over 100 tragedies and satyr plays, of which seven survive intact.

ca. 460–377	Greek physician Hippocrates initiated the rise of rational medicine; disease was a consequence of nature and individuality. He considered imbalance of the four humors (blood, phlegm, yellow bile, black bile) the cause of disease.
ca. 450–385	Greek dramatist Aristophanes included choruses and solo voices that were relevant to the action of the tragedy.
429–347	Plato equated music with spoken language and argued that music should be used by intelligent people to heal the soul. He approved only two of Damon's six modes: Dorian and Phrygian. In *Republic*, he emphasized sound interaction between mind and body, insisted that all people should take part in choruses, and argued for the importance of preserving traditional music. In *Republic* and *Laws*, Plato banned the aulos from the ideal city-state because it was an alien element in Greek religion.
414–412	Euripides's *Iphigenia in Tauris* described magician's spells in the form of incomprehensible songs.
Late 5th century	Choruses no longer held the main role in Greek tragedies.
ca. 400–100	The *Bhaqauadqiitaa* (part of the Hindu epic narrative *Mahabharata*) used vocal performance to present a text.
ca. 375–360	Aristoxenus separated music from arithmetic and astronomy, arguing that music was an autonomous discipline. He remarked that Pythagoreans affected the "katharsis of the body by means of medicine and katharsis of the soul by means of music."
ca. 372–287	Greek philosopher Theophrastus (ca. 372–287 BCE) was opposed to the idea of attributing medical powers to music.
4th century	In China, drink-induced singing, dancing, and trance may have been involved in Shang dynasty divination.
ca. 384–322	Aristotle's *Politics* described two uses of music: exciting music was used at rituals and festivals and contemplative music was used for recreation. He believed learning an instrument would help young people make better musical judgments later in life.
339–314	Xenocrates of Chalcedon, pupil of Plato, was head of the Greek Academy. He is said to have practiced music therapy and used instrumental music to cure hysterics.

ca. 300	The Dead Sea Scrolls were recorded. They included information about responsive singing between male and female choirs.
ca. 300–240	The Daoist holy book, *Daodejing*, was written by Lao Zi. It referenced ancient Chinese concepts such as ying and resonance. Sacrificial music relied on ying to contact departed ancestors in ritual music.
280–240	Hibeh (Egypt) musical papyrus stated that different types of music produced different ethical states.
ca. 200	*Argonautica* by Greek epic poet Apollonius Rhodius reiterated the legend of Orpheus singing in order to save Argo's company from sirens.
ca. 200	Epicurus believed music was a source of innocent pleasure.
ca. 200 BCE–200 CE	*Natya Shastra* is an important record of Indian musical lore. It lists the ten meritorious qualities of singing: color, abundance, ornament, clarity, distinctness, loudness, smoothness, evenness, great delicacy, and sweetness. The faults of singing are: lack of confidence, timidity, excitement, lack of clarity, nasality, a shrill tone, a tone produced too high in the head or in the wrong register, a discordant sound, tastelessness, interruptions, rough enunciation, confusion, and inability to keep time.
128	The Delphic Hymns were written by the Athenian composer Limenius (fl. 128 BCE) in honor of Apollo.
ca. 100 BCE–100 CE	A collective of Indian sages known as Patanjali codified known yoga practices in a book of aphorisms: *The Yoga Sūtra*.
ca. 70	Asclepiades (124–40 BCE), a Roman physician, calmed seditious mobs and cured insomnia with harmonious strains of music heard at a distance.
ca. 43 BCE–17 CE	Roman poet Ovid wrote *Metamorphoses*, in which he detailed the mythological stories that credited the invention of the pan-pipes to Pan and the invention of the lyre to Mercury. He further established the image of Sirens as bird women.
ca. 20 BCE–40 CE	Philo of Alexandria described a healing and singing order of monastics, the Therapeutae.

ca. 4 BCE–65 CE	Roman statesman Lucius Annaeus Seneca wrote in a letter: "I heard, about midnight, a furious clamor. I asked what it was, 'Vocal exercises,' was the answer."

CE

ca. 30	Christianity, called a religion of healing, is established.
ca. 30–60	Greek historian Diodorus Siculus wrote *Bibliotheca historica*, which relates that Osiris taught the arts of civilization through speech and song.
ca. 95	Greek orator Quintilian wrote *Institutio oratoria*, in which he suggested using music as a tool for training orators. This training would make speech more musical.
ca. 100	The Epitaph of Seikilos, containing a Greek diatonic vocal melody, was inscribed on a tombstone.
ca. 100–800	Healers in Peru were pictured playing flutes, pan-pipes, and drums.
ca. 120–200	Lucian of Samosata described solo singing in his treaty "On the Dance."
131–200	Claudius Galen developed a system of medicine based on anatomy rather than on philosophy. He incorporated the teachings of Hippocrates, including the four humors. Galen believed music could be an antidote for viper and scorpion bites.
ca. 155–222	Tertullian, a Christian author from Carthage, promoted the use of responsorial psalmody.
ca. 185–254	Origen, an early Christian theologian born in Alexandria, testified to the wide use of song in worship.
ca. 200	Athenaeus referred to a choir of 600 with 300 harpers in the reign of Philadelphus (285–246 BCE).
ca. 250	Athenaeus' *Deipnosophistae* warned against using musical instruments, which the author believed would interfere with the act of singing. He wrote that declining to sing was a disgrace.
ca. 300–600	The rabbinic period, after which Jewish liturgical singing in orthodox environments was performed by males only.

330–379	St Basil the Great wrote that singing of the psalms had the power to calm the soul, but that instrumental music could lead to destruction.
ca. 340–397	St. Ambrose wrote that women were to be silent in the congregation.
354–430	In *Confessions*, St Augustine wrote that songs inspired great religious fervor, but warned Christians to take care not to let the music be more prominent than the spiritual text. He also recorded his own moral dilemma regarding singing in worship.
ca. 400	St John Chrysostom claimed work songs eased the necessary toil of daily human existence.
ca. 400	Ammianus Marcellinus described the barritus (barbarian war song) as a soft hum which increased in volume until it "thundered like waves breaking on rocks."
ca. 400	*De nuptiis Philologiae et Mercurii*, by Latin writer Martianus Capella, described the ethical power of music. He recorded that one of his students calmed a group of drunks by making them sing along with a flute accompaniment.
ca. 400–900	Greek learning returned to Western Europe, medicine recovered its philosophical foundation, and the demand for music therapeutics increased as a way to moderate the passions of the soul.
ca. 450	Roman physician Caelius Aurelianus used specific keys to cure ailments: Phrygian cured dejection and rage; Dorian cured excessive laughing and giggling.
476–1476	In Christianity, music was viewed as a servant of the Church to be regulated.
ca. 490–585	Roman statesman Cassiodorus wrote a letter to Boethius describing the powers of music. He claimed the Phrygian mode stirred fighting and wrath, the Aeolian mode calmed the upset, and the Lydian mode soothed a heavy soul.
ca. 500	In *De Musica*, Roman statesman Boethius (ca. 480–524) wrote of the individual soul (musica humana), which could be returned to cosmic harmony through the intermediary use of appropriate instrumental or vocal music. *De Musica* became the principal document by which the ancient philosophy of music therapy was transmitted to medieval Europe.

ca. 540–604	Pope Gregory the Great's music reforms placed Rome at the center of sacred music development. Music was used as a tool to spread the beliefs of Christianity.
ca. 578	Women were excluded from Christian choirs, except in convents.
813	The Roman Catholic Council of Tours promoted the belief that magical spells could not cure illness. The Church claimed that anyone relying on magic had fallen victim to the illusions of the Devil.
ca. 850–1000	During the Islamic Golden Age, both music and medicine developed as scientific areas subject to systemization. Writing in Arabic, philosophers expressed understandings that the sonic arts had great power over the body and soul alike. In general, adhān (call to prayer) and tajwīd (recitation of the Qur'an) are not considered music.
ca. 900	Islamic philosopher and music theorist Al-Fārābī wrote *De ortu scientiarum*, in which he observed music's power to heal various maladies. He recounted the use of extremely high pitches for curative and poisonous means. Al-Fārābī's works were translated in the 12th century by both Gerard of Cremona and John of Seville.
ca. 900–1000	Ikhwān al-Ṣafā', a group of Islamic encyclopedists, adhered to a philosophic and metaphoric approach to music therapy. As described in *Epistles of Music*, they used music in hospitals to alleviate pain, calm violent patients, and cure illness.
ca. 950	*Bald's Leechbook* was the primary manual for English physicians. The text recommended the use of incantations along with other treatments to cure ailments.
ca. 1000–1073	The Persian Shaykh 'Ali al-Hujwiri wrote *Kashf al-mahjub* (Revealing the Mystery). This Sufi treatise discusses the potentially fatal influence of music on the neophyte. Al-Hujwiri described a treatment in which patients were forced to listen to the anghalyun (a string instrument).
11th century	Arabs further refined the theory of the four humors.
11th or 12th century	The iconic image of sirens changed from bird women to fish-tailed women.

1098–1179	Hildegard of Bingen, composer, abbess, and preacher, enjoyed widespread notoriety for her vocal and instrumental compositions, along with her miracles.
ca. 1100	Eadmer, a monk of Christ Church in Canterbury, wrote a biography of St Dunstan (d. 988) that contained Dunstan's advice to find the healing of celestial harmony through the power of words interspersed with melodies.
ca. 1126–1226	*Tibb al-Nufus* (Hygiene of Souls) by Yosef ibn 'Aknin (d. 1226) claimed music had the power to remedy mental illnesses. Patients could be cured by listening to performances of poems sung with the accompaniment of lyres, rattles, cymbals, and wind instruments.
1128	French theologian and mystic Bernard of Clairvaux (1090–1153) founded the Knights Templar. He wrote that the chant should please the ear only that it move the heart.
1159	John of Salisbury suggested in *Policraticus* that polyphonic singing, like that of sirens, undermines religion.
ca. 1200	Scholars began recording empirical observations about the curative power of music.
1215	Pope Innocent III convened the Fourth Lateran Council in order to reform the church; the Fourth Lateran viewed confession as a medical process.
ca. 1216	Thomas Chobham, an Englishman from Surrey, wrote the manual *Summa confessorum*, which provides insight on the music used to help patients at St Augustine's Abbey. He recommended the use of narrative songs that recounted the lives of saints and princes.
ca. 1220	John of Erfurt wrote *Summa de Penitentia*, a manual compiled for confessors or "physicians of souls." The manual detailed the Fourth Lateran requirement that physicians should advise patients that treatment would not begin with the work of the physician, but the priest.
1231–1236	William of Auvergne, Bishop of Paris, wrote the treatise *De universe*, which contains a chapter on the curative powers of music. He claimed that many mental illnesses have been cured by musical sounds.
ca. 1240	The *Saṅgīta-ratnākara* (*The Jewel Mine of Music*), one of the most influential treatises in the history of Indian music,

described God as the embodiment of music, and described music as an integration of science, art, and yoga. According to the treatise, flawless singing of a raga can bring it to life in a visual form.

1266–1268	Richard of Ware, an abbot of Westminster, wrote a *Customary* for St Augustine's Abbey. It contains a section on the duties of the Infirmarius, the person in charge of the monastic hospital. The Infirmarius was instructed to lead the sick into the chapel where music would lift their spirits. The *Customary* banned music outside of therapeutic purposes.
ca. 1300	Turkmen tales portrayed the bagşy-shaman, a man with magical power and wisdom, a healer, musician, and poet.
ca. 1300	The *Tractatulus de differentiis et gradibus cantorum* by Arnulf of St Ghislain described "earthly Sirens" who used microtones to enchant their listeners.
ca. 1300	Music theorist Johannes de Grocheio declared that certain types of songs, when performed by young people on feast days, had the power to quell excessive erotic desires.
ca. 1300	*Astesanus*, a book by an Italian Franciscan, contained dialogue in which a friar was asked whether musical sounds could drive away devils and cure maladies. The friar explained that herbs and melodies could mitigate the demons' effect by lifting the patient's spirits.
1300–1700	Philosophers during the Renaissance began to research medicine with science. Ideas from antiquity, such as the four humors, were sources of inspiration and knowledge. Disease was viewed as a disruption to the body's naturally harmonious state.
1318	A passage in the register of Adam of Orleton, Bishop of Hereford, revealed that wanton songs were played when patients were being bled in the infirmary.
ca. 1320	Clergy operated institutions to treat the mentally ill in Spain.
1350–1600	Humanism, the study of linguistic and rhetorical traditions of classical antiquity, flourished first in Italy, and eventually spread throughout Western Europe. Vocal inflection was mirrored in non-vocal musical forms.
1433–1499	Marsilio Ficino's *De vita triplici* contains theories of music's effects on the human "spiritus." An Italian scholar and Catholic

	priest, Ficino believed music helped restore the proper balance of the humors. He translated the Hymns of Orpheus into Latin.
ca. 1453	Greek medicine was rediscovered during the crusades. The invention of printing further disseminated this information.
1486	*Malleus malificarum*, a treatise encouraging the persecution of individuals who practiced witchcraft, was compiled by Dominican monks Heinrich Kramer (ca. 1430–1505) and James Sprenger (ca. 1436–95).
1493–1541	Paracelsus combined practical and folk medicine, alchemy, and the teaching of several bishops. Paracelsus was a Brotherhoods adherent; religion, healing, and singing remained joined in the Brotherhoods tradition.
ca. 1500	Naik Gopal, a singer at the court of Abkar the Great in India, was ordered by his monarch to sing rāga Dīpak. This raga creates fire, and when Gopal sang it, he burst into flames and perished. Prison wardens taught these melodies to prisoners for a fee, because the prisoners believed it would melt the stones of the prison walls.
1500s	Magic was considered an art that affected people by occult (supernatural) means. Members of the clergy were often involved in the practices of magic; physicians, engineers, painters, and musicians attempted to affect people and things through occult means.
1500s	Composers began to reflect on music's capacity to affect emotions.
ca. 1500–1700	Renowned string instrument builders in Cremona, Italy, strove to perfect string instruments that could effectively imitate the human voice. These builders included the Amati (ca. 1530), Stradivari (ca. 1666), and Guarneri (ca. 1690) families.
1514–1564	Belgian physician Andreas Vesalius published *De humani corporis fabrica libri septem* in 1543. The text detailed the process of human dissection that Vesalius used to correct errors in the four humors theory.
1517–1590	Italian music theorist Gioseffo Zarlino believed that musical understanding could improve a physician's understanding of the human heart rate, and that music could be used in addition to preventive medicine.

1520–1591	Vincenzo Galilei believed that Greek humanism was manifested in monody (accompanied song) and heterony. He concluded that music was congruent with rhetoric.
1561–1626	Francis Bacon's *The Advancement of Learning* introduced a systematic structure for the disciplines of knowledge. The practice of music was classified in the category of the "voluptuary arts" due to its direct effect on the passions of the mind and morals.
1564	The Tridentine Index (list of prohibited books authorized by the Council of Trent) imposed a general ban on works of magic. The practice of witchcraft was a statutory offence in England. However, interest in witchcraft increased during the 16th and 17th centuries.
1573–1602	The Camerata (especially Giulio and Francesca Caccini, Vincenzo Galilei, and Pietro Strozzi) frequented the salon of Count Giovanni de' Bardi in Florence; opera, inspired by their reading of the Greek classics, was the result of their discussions.
1574–1637	Robert Fludd's *The History of the Macrocosm and Microcosm* disputed Bacon's classification of music. Fludd claimed music was an organizing force on the universe and a manifestation of cosmic harmony.
1598	*Introduction to Practical Music* by Thomas Morley (ca. 1557–1602) divided music into two categories: the science of music (theory) and the art of music (practice). This coincided with the division of the English educational system of the time, in which speculative music theory required philosophical training and practical music theory required technical training in performance.
Late 1500s	Syrian pharmacist and physician Da'ūd al-Antakī, active in Cairo, wrote a medical encyclopedia called *al-Tadhkira* (Memorial for Wise Men) which introduced medical applications for the eight rhythmic modes.
ca. 1602	Instigated a transition from "symbolic to mimetic" musical expression and demanded a new language of music. The earliest composers of opera used the mythological story of Orpheus as subject material: *Euridice* (1600) by Jacopo Peri; *Euridice* (1602) by Giulio Caccini; and *Orfeo* (1607) by Claudio Monteverdi.
1600s	Science was considered a body of theoretical knowledge about a subject. Music was classified as a discipline of science and art, because it comprised both theory and performance.

1648	Evliya Chelebi visited Nur ad-Din Bimaristan (hospital, built in 1154) in Damascus and reported that concerts were given for patients three times a day. The Mansuri Hospital in Cairo also hosted troupes of musicians that performed for patients.
1649	*Passions of the Soul* by René Descartes explained the six passions—wonder, love/hate, joy, sadness, desire, and virtue—in physiological terms. Descartes claimed passions are caused by spirits managed by the brain's pineal gland and are disseminated throughout the body by the blood. In *Compendium*, Descartes distinguished between sound as a physical phenomenon and sound as understood by the human conscience, which would inspire late-seventeenth-century German philosophers in the conceptualization of *Affektenlehre* (doctrine of the affections).
1650	*Musurgia universalis*, by the Jesuit Athanasius Kircher (1601–80), was the first account of the "doctrine of affections." This complex system by which rhetoric and music were joined influenced early opera and oratorio composers and later giants such as Bach and Handel. Kircher included eight songs (dances) used to cure tarantism (illness supposedly caused by the bite of the wolf spider) in the early 17th century in his *Magnes, sive De arte magnetica* (1641).
1654	In *Physiologia*, Walter Charleton wrote that victims of tarantula bites who succumb to violent fits of dancing could only be cured by listening to harmonious strains of music.
1655	Thomas Hobbes's *Elements of Philosophy* included a discussion about using music to cure the venom of tarantula bites.
1668	Jean Baptiste Tavernier (1605–89), a French merchant, traveled to the Ottoman Empire and wrote about the seraglio (women's apartments in an Ottoman palace) in Constantinople. He described patients being treated in infirmaries with unpleasant vocal and instrumental music.
Early 1700s	Mimesis (varying theories of imitation in music) overtook the ethos theory.
1717	Modern Freemasonry was revived. Musical specifics of the Masonic ritual are shrouded in secrecy, though it appears that hymns and songs appropriate for unison singing were used in lodges.
1737–1749	Carlo Broschi, aka Farinelli (1705–82), an Italian castrato singer, was appointed "royal servant" to the Spanish king,

	PhilipV (1683–1746). Farinelli serenaded the king every night in hopes of improving Philip's debilitating depression.
1751–1772	In the *Encyclopédie*, Swiss philosopher Jean-Jacques Rousseau wrote that music no longer held power over the affections of the soul as was believed in Greek antiquity. In another *Encyclopédie* article, the physician Jean-Joseph Menuret de Chambaud (1739–1815) maintained that music could affect the human body or stir the passions. Menuret believed sound created a movement that was transmitted via air to the human body.
1761	In Rousseau's novel *Julie* (*La Nouvelle Héloïse*) the St. Preux character believed music directly affected the soul, and that the singing voice had the power to "agitate the heart." The author believed that human emotions should be attributed to moral rather than physical being.
1775–1835	Life of Muttusvāmi Dīkṣitar, a South Indian composer and musician, who composed a cycle of nine songs for therapeutic purposes, *Navagraha* (the nine planets).
1776–1789	English musician, composer, and historian Charles Burney published the *General History of Music*, which divided the roles of music therapy into three categories: music to promote civilization, soften, and humanize society; music to excite or repress the passions; and music to cure disease.
1777	French music critic Jean-François de La Harpe (1739–1802) criticized Gluck's opera *Armide*, claiming that it harmed the emotions of the soul because it sounded like screams of pain.
1800s	Theories of mimesis were gradually replaced by the belief that music is significant for its own sake (formalism), not for its function.
1800s	Music was considered an interplay between music and philosophy. Music was considered an analogue for life.
1802	By this point, the erosion of the Church's control over medicine was nearly complete.
1804–1806	*An Inaugural Essay on the Influence of Music in the Cure of Diseases* (1804) by Edwin Atlee and *On the Effects of Music in Curing and Palliating Diseases* (1806) by Samuel Matthews were written from the medical, instead of the philosophical, perspective. The authors, both students of Benjamin Rush (US founding

	father), relied on the cause-and-effect model in order to link music to the health of the patient.
1835	The Finnish national epic *Kalevala* was first published. The text was a compilation of Finnish runic lore weaved together into an epic by Elias Lönnrot (1802–84). The poem often references magic spells that were sung.
1840s	The Illenau Asylum in Achern, Germany, hired a full-time instructor to establish singing and instrumental groups for the patients. The asylum published a hymnal that was later adopted by other asylums.
1857	"On the Origin and Function of Music," an essay by philosopher Herbert Spencer (1820–1903), described music as a refined language of the emotions and suggested that music has evolutionary roots in the excited speech of primitive ancestors.
1865	Jean-Baptiste Bouillaud (1796–1881) published discoveries that helped locate the musical centers of the brain.
1871	Charles Darwin (1809–82) published *The Descent of Man*, in which he stated that the art of singing was perfected in relation to the propagation of the species.
1893	American ethnologist Alice Cunningham Fletcher (1838–1923) published *A Study of Omaha Indian Music* after extensive field research among the Great Plains Indians. During her study, she reported being successfully treated by native healing songs during an illness that kept her close to death for five weeks.
1893	*Primitive Music*, by Austrian pioneer in musical psychology Richard Wallaschek (1860–1917), analyzed musical instruments of ethnic groups and set forth a naturalistic theory of music. He described the performance of music for medicinal purposes.
1903	National Therapeutics Society of New York, aka International Society for Musical Therapeutics, was founded.
1909	In the article "The Anglo-Saxon Charms" (*Journal of American Folk-Lore*), Felix Grendon documented instances when "respectable" Americans resorted to incantations to treat health issues.
1913	*Chippewa Music*, by ethnographer and anthropolgist Frances Densmore (1867–1957), reported successful shamanistic

treatments using song, including one instance in which a patient with a serious gunshot wound was healed with song.

1918	The modern profession of music therapy evolved after provision of music in post-First World War veterans' hospitals. Originally considered to be a valuable distraction from psychological and physical traumas, music therapy was soon recognized to provide notable benefits to patients.
1918–	British cognitive specialist Brenda Milner (b. 1918) pioneered the field of behavioral neuroscience.
1919	Margaret Anderton, an English pianist, taught a course titled "Musicotherapy" at Columbia University which was aimed at training those offering musical experiences in veterans' hospitals.
1922 or 1924	Esther Kahn established the International Society for Musical Therapeutics in Australia.
1926	Lionel Logue's speech therapy, which included the method of singing difficult words, helped King George VI of England overcome speech disfluency (stammering).
1926–1933	Swiss archeologist Gustave Jéquier (1868–1946) discovered incantations at four Egyptian royal burial chambers that dated back to the sixth through eighth dynasties (ca. 2345–2055 BCE). These incantations were spells intended to resurrect dead rulers into the afterlife.
1927	Danish explorer Knud Rasmussen describes Eskimo (Inuit) cultures and especially angakoqs, or wizards, whose rituals involved travelling to the heavens. For these shamans, music provides a portal to the spiritual world.
1929	Hans Berger began publishing a series of papers that described a rhythmic oscillation of electricity detected by electrodes on the human head — the "Berger Rhythm." This research stemmed from Berger's invention of electroencephalography (EEG) in 1924.
1930	Scholar R.A. Fischer published the theory of runaway sexual selection.
1934	E.D. Adrian and B.H.C. Mathews explored the effects of rhythmically flashing lights on the brain. They discovered that the brain would adapt in response to changes in the rhythmic speed of the light.

1936	*Music in Institutions,* by music educator Willem van de Wall, helped pioneer the use of music therapy in state-funded facilities.
1944	Michigan State University opened the first program for a degree in music therapy.
1948	The National Music Council started the *Hospice Music Newsletter* in response to a growing number of music programs in healthcare facilities.
1950	The (United States) National Association for Music Therapy was founded. It gave structure to practices in music that aimed to help the ill.
1951	*Le Chamanisme et les techniques archaïques de l'extase* (Shamanism: Archaic Techniques of Ecstasy), by Romanian religious scholar Mircea Eliade (1907–86), described many different traditions of shamanism from around the world. The text was translated into English in 1964.
1957	The "Tomatis Effect" was formally recognized by the French Academy of Science. Alfred A. Tomatis (1920–2001) was an ear, nose, and throat doctor who developed an auditory treatment for a variety of problems such as autism and dyslexia. He also treated vocalists; his theory revolved around retraining hearing in order to retrain the voice.
1958	The British Society for Music Therapy was founded.
1964	The *Journal of Music Therapy* began publishing peer-reviewed research.
1967	Phacoemulsification, a surgery that uses ultrasonic waves to break up cataracts, was introduced by ophthalmologist Charles Kelman. Since its introduction, neurosurgeons have adopted the Kelman phacoemulsification machine for use in dissecting tumors from delicate brain and spinal cord tissue in children.
1969	Paul Bach-y-Rita (1934–2006) conducted the first experiments addressing brain plasticity.
1970s	Scientists posited that the average human fetus can hear during the last trimester of pregnancy.
1971	The American Association for Music Therapy was established. This group merged with the National Association for Music Therapy in 1998.

1978	*Yuman Tribes of the Gila River* by Leslie Spier noted that many healers typically specialize in curing only a single sickness. Healers' songs are considered gifts from the deities and they are usually intended for one illness only.
1980s	The Tuvan shamanic tradition of throat singing, or khoomei, was revived as a national art-form in Mongolia and Russia. This ancient art-form was banned by communist regimes during the first half of the 20th century. Tuvan herders developed this tradition out of the belief that living creatures manifest spiritual power through sound.
1983	The Certification Board for Music Therapists was incorporated. The board developed a certification exam for music therapists (first administered in 1985) and strengthened the credibility of the profession.
1985	Extracorporeal shockwave lithotripsy was introduced as a treatment to break down kidney stones using pressure waves.
1985	Non-invasive brain imaging technologies were first used, allowing the research for brain mapping to begin.
1992	In the essay "White Mountain Apache Dance: Expressions of Spirituality" in *Native American Dance: Ceremonies and Social Traditions*, Cécile R. Ganteaume described how the songs of the White Mountain Apache Indians are revealed to individuals in dreams. She explains that almost all people who receive songs go on to become healers.
1994	Scientists confirmed that the mother's voice is the most intense acoustical signal in the amniotic environment.
1994	"Zaman el Salaam" was performed in three languages by 50 Palestinian, 50 Israeli, and 100 Norwegian children. This performance, produced by Amnon Abutbul and Fatchi Kasem, demonstrated vocal music's reconciling power.
1994	Music therapy services were included under the Partial Hospitalization Program in the US.
1994	Joanne Loewy founded the Department of Music Therapy at Beth Israel Medical Center in New York. Loewy has successfully utilized music therapy to reduce reliance on anesthesia in pediatric patients.
1994	*Magic in Ancient Egypt* by Geraldine Pinch described the gendered roles of magical healers in ancient Egypt. Pinch noted

	that while male magicians worked alone, female magicians worked in groups, often utilizing dance and simple musical instruments.
1996	*The Sound of Healing*, by music therapist Judith Pinkerton, included an appendix that suggests particular songs for various mental maladies.
1999	Heaton and others showed that children with an autism spectrum disorder do not differ from neuro-typical children in their abilities to perceive happy and sad affect in musical excerpts.
2005	Thaut, Peterson, and McIntosh found that singing can break data into memorable portions and access substitute pathways for memory tasks.
2005	Hillecke, Nickel, and Bolay published five general factors that contribute to the success of music therapy.
2005–2009	Galbally and others performed a meta-analysis of sixty-nine oxytocin studies conducted between 2005 and 2009, each of which focused on mother–infant relations.

INDEX